Table of Contents

v

Facilitating Learning

Best wishes
Bill Daggett

Sam Houston
6-30-98

MORENO VALLEY UNIFIED SCHOOL DISTRICT
13911 PERRIS BLVD.
MORENO VALLEY CA 92553

Facilitating Learning

By
Willard R. Daggett, EdD
and Sam Houston, EdD

with Benedict Kruse

Published by:
LEADERSHIP PRESS
an activity of
International Center for Leadership in Education, Inc.

This is a publication of
Leadership Press
an activity of the
International Center for Leadership in Education, Inc.

Printed in the United States of America
98 99 00 01 02   6 5 4 3 2 1

Library of Congress Catalog Card Number: 98-66046

ISBN: 0-9656553-1-8

Part 1

Educational Basics: Some New Outlooks

Chapter 1
The Educational Transaction

There's an old business slogan: "Nothing really happens around here until somebody sells something or delivers something that satisfies a customer."

MODEL FOR SUCCESS

Recognition of this simple reality led, during the early 1980s, to a highly effective revision and upgrading of the business education curriculum in New York State. A team of educators and experienced managers/executives was revising the State's recommended business education curriculum. More specifically, the job at hand was to broaden the content coverage of the curriculum to recognize the advent of computers and their impact. We wanted students to be prepared for demands of the information-dependent workplace into which they were transitioning.

The initial temptation was for members of the study team to immerse themselves within the high-tech fine points of computer equipment (as, unfortunately, many educators did in subsequent programs for introduction of computers into schools). Fortunately, this group—at that particular time and place—chose to focus on business education rather than technological elegance.

Members of the New York State team modeled their efforts after those of corporate information specialists and consultants involved in information system development. Emphasis in the new curriculum was placed on information and its value for decision making and problem solving. Specific units of equipment that accepted and handled data were a secondary concern.

3

(Note the distinction between information and data. Information was treated as a compilation of data items which, in turn, represented the lowest level of detail within an information system. For example, data items covered individual product sales or new inventory receipts. When compiled to represent overall business transactions, the collected data contributed to information reports on the status of the affected business.)

The fortunate students exposed to courses based on the resulting curriculum learned important lessons about business and about computers as tools. The principle stressed was that computers model, through accumulated information, the functions and condition of a business. Accordingly, the courses led students to a real understanding about what happens in a business and what results are realized. The students learned that transactions are at the core of any business operation—the proverbial point where the rubber meets the road, where business actually happens.

The objective of this curriculum-design decision was to impart an understanding of the cause-and-effect relationships that drive business and some governmental operations. Another value for students: By learning about the mountains of data that inundate businesses, students could appreciate the rate and explosive nature of change in the business world. Within New York State, the programs resulting from this curriculum development project were among the most successful units of vocational education offered to our students in more than a half century.

One of the major successes came from the practicality of this approach, which introduced students to the vital role of systems in the real world. By overviewing the transition of data into information, students learned that information workers operate within a series of connected functions—interdependencies. That is, a modern business organization or other entity consists of a series of related parts; and the total system that results is greater than the sum of those parts. It follows that survival in the ever-expanding information society requires **teamwork.** Thus, in understanding human-computer interfaces, students learned that their futures required that they understand and be prepared to function as members of teams.

Now, as educators prepare to gear our curricula toward the twenty-first century, it's time to challenge our expectations about student achievements. The same kinds of realities that led to design of the New York State business courses during the early

1980s are being expanded to the full core of content curricula of the future. The same kind of needs analysis is now necessary in the knowledge-mainstay areas of English, science, and math. In the twenty-first century, kids also are having to acquire a better understanding of their traditions and the meaning of being an American. In times of sweeping societal change, schools are going to have to change themselves to keep pace.

CHALLENGING ASSUMPTIONS: THE CHANGE IN EMPHASIS

These challenges emerged and their urgency was accented by pressures from business and international trade competition that became increasingly fierce during the 1980s. By the 1990s, everybody had computers. So competition had to shift to new venues. As computer capabilities became universal, technology diminished as a competitive make-or-break factor and the battle lines of commercial combat shifted to the marketing front. Companies increasingly differentiated themselves from competitors through the quality of their products and the customer satisfaction evoked by their services.

With these trends, business transactions acquired new dimensions of importance and new standards for evaluation. In the current parlance, transactions are skirmishes in fierce commercial wars. A completed, or *perfected,* transaction is a victory, a measure of success, a measure of the confidence that an organization has achieved in its marketplace.

Marketing success, in turn, results from astute positioning of an organization on a number of competitive fronts:

❑ Targeting of customers to be served.
❑ Identification of the elements by which customer satisfaction is to be measured.
❑ Design or adaptation of products or services to assure customer satisfaction.
❑ Delivery of goods or services at the point of transaction.
❑ Follow-up to assure continuity of a satisfactory relationship between customers and providers.

The emerging emphasis during the 1990s on identifying and satisfying customers is a normal outgrowth of the emergencce of service as the dominant factor in American commerce and society. Success now depends upon the existence of teams and systems that identify, serve, and satisfy customers. Today, the authors submit, the growing emphasis on assurance of customer satisfaction has direct parallels applicable to managing what has become the country's single largest customer-service enterprise—education. The demands that lie ahead for today's students must lead us to change our assumptions about achievement expectations of students—the basis for the results we will have to deliver during the twenty-first century.

To paraphrase the statement that opened this chapter: ***In education, nothing meaningful happens until a student learns something.***

SCHOOLS ARE SERVICE ENTERPRISES

This line of thinking has evolved within the International Center for Leadership in Education (ICLE) as a natural progression within concepts and programs designed for the management of educational change. The reasoning conforms to program objectives that call for a transition of schools from their traditional, adult-based emphasis on teaching to a new, student-oriented accent on learning. In this light, the school should be viewed as a service enterprise whose managers must measure their success in terms of identifying and satisfying customers. The criteria for satisfaction, in turn, depend on the development of rigorous, relevant curricula that satisfy multiple stakeholders. Change has to happen for all participants in the educational process. Members of diverse constituencies must establish new, meaningful relationships. And old constraints, particularly those that require school facilities to remain empty and unused for up to three months each year, must be overcome.

The net effect is that schools must be measured by the achievements of their students rather than seat time in classrooms. In other words, the measure of success centers on the learning achievements of students. In turn, the role of teacher changes from that of a lecturing information deliverer to a facilitator of content understanding and knowledge acquisition. As a school completes its transition from a teaching to a learning environment, students must be provided with opportunities to learn under conditions that permit each of them to apply the combination of sensory skills and capabilities natural to each individual. Beneficiaries of a transition to a learning-oriented environment include all constituents of American schools: their students, teachers, administrators, and other adult stakeholders.

Recognition and organization of educational institutions as service enterprises to meet demands of the twenty-first century are part of an ongoing commitment at ICLE and the scores of districts we serve. Improved service to educational publics is a primary target of the ICLE system aimed at managing educational change. At this writing, districts implementing the Management of Change methodology are well along in a multi-stage process that calls for redefining curricula for student achievement, setting goals to be implemented within a learning—rather than teaching—environment. As these programs have progressed, a marketing-oriented outlook under which schools regard themselves as service entities has become an apparent requirement, a need defined by community-based task forces. Under this orientation, identification of and service to educational customers becomes critical to the success of schools in delivering workplace-ready graduates whose achievements match or exceed community-defined standards.

THE EDUCATIONAL TRANSACTION

From the beginning, the ICLE Management of Change process, reviewed in subsequent chapters, has focused on participation by community members with a direct stake in the quality of local education and the capabilities of graduates. Each program for educational change, necessarily, is driven by a consensus of local business and political leaders, members of civic organizations, parents, and students—with active participation and guidance from teachers and school administrators.

Each of these groups has a distinctive role in the shaping of satisfactory educational transactions. For the purposes of reshaping or refocusing educational emphasis, a ***transaction*** can be defined as ***an interaction between student and teacher in which the student enlarges his or her knowledge base, enhances the ability to analyze situations and reach effective decisions through processing of information, and/or develops attitudes and character traits that will contribute to lifelong success.***

This standard of achievement renders the educational transaction particularly unique in that the recipient of interaction and/or service—the student—is not the primary customer of the education system. *Think about this!* ***The student is the primary recipient of educational services but not the main customer.***

Why? For one thing, students, especially those in early primary grades where the most critical elements of educational success are established, are not qualified to create standards or measure their own achievements. That job belongs to adults, adults who are not part of the educational system. School employees are, increasingly, looking to these constituents for guidance on what students should learn and be able to do.

As demands of job markets continue to change at an accelerating pace, prospective future employers are in the best position to define future educational standards and expectations. Thus, **adults qualified to determine essential knowledge and skills for future employment become the primary customers for determining what educational content should be.** In this sense, it becomes essential for managers of a program for educational change to seek participation and follow the recommendations of businesspeople. The student, then, is the product of educational services. Each student's achievements, in turn, provide a composite for measuring the effectiveness of the school, its faculty, and the administration.

In this respect, a word of caution is appropriate and important: The business managers, community leaders, and policy makers who help to define educational content and performance standards should be capable of projecting their recommendations toward the future. A person who is focused entirely on traditional, established workplace skills may be qualified only to advise on methods that condemn today's students to future obsolescence. The advisers given the strongest voice should be those who understand the dynamics of technological and economic forces and the challenges they represent for students.

The other major adult customers of an educational system are **parents, guardians,** or agencies responsible for the rearing the children. This is assured by the basic responsibility implicit in parenthood: Parents are fully and totally responsible for determining the values and setting the goals related to raising their children. Education is a critical part of this picture. Parents have both responsibility and authority for determining what their children learn and for guiding them to adulthood. Further, as customers, **parents control selection of the schools their children attend.**

In effect, then, prospective employers provide qualitative input to the setting of educational standards while parents have control over student enrollment in specific schools. The parent role promises to become increasingly critical as demands for choice resound through the educational system. Both prospective employers and parents are thus different but major customers an educational system should serve. This is a major shift from the traditional outlook that sees teachers and other adult staff as the primary shapers of educational activities.

Where does that leave teachers and administrators? Teachers in particular are the professionals who make learning happen. The system must recognize their vital roles and support their education, development, and classroom activities. Within an effective program for management of change, administrators assume the role of coordinators and facilitators akin to operating officers of corporations. With roles defined clearly, there is neither need nor excuse for teachers to be placed in adversary roles in their relationships to students, parents, community leaders, or school administrators. Mutual respect becomes the lubricant for a smoothly rolling educational operation. From the teachers' viewpoint, recognition of future employers as prime customers has a potentially positive connotation that should be recognized: Future employers tend to be influential policy setters in their community. They are also trained to recognize the value of professional services and to compensate contributors accordingly. Therefore, these participants represent an opportunity for teachers who feel the value of their services merits increased compensation.

A GAME OF CATCH-UP

The ground-swell demand for school change needs little explanation or elaboration today. Most of the complacency about education disappeared with publication of the 1983 report entitled *A Nation at Risk.* The dramatic title itself made this report the grist for crisis-instigating front-page and broadcast stories.

In retrospect, *A Nation at Risk* can be regarded as a wake-up call that incited a commitment to action. Unfortunately, the main reaction to the dramatic warning proved prototypically American: We threw mounds of money at what proved to be a misdefined problem. The heralded solution called for a massive *Back to Basics* effort under which schools were to stress content and methods assumed to have been proven in the dream world of education's "good old days." The theory: American schools did just fine in the days when curricula stressed The Three 'Rs. The resurrected basics, then, consisted of return to nineteenth-century-type emphasis on reading (some schools actually reinstituted use of *McGuffy's Reader*), writing, and arithmetic. Not only did these efforts waste a lot of money, but they also drained other valuable resources essential to a sound education, such as time, motivation, and commitment to achievement.

A second, even more serious wake-up call came with realization in the late '80s and early '90s that the old times weren't really great after all. The truth was that America and American society had undergone massive changes at a pace that far exceeded the ability of existing educational mechanisms to keep up. The system that engendered all the retrospective pride and fond memories turned out to be rudimentary and outdated. The American system of education had been created to serve an agrarian country whose citizens required little in the way of education beyond the ability to sign their names, do some basic sums related to dealings with merchants, and perhaps read a few verses of the Bible on Sunday morning. That system of the early 1800s was noteworthy in that it made instruction in basic literacy and computational skills available universally—and free.

For almost a century and a half, this system was good enough as agriculture was gradually mechanized and the Industrial Revolution led to a transition in which a nation of farmers became predominantly a nation of factory and construction workers. Throughout this entire period, which continued through the first half of the twentieth century, the self-deceit that mastery of the Three 'Rs constituted an adequate, basic education held sway. In truth, rather than representing the level of excellence assumed by many, the low levels of academic standards and achievements were only good enough, through much of our history, for many Americans to scrape by on. During the eighteenth and nineteenth centuries, farmers needed little more than rudimentary levels of education. Construction and factory workers needed little more than the ability to wield picks and shovels—or to follow orders on assembly lines designed to utilize untrained help.

Again, the answer of the '80s and early '90s was prototypically American: **more.** Since the basics of reading, writing, and arithmetic were no longer adequate, American educators entered into a frenzy of adding academic topics to the curriculum. This led to situations where curricula for American schools contained topical lists that were as much as five times those in countries like Japan and Germany. The expression coined to cover this situation is that the typical curriculum was "a mile wide and an inch deep." At this writing, some serious re-evaluation is underway about the depth and appropriateness of curricula imposed on American kids. The principle: If learning is really going to happen, the achievement expectations imposed on students are going to have to be reachable and are going to have to be structured to promote learning. In looking to twenty-first century education, educators should pay serious attention to curriculum standards that set the framework within which everything else happens.

CHANGED EXPECTATIONS

A rude awakening occurred when computers and other technologies brought to life during World War II began seriously impacting farming and industrial operations in the late 1950s and throughout the 1960s. On farms and elsewhere in the countryside, developments like automatic harvesters or cotton pickers and chainsaws displaced millions of workers. In factories, large companies undertook major changes in production techniques, changes that required massive retraining of employees. To master use of the new equipment and to learn new procedures, employees had to be able to read well enough to decipher and follow instructions.

That's when the true shortcomings of our complacency-burdened education system came to light. The shortcomings became most painfully apparent in their impact on jobs in places like Detroit automotive plants. One of the Big Three auto companies discovered, as plans were being formulated for retooling and re-engineering a large factory, that an estimated 27 percent of its production workers were functionally illiterate. That kind of discovery, among others, led to a clamor for improved educational results. This type of discovery, in turn, led to the study that produced the *Nation at Risk* report.

At that point in the history of educational change, the spirit was more willing than the system was capable. The *Back to Basics* movement did prove to be a backsliding activity. The multi-billion-dollar program, in effect, threw the mechanisms of education into reverse, re-instituting and re-emphasizing all of the techniques and instructional emphasis that had gotten American education into trouble in the first place. Fortunately though, this experiment led to the discovery that perhaps the good old days weren't that great.

REALITIES OF CHANGE

As the ongoing movement for educational change took new directions in the 1990s, one of the first points of attack for innovators was to create a climate of cooperation between educators and the communities they serve. In many places, education had fallen into the grip of a severe **us and them** mentality. The image created for schools, justly or not, was that most schools were fiefdoms in which public participation was unwelcome.

For their part, many teachers and administrators tended to accuse parents of being disinterested in the education of their children and unsupportive of their schools.

The tensions, inevitably, led to unproductive blame placement and finger pointing. That condition has been analyzed as one of the things about education that needs fixing: Education, critics hold, has become a political system that attempts to teach children, a place where student achievement does not get the priority it must enjoy.

The structure of the ICLE system for managing educational change is reviewed in subsequent chapters. However, some discoveries and conclusions concerning effective approaches to educational change are appropriate to this discussion. These findings identify characteristics of schools that provide quality learning experiences and graduate students prepared for successful transition to college or the workplace.

COMMITMENT TO LEARNING

Education happens primarily as a result of learning, not teaching. Regardless of how much a teacher may lecture or how many assignments are mandated, each student will master educational content as an individual. Each student will use separate sensory skills in the learning process and each will progress at an individual pace. The system must adjust to these realities of student performance. One-size-fits-all delivery systems and achievement expectations are both unrealistic and unworkable.

In a learning-oriented school, the teacher functions as a coordinator and facilitator of learning, using a variety of resources and methods that are different from traditional lecture-based instruction. These methods serve to establish a kind of partnership encompassing students, teachers, parents, and other contributing adults—a partnership under which students and teachers make commitments to accommodate individual learning styles and to enable each student to learn at his or her own pace.

When realistic expectations for student performance are in place, it becomes possible to incorporate meaningful assessment into the learning process. As a result, each student and every teacher gains a running measure of learning achievement—and of any knowledge needs to fill in gaps or shortfalls. The process establishes a new degree of equity in determining expectations for and measuring performance of teachers. When this happens, teachers are accorded professional status and recognition not possible under the antiquated organizational structures that rely primarily on multiple-choice tests for assessment. Under traditional systems, teachers waste their knowledge and experience as they labor to prepare students for tests that do little to measure their abilities to use reasoning power to apply knowledge.

ACHIEVING A LEARNING ORIENTATION

Methodologies for establishing and implementing learning-oriented programs are known, proven. Admittedly, however, these techniques require extensive rethinking and retraining of teachers. This is because each teacher needs to develop an individual approach to the job of learning facilitator.

In other words, while learning is the logical, most effective basis for enhancing educational performance, nobody claims implementation will be easy. A number of significant changes must occur if a school is to complete a successful transition to a service-oriented, customer-satisfying enterprise. A school organized to facilitate learning should display a series of positive organizational characteristics, including those identified below and discussed further in later chapters.

Customer Identification and Service

The staff of a school must identify its real customers and their expectations, then compare these criteria with existing performance. Customers must participate in setting goals for a school and must be part of an ongoing process to monitor progress toward achievement of those goals.

Once customers and their aspirations are identified, programs must recognize that achievement of educational goals requires **motivated** participants, with students presenting the most critical challenges. Values and opportunities for learning must be inherent in all plans for and commitments to education.

There's a lot to overcome in dealing with misguided good intentions of the past. Traditionally, education has been organized and structured for the self-perpetuation of a status quo that treated adult employees of schools as customers rather than service providers. Teachers committed to change still face, in many cases, demands of curriculum content subdivided and fractionated into disciplines established more for the convenience of adults than the logical learning patterns of students.

Possibly the most damaging example lies in the segregation of reading from instruction in other English-language skills. By isolating reading from corresponding skills in writing, listening, and oral presentation, the system has diminished its ability to encourage and impart communication capabilities. Once this artificial delineation was established, specialists created further isolation from practical use of language by stressing phonics as though the ability to decipher and recite syllables was the totality of reading requirements. In reality, phonics is a subskill for effective reading. Phonics is to reading approximately the same as spelling is to writing. Under most existing methods, *elementary students are taught recitation rather than reading.*

Meaningful Time Allocation and Activity Scheduling

Learning opportunities should not be constrained artificially by limitations upon the time available for learning. Existing obstacles to be recognized and dealt with should include the length of the school year, the time available in a school day, and the structure of classes into arbitrary periods that treat all content subjects equally regardless of importance to student success or their degree of difficulty.

Further, and possibly most important of all, time allocations should recognize that each student learns individually, in a unique way and at a different pace from all others. In a successful school, *time must become a variable while projected student achievements are the fixed elements within the operation.* The lockstep structure that demands completion of course materials within fixed time limits must be broken.

A well known obstacle to learning retention is the interruptions built into school schedules. Where knowledge is concerned, the guiding principle is *use it or lose it.* When students return to school in September, teachers invariably find that a significant portion of the knowledge base that existed in June has been dissipated through lack of use. The system suffers severe penalties as a result of its own artificial scheduling traditions.

The typical school year is still built around a three-month summer hiatus intended some 200 years ago to provide time for kids to help out on farms during planting, growing, and harvesting seasons. Rethinking of this antiquated practice is more than a century overdue. In the current economic and competitive climate, learning must be regarded as a full-time, year-round, lifelong necessity. School schedules should reflect this current reality.

Curriculum Content Priorities

Priorities must be established to govern the content of a school's curriculum. The principle applied in setting these priorities should establish that some content, generally identified as **core** courses, deserves a priority in use of instructional time. Also, because students learn at different rates and in different ways, some students may have to be provided with special or extra opportunities to reach learning levels that match curriculum standards.

Specifically, a basic, nonvariable priority must apply to the acquisition of communication capabilities and skills *in the English language.*

Reading should be considered part of this capabilities mix. But reading should no longer be isolated from the other requisite language communication skills. It must be recognized that reading competence should be paired naturally with writing performance and that students also need to develop capabilities for listening and speaking in English.

Further, it must be recognized that these communication requirements have application to all content areas of a curriculum. Reading and writing should be emphasized in courses in all subject areas that require communication between student and teacher and among students themselves.

Reading instruction in the early grades is a threshold that determines, totally, whether a student will acquire a level of education adequate for successful transition into society and the workforce. A student who falls behind in reading in early grades will almost surely begin to falter in math, since word problems are typically introduced into math curricula at third or fourth grade. Later, as science instruction increases, any lack of reading proficiency will penalize students further. The same, of course, applies in history and the social sciences, where comprehension is the most critical reading skill, and where students who have been taught to pronounce rather than understand what they read are doomed to substandard performance.

All courses and subjects are not equal in educational importance. Certain core subjects should be given priority in time and attention because of their relevance to the student's total educational experience, as well as to ultimate success in society and the workplace. A recent report by the National Education Commission on Time and Learning recommends that a series of identified core courses be prioritized above others through inclusion in what the Commission calls an academic day, or the hours of requisite attendance. The academic day is distinguished from the school day, which encompasses the total attendance hours students are in school, including for voluntary, nonrequired activities. Subjects singled out as core courses are English and language arts, mathematics, science, civics, history, geography, the arts, and foreign languages.

The Commission report stipulates: "Regular assessments at different stages of students' lives should require every student to demonstrate a firm grasp of demanding material in each of these areas, a grasp extending far beyond the trivial demands of most multiple-choice tests. They should assess not only the mastery of essential facts, but also the student's ability to write, reason, and analyze."

The report suggests that course offerings outside of this core be scheduled for later portions of the school day to avoid conflict with the priority to be accorded to the academic day. While the report is specific in delineating the areas of knowledge to be acquired by students, it also places clear responsibility for determining the exact instructional content in the hands of local school officials—with a recommendation that a community resources task force be set up to advise and participate in the setting of achievement goals and the organizational structure that facilitates their attainment.

Advancement should be on merit rather than age. Social, lockstep promotions should be ruled out and diplomas should be earned. Progress should be on the basis of achievement and should be independent of time frames. Plans and schedules should be flexible and adaptable to accommodate the wide variations in learning rates and styles among students. The environment in the school should recognize learning-pattern differences and eliminate any possibility of stigmas relating to the amount of time it takes a student to master prescribed content.

For students who require special help, including those with a native language other than English, ICLE recommends creating a **PAR (Progress Assurance and Reinforcement)** program that provides tutoring or special work in areas where individual students need help to bring their achievements up to standard.

By breaking out of what has been called a "Prison of Time" that has severely obstructed educational excellence in America, it becomes feasible to develop programs that enable each student to realize his or her full intellectual potential. The principles that underlie such programs recognize that all students are not equal in their learning potential, that rates of progress and levels of achievement will vary, but that every student deserves an opportunity and support from the system to assure that each reaches his or her full potential. The longstanding, fictitious "one size fits all" principle of education must be replaced by programs that assure flexibility and adaptability to specific student needs.

Direct relationships exist between physical exercise and mental achievement. This does not necessarily mean that physical education or sports require a priority in curriculum time allocations. The most beneficial kind of exercise is integrated into routine learning activities and class sessions.

Both in schools and on the job, periodic breaks for simple exercise routines are mandated for students and workers in Japan, Germany, and other countries. These activities take place right in the classroom or factory. Many successful companies in America provide exercise facilities in their plants or offices. Experience proves that interspersing brief periods of exercise into the work or study routine enhances learning experiences and on-job productivity.

Recognize that education is a complex field served by a variety of institutions, any of which can contribute innovative, valuable ideas or methods. Alternate approaches from either public or private entities can contribute to enhanced learning opportunities. Constructive review and open-minded willingness to accept improvements can advance all facets of education. Potential contributions can come from a wide range of sources, including but not limited to private schools, charter schools, specialized public schools or programs, contract public school operation, private tutorial organizations, home study, or even voucher plans. Diversification is a fact of organizational life in education. Alternatives should be reviewed positively rather than from a negative, competitive attitude.

Ask yourself: What would happen to public education if all private, contractual, and other alternatives disappeared? Public education, already overcrowded and facing rapidly growing student populations, would undoubtedly be swamped to a point of inadequacy. A number of different forms of education have a place in the increasingly diverse educational marketplace. This reality should be recognized by all professionals involved in education. Focus should be more on student progress than competition among different sources of education.

SET HIGH, UNCOMPROMISING STANDARDS

The best conceived schemes for improvement of educational content, methodologies, facilities, or organizational structures can be rendered useless and subject to assured failure if a system does not insist on and maintain high standards. *Quality should never be sacrificed,* not even on an altar of time constraints, political pressures, or compassion for students with extenuating circumstances or convincing stories.

Throughout its successful involvement in management of change programs, ICLE has enunciated and supported policies that insist on *rigor and relevance.* Rigor means that all students should be held to the same standards of achievement. Relevance means that every portion of a curriculum should contribute to the full, overall development of students as future, productive members of society and participants in an increasingly demanding and competitive workplace.

Many schools, for example, are still groping with issues of rigor and relevance in relation to installation and application value of computers. There's a tendency to wrap computers in a technological mystique. Almost defensively, many schools are teaching use of computers as machines, with the focus fixed on which buttons to push. Faculty and students should refocus on the computer as a tool for creativity and productivity, stressing capabilities and values for the varied and valuable outputs they can generate. Each computer is part of a system. Educators and students need an open-minded approach that encourages use of computers for the learning they can stimulate and for the achievements they make possible. In any program oriented toward building twenty-first century skills, the computer has to play a vital role.

The elements of rigor and relevance are stressed throughout the discussions in this book and should be integral parts of all learning standards and activities.

DIVERGENT VIEWPOINTS CAN BE HEALTHY

In undertaking change—any significant change—within a school system, *anticipate disagreement.* The constituencies within any school or district are bound to come to a program of change with different values, viewpoints, allegiances, and expectations. Easily, all too easily, disagreements can deteriorate into vituperative arguments which, in turn, lead to obstinate defenses of opposing opinions. Also all too often, antagonism blocks action, contributing to worsening situations that become complicated with bitterness.

If progress is to be realized, it is vital that **all parties respect one another's positions,** regardless of whether or not they are sympathetic or agreeable. Then, in negotiation for an acceptable position or program, the ICLE philosophy accentuates the positive (and possible). We recommend that all contentious recommendations or items of disagreement be tabled in favor of a search for positions on which there is mutual acceptance.

To illustrate, this outlook has served well in facilitating development of character education programs in a number of districts. Invariably when community representatives and parents enter the picture to establish parameters for character education, points of irresolvable contention arise in such areas as religion, sex education, and/or politics. By setting such issues aside, it becomes possible to concentrate on content about which agreement is readily attainable—areas such as honesty, integrity, loyalty, consideration, and others. Extensive and highly effective educational programs have been and are being built around these mutually acceptable areas, without even dealing with disagreements.

Experience has shown that there is enough agreement in American communities about expectations for educational achievement—including content and methodology—so that it is unnecessary to dwell unproductively on areas of rancor.

BE SKEPTICAL ABOUT GLOWING PROMISES

Recent educational history is replete with negative examples of elaborate programs that fail to deliver promised benefits. Too often, changes have been instituted without regard to which problems they were supposed to solve or even to whether problems actually existed. Consider such examples as new math and new grammar. By the time these programs were abandoned as failures, entire generations of students were processed through the educational assembly line without benefit of the knowledge or skills they should have acquired.

In education, it is common to encounter **solutions that are seeking to solve unidentified, possibly nonexistent problems.** The lesson: Avoid grasping solutions before problems are adequately defined. Consider all changes from a vantage point that sees education as a service enterprise. Insist that value be proven before change is institutionalized.

Also to be avoided is the pettiness and rancor that comes

with criticism of existing programs along with focus on placing blame rather than on achievement of improvement through change. To improve education, all involved parties need to look forward, not backward. Keep your eye on the twenty-first century, on the future, not the past. All educational progress needs to be future oriented.

Mechanisms for setting goals and standards for educational programs through evaluation under a proven taxonomy are covered in the chapter that follows. Following that presentation, succeeding chapters review a standard process for managing change, leading up to reviews of elements and examples for organizational structures and methods for promoting a learning environment in any school situation.

Chapter 2
Measuring and
Assuring Educational
Quality

W hen a physician pledges to observe the Hippocratic oath, the ancient set of commitments to the practice of medicine, he or she promises, first of all, to ***do no harm.***

A WASTED LESSON

This simple prioritizing of commitments should be a valuable guideline for educators. But it isn't! As our academic achievement scores and dropout rates attest, too many students are being harmed, too often irreparably.

To demonstrate how harm can be inflicted on the innocent, consider an unfortunately typical scenario that can occur on day one in first grade. The entering first grader—a normal child with a typical level of intellectual curiosity—comes to school speaking in sentences, describing experiences, and questioning the meaning of oral and visual stimuli. He or she may even display a soon-to-be-objectionable trait—a sense of humor. In other words, before a kid ever shows up to register for elementary school, a lot of knowledge and experience have been accumulated and a considerable amount of learning has happened. If the kid enters a modern school that has established a learning-oriented environment, the student's knowledge and skill levels would begin from this base and build at a pace that reflects his or her abilities.

But that doesn't always happen, at least not in too many of our schools. Harm may be done if the six-year-old is forced to focus on lesson materials so simplistic that they represent a return to a cradle-level mentally. Too many programs attempt to **teach recitation rather than reading.** Considerable harm may be done if the child is immersed in rote instructional practices that stifle curiosity and imagination and cause atrophy to most pre-education knowledge. If this kind of scenario is acted out, the education system can, in fact, do significant harm. Invariably though, the adults involved in the system are acting with high levels of good intent. They are unaware that they are doing harm. The negative results, in such situations, have been described as responses to a **law of unintended consequences.**

The type of damage that can be inflicted is even measurable on a standard scale of educational performance, Bloom's Taxonomy. The as-yet-unschooled student will typically acquire language orally and process instructions or information at a level of perhaps 4 or 5 on the Bloom's scale, reflecting the ability to analyze and synthesize acquired knowledge elements. Now, suppose this same kid is immersed into a system that purports to teach reading through a traditional recitation approach. The methodology in use presents reading materials that, typically, require intellectual processing at levels 1 or 2 in language skills, possibly a 3 in exceptional cases. After that, it may take years to undo the initial harm. In too many instances, children never do progress to their full potential. This disparity between incoming intellectual level and acquired reading skills could account at least partially for the 40 percent of third graders whom President Clinton singled out as nonreaders. Regardless of total cause, the very fact of language inadequacy provides evidence that at least some youngsters are being harmed.

This kind of performance, replicated year after year for some portion of the student population, does not represent an acceptable level of customer satisfaction for learning transactions. If educational achievements are to improve, we must create an environment, a set of basic organizational structures that recognize the need for and promote the meeting of reasonable learning expectations. Results must satisfy the students who are the products of education and whose achievements must satisfy our principle customers, future employers, other community leaders, and parents. Of particular, critical importance, we need a way to evaluate student potential, adapt learning-oriented programs to their needs, and measure student achievements, which are the outcomes of learning transactions and the results by which educational effectiveness will be judged.

Rudimentary tools for applying these measurements, such as Bloom's Taxonomy, have been available for some time. But, back in the early 1990s, ICLE determined that adaptation from its original application context was necessary to develop a tool adequate for use in today's more complex society. ICLE analyses identified two primary requirements that could be met by adapting and expanding Bloom's Taxonomy:

1. Following an extensive survey of educational curricula in a number of other countries as well as the U.S., ICLE concluded that communication of results and new concepts required a graphic comparison tool to illustrate levels in student achievement for comparison with expectations.
2. In designing new, more productive curricula for American schools, officials needed methods for representing current levels of achievement and to illustrate the advanced capabilities to be reached within new programs based on a learning orientation.

These requirements evolved from a series of ongoing programs for management of change in scores of school districts. If changes resulting from the challenging of assumptions about educational achievement were to be delivered, tools were needed to express goals and monitor programs for their attainment. Bloom's Taxonomy, on its own, wasn't adequate.

MEASURING RESULTS OF LEARNING TRANSACTIONS

A **taxonomy** is a presentation method commonly used to **classify information and/or knowledge,** a tool for describing educational content. Bloom's Taxonomy establishes six levels that represent the extent or degree of sophistication for an academic course objective, performance standard, or actual student achievement. These levels are intended to classify the extent of knowledge and related degrees of skill acquired by students as they progress through school. Thus, typical, rudimentary first-grade instruction in a subject might be at level 1 or 2 while a high-achieving high school senior or college student might be expected to reach the greatest depth or degree of content-area knowledge, which would be level 6 under Bloom's Taxonomy.

Note that these references are to typical, traditional school curricula. The traditional application of these measures, as noted earlier, tend to ignore natural student intelligence and instinct. Instead, they are generally confined, or limited, to typical academic achievement levels, thereby accomplishing what is often described as a "dumbing down" of students. Now, to avoid blaming the messenger in this instance, let's recognize that Bloom's Taxonomy is a valid measurement tool that can provide vital guidance in an era of widespread interest in upgrading our schools. The six levels of Bloom's Taxonomy are:

1. Awareness
2. Understanding/Comprehension
3. Application
4. Analysis
5. Synthesis
6. Evaluation

APPLYING BLOOM'S TAXONOMY

To apply a taxonomy to levels of knowledge or skill acquired through learning transactions, think of the set of numeric values as part of a chart in which the first level is at the bottom and the sixth is at the top. These levels track acquisition of knowledge about a specific subject or academic discipline. That is, the Bloom's scale might measure degree of knowledge in math, language, science, or other area—but never across disciplines or knowledge segments within disciplines.

To illustrate, consider knowledge and skill in language. A toddler is aware of language from shortly after birth. Bloom's level 1 could apply from the point at which a child begins ascribing meaning to sounds uttered personally or by care givers through the acquisition of simple, basic words. At this level, the child is still short of phrase or sentence building.

Level 2 would cut in even before the child's preschool experience, extending to the ability to form phrase and sentences and to hold rudimentary conversations.

Level 3 might begin with telling or hearing or relating simple stories and extend to recognition of printed words, relating them to objects or images, and possibly to drawing those images and printing some words. For children who are natural learners, this stage might encompass rudimentary reading and writing and run through the ability to read simple stories and write basic descriptions of objects or experiences. However, at this level, reading and writing are not essential. Language comprehension and use, skills attained by most children, are the key elements of achievement.

Level 4 would incorporate the ability to read or listen to relatively complex presentations and break them down into understandable components. A Level 4 student would be able to explain meanings of ideas to which the learner is exposed so that peers or persons with either lower or higher levels of sophistication could understand.

Level 5 calls for synthesis, the point at which a person can relate multiple ideas or concepts already known and understood to express or describe a larger idea. Making up stories or relating ideas from different sources are examples of synthesis. For example, a student might be able to make up and tell stories that are adaptations of fables that have been read to him or her by adults.

Level 6 involves evaluation in language presentations. Persons who present critical reviews of political, literary, theatrical, or societal statements are operating at this highest level on the Bloom's scale. For classroom purposes, the highest, or evaluation, level is reached when a student can intelligently compare the works of different writers, possibly in a critical essay.

BLOOMING REALITY

Applying this Bloom*ing* evaluation tool to the experience of the hypothetical first grader cited earlier, it's readily apparent that almost any six-year-old kid should be able to process language-borne information and ideas at a level of perhaps 3 or 4. A bright, precocious kid might even weigh in with a level 5 rating.

Now consider language-related teaching (certainly not learning) transactions in grades 1 and 2. Think about the degree of required sophistication and information-integration skills. On that basis, where would you put the language program to which this hypothetical child is exposed? If you said 3 or 4, you estimated way too high. How about a 1 or 2? This is the typical rating assigned to introductory language instruction content by qualified people asked for impartial judgments.

This kind of practice inevitably leads many critics to comment about the "dumbing down" of instruction and, as a result, children.

ONE SIZE DOESN'T FIT ALL

How bad are things when it comes to challenging the intelligence potential of American students? In considering an answer to such a question, it's hard to know where to begin. For one thing, bear in mind that Bloom's Taxonomy is limited to a single discipline. It is suitable for application to only one dimension of learning achievement at a time, be it an academic discipline or a performance competency. Thus, if you wanted to prepare a graphic showing a student's profile, you would wind up with a series of bar charts unrelated to one another. As shown in Figure 2-1, you'd be looking at a series of parts that resist combination into a composite picture of the standing of the whole child. Extensive research, backed by practical common sense, establishes that today's jobs and career opportunities are multidisciplinary in nature. When today's students eventually go to work, their performance will be judged largely on their ability to integrate multiple dimensions of knowledge into their lifelong learning and decision making activities.

For a number of decades, this single, linear form of measurement sufficed; it did everything that educators required in their communication about the relative sophistication of achievements and/or course offerings. However, for a world in which the primary goal is to prepare students to assume adult roles, Bloom's Taxonomy by itself is not sufficient to represent the multidisciplinary challenges of the modern workplace. This is because Bloom's Taxonomy is a one-dimensional measuring system in a world that requires multidimensional development and performance from our future adults.

To illustrate, suppose a student is asked to describe relationships between literary works, fine arts, music, and architecture as they reflect the growth of democracy or the incidence of wars during an era, Bloom's Taxonomy, used in its traditional, single-dimension format, is not suitable as an evaluation tool.

The Bloom's method could be used to represent multidis-

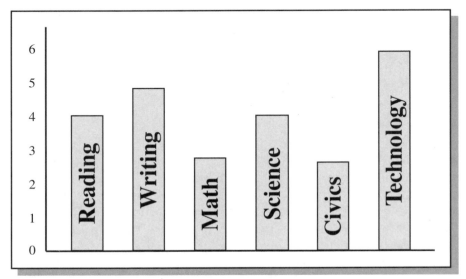

FIGURE 2-1. BLOOM'S TAXONOMY IS LIMITED TO EVALUATION OF A SINGLE DIMENSION OF ACHIEVEMENT. THERE IS NO CAPACITY FOR A MULTIDIMENSIONAL UNDERSTANDING OF A STUDENT'S CAPABILITIES OR POTENTIAL.

ciplinary knowledge only if content is predefined. For example, a single scale could be used to represent a composite of capabilities in areas such as math and physics or, separately, in comparative French and English literature. Under such applications, the highest levels of achievement represent cross-topical analytical capabilities. As another example, a person with a level 4 knowledge base in math may also develop expertise in preparation of business budgets. Even if such ratings were attempted, it would be difficult, if not impossible, to represent all the facets of a student's learning achievements or performance potentials in a single number on the Bloom's scale.

Therein lies a major shortcoming. ***People are not one dimensional in their intellectual makeup. They hold complex combinations of beliefs, capabilities, acquired knowledge, and variable motivational levels.*** In other words, every person—each child in every school—is a unique individual. In guiding students and evaluating their progress, we can no longer rely on one-size-fits-all academic programming or fixed curricula that apply to all students. We need a way to recognize and encourage individuality. Among other benefits, a multidimensional evaluation and measurement capability can be a powerful tool in breaking the time-based constraints that now limit and inhibit just about everything that happens in education.

SPREADING OUT

These Bloom's shortcomings surfaced during a multi-year, ongoing project initiated by ICLE in 1992. Massive amounts of data were accumulated on educational practices and achievements from as many as 16 countries. The purpose was to measure accomplishments and to identify strengths and weaknesses of American schools, then to pinpoint areas where restructuring and improvement could be deemed necessary if American education was to compete in a multinational marketplace.

One objective for the study was to develop a technique to enlarge the Bloom's single-number rating with graphic representation of the collected data. The purpose was to demonstrate the difference in content emphasis and applied skills achieved by respective curricula. In the 1992 analysis, the challenge was to show how countries like Japan, Germany, Denmark, and China were stressing practical, work-related applications of acquired knowledge while American schools maintained their longstanding emphasis on theoretical, academic content.

To establish a broader basis for demonstrating both the

practical, application value of acquired knowledge and to show, at the same time, achievements in traditional, academic content, the ICLE staff added a new dimension to create a model with broader range than Bloom's taxonomy. A second classification system was established, this one based on the application, or practical, value of acquired knowledge and skills. This application-based evaluation model, created in 1992 by Dr. Willard Daggett, uses five categories:

1. Demonstrate knowledge of one discipline.
2. Apply knowledge in discipline.
3. Apply knowledge across disciplines.
4. Apply knowledge to real-world predictable situations.
5. Apply knowledge to real-world unpredictable situations.

At the time, the Daggett Application Model was, as has been true for the entire ICLE educational enhancement program, a work in progress. Accordingly, the model was renamed more appropriately and expanded on the basis of experience in the course of subsequent work. Currently, the designation for the graphic technique for representing concurrent achievements in knowledge and application skills is the **Relational Model.** This name comes from a computer-oriented database structure, a method that establishes files for multiple, unique, related, sets of data, then extracts and relates information from multiple files to produce meaningful, related information. In computer parlance, separate sets of data that can be processed and accessed concurrently are called **relations.** The dimensions of this Relational Model are designated as the Knowledge Axis and the Application Axis.

The ICLE Relational Model also expands the number of levels in the Application Axis from five to six. The sixth level is for **Innovation.** Though the illustrations covering pre-1996 comparisons still use the five-level application scale, the sixth is being added to new and future projects. Innovation goes beyond the problem-solving implications of Level 5 (Apply to Unpredictable Situations) to include such capabilities as predicting or anticipating future problems or creating entirely new products or procedures to enhance a process or improve services to customers. Also encompassed in this sixth level are literary and artistic creations.

MAPPING EDUCATIONAL CONTENT

Along the Application axis, level 1, for knowledge of one unique discipline, matches the Bloom's (Knowledge axis) bottom-level rating, for awareness of a single subject. To demonstrate relative comparability between basic knowledge and applied skill as an educational outcome, the ICLE staff devised the chart format shown in Figure 2-2. This structures the Knowledge (Bloom's) axis on a vertical scale while the skills of the Application axis are represented on a horizontal scale at the bottom of the chart. For program evaluation, a series of content areas, individuals, or groups of people can be assessed to determine where, within this spectrum, the content or performance level fits. For each response, a mark is placed on the graph in the appropriate location. The collection of these marked positions is called a ***scattergraph.***

As an evaluation aide, the graphed area is divided into four quadrants, A through D. The greater the current relevance of an educational curriculum, the greater the portion of area D will be encompassed within a scattergraph representation of educational achievement.

In its initial application, this system was used to establish meaningful, dramatic comparisons between curriculum content in the United States, Europe, and Asia. Evaluations were collected from thousands of constituents in each geographic region. These evaluations were marked as points on respective scattergraphs. Then curves were drawn to represent the esti-

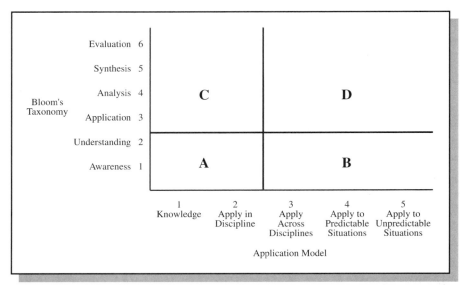

FIGURE 2-2. GRAPH FORM USED TO CHART EDUCATIONAL ACHIEVEMENTS ON THE RELATIONAL MODEL TO SHOW BASIC KNOWLEDGE AND PRACTICAL APPLICATION SKILLS.

mated areas of content coverage. Results are illustrated in Figures 2-3 through 2-5. Figure 2-3 represents topical content for an average United States curriculum. Figure 2-4 reflects similar evaluations by observers of the European curriculum, while Figure 2-5 models curriculum content in Asia.

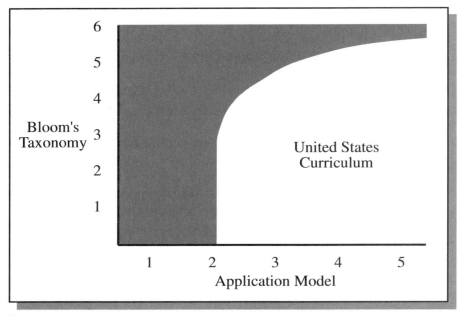

FIGURE 2-3. KNOWLEDGE-SKILL RELATIONSHIPS, UNITED STATES CURRICULA.

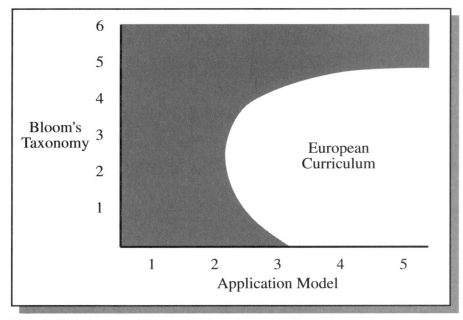

FIGURE 2-4. KNOWLEDGE-SKILL RELATIONSHIPS, EUROPEAN CURRICULA.

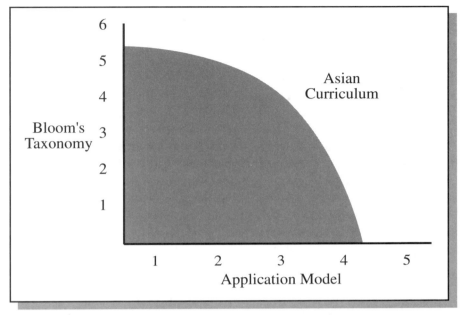

FIGURE 2-5. KNOWLEDGE-SKILL RELATIONSHIPS, ASIAN CURRICULUM.

COMPARISON TOOL

These charts compare and demonstrate significant differences among curricula. The curve for the European survey approximately parallels the American model but encompasses greater areas of application relevance at the lower and upper ends. This reflects the greater emphasis on vocational education and apprenticeship programs common in Europe.

By comparison, the chart for Asian schools reflects the culture and discipline typical for that part of the world. The graph shows solid coverage in both basic knowledge and application relevance, but within a more limited range. The Asians evidently place less emphasis than Americans and Europeans on the ability to evaluate acquired information or to apply analyses to unpredictable situations. This would seem to reflect a cultural focus on organizational values and loyalties, creating a society in which few people question authority or established customs.

RELATIONAL MODEL AS PLANNING TOOL

Within projects aimed at educational change and improvement, ICLE Relational Model graphs are used regularly as part of programs for management of change to chart both current status and targeted achievements. The questions addressed:

Where are we?

Where do we want to—or must we— be?

Evaluations are sought from a wide range of participants, including all adult constituencies: parents, community leaders, business advisers, teachers, administrators, and any consultants who may be involved. Scattergraphs are prepared for each of the competencies identified for the program under development. For each competency, separate profile graphs are prepared to depict current and desired achievements.

To demonstrate, Figure 2-6 is a graph of composite data gathered at 10 geographically scattered pilot sites in Michigan under a project initiated and monitored by the state legislature and managed by ICLE. Note that the configuration of the curve in Figure 2-6 is similar to the one for the United States in Figure 2-3. However, the Michigan curve for then-current achievement levels shows a greater coverage of applied skills, possibly because of extensive vocational education programs to prepare students for work in heavily industrialized areas.

In extreme contrast with the existing picture depicted in Figure 2-6, Figure 2-7 represents responses to questions on where constituents felt the content of Michigan school curricula **should** lie. In effect, respondents indicated a desire to deliver results that are almost directly opposite of what they are currently getting.

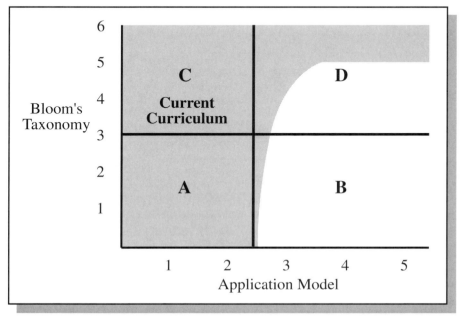

FIGURE 2-6. GRAPH REPRESENTING EVALUATION OF EXISTING EDUCATION SYSTEMS IN TEN MICHIGAN DISTRICTS.

Figure 2-7 reflects the kinds of requirements identified by constituents in scores of districts across the country where the same kinds of evaluations have been made and continue to be made. The message is clear: Constituents expect a greater degree of practical skills from graduates of their schools.

An important caveat: This finding, and any others that might emanate from an educational restructuring project should assume an underlying requirement that is so obvious that public recitation is sometimes overlooked. That is, the American public demands, first and foremost, that students acquire high competencies in areas of basic education—language, computation, science, citizenship, and culture and art. Acquisition of practical skills must be added to this knowledge base, for which quality and achievement levels have to be vastly improved. Virtually nothing can be accomplished educationally if schools fail to impart competencies in the standard academic basics, those referred to as core courses in the *Prisoners of Time* report. In other words, students can't apply knowledge and skills they don't have and haven't gained from their educational experiences.

It follows also that, where significant numbers of students are found to be deficient in basic reading, writing, and computational skills—and where a school is committed to eliminating social promotions—high priority remediation efforts must kick

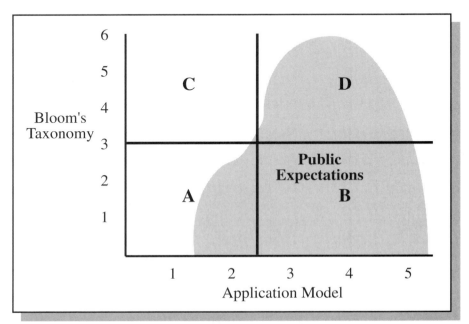

FIGURE 2-7. THIS GRAPH REPRESENTS RESULTS MICHIGAN RESPONDENTS WOULD LIKE TO SEE FROM THEIR SCHOOLS.

in. One approach for accomplishing this is to conduct PAR programs during the latter part of the school day. This option is covered in Chapter 1 and elaborated in a subsequent chapter. Nothing meaningful can occur in the delivery of results like those diagrammed in Figure 2-7 unless adequate proficiencies in language, math, science, and technology are present to form a strong foundation.

Crash programs in literacy can be highly effective if their purpose is clearly understood and participants are constructively motivated. Unless basic academic competencies are achieved, drastic measures may be necessary to avoid conditions in which unprepared students inhibit progress of a class or school's entire population. Further still, skills like those demanded in the Michigan survey cannot be achieved unless a basic knowledge foundation is established. The most effective way of achieving this end is through a commitment to a learning orientation for each school and every classroom.

CHARACTERISTICS OF THE LEARNING EXPERIENCE

Any time a student acquires knowledge, learning happens; an educational transaction is *perfected.* A completely individual experience has taken place. A single student in a group of 20 may be the only one who has achieved a learning experience. Or, some others might learn too, but not the same idea or information in exactly the same way.

Some learning, of course, does involve groups. An assembly line in a factory requires coordination, as does execution of a play by a football team. But even then, each worker or player must master a different role and set of responsibilities, in a different way, with different intellectual equipment and capabilities.

RECOGNIZING INDIVIDUALITY

Education, if it is to happen effectively, must recognize and accommodate every learner's individuality while also building an understanding of demands for teamwork in the workplace and in society as a whole. Of necessity, education is universal and multidimensional. But the basic process that underlies educational achievement is individual learning.

The special property of the approach to learning proposed in this book is that individual learning becomes the driving force of education. Acquisition of knowledge is approached from a direction opposite to that pursued in many classic, teaching-oriented systems. Teaching happens in a top-down order; initiative comes from the teacher and is directed downward—too often condescendingly—toward a group of students. As long as teaching takes the form of a group presentation, there is no sure way of knowing how much or what knowledge is being understood or absorbed, by which students—and also no way of assuring or assigning responsibility for educational achievement.

When learning becomes the driving force for acquiring knowledge and for skillbuilding, the process follows a bottom-up route. That is, the student's application of human senses both guides and controls acquisition of knowledge. This approach recognizes that each student, no matter how large the group in which he or she is positioned, learns differently and at an individual pace.

HOW LEARNING HAPPENS

Regardless of how information is presented, each student functions individually in using human senses to incorporate new content into an existing, continually growing body of knowledge. All of the five senses—hearing, sight, touch, smell, and taste—can play roles in the learning process. However, three of these senses predominate where acquisition of knowledge is involved:

1. **Hearing.** It is the student who converts sounds such as the spoken voice to meaningful information. The most common application of hearing to the acquisition of knowledge, at least in school settings, is the spoken lecture. Ideally, discussions or exchanges among students, with faculty coordinating or facilitating rather than lecturing, should play an ever-increasing role.

2. **Sight.** Visual stimuli can generate information on their own or can be combined with spoken messages to add a dimension to the learning process. In education, the most common sight-learning experiences are reading or viewing pictorial and/or projected images.

3. **Touch or feeling.** Some people and certain skills require an act of doing, a physical dimension, to establish or perhaps reinforce the acquisition of knowledge. A piano player acquires skill by playing and replaying a musical piece. A basketball player may shoot hoops for hours each day to enhance scoring percentages. Skills such as spelling and math are reinforced and enhanced through written exer-

cises. Skill in writing is enhanced by practice; a kind of mental dexterity evolves as a person produces written messages that communicate with pre-identified audiences which, in turn, provide feedback and criticism that enhance further learning and skillbuilding. Writing practice, unfortunately, is one of the underemployed curriculum elements in many schools. This is a double pity because practice in writing enhances skills in reading as well.

The senses of smell and taste also lead to acquisition of knowledge. But these senses are less active in a school-centered environment, since it is possible for learning to happen without these senses being applied.

A skill that is critical to learning and is related to—but is not a direct part of—the sense of touch is **speech.** Speaking is a doing-type skill in the same sense as writing, playing a piano, or dribbling a basketball. Speaking applies knowledge and, in doing so, requires references to the student's mental memory and also helps to reinforce existing knowledge. Thus, **there are really four natural activities or functions involved in the process of learning—hearing, sight, touch, and speech.**

Though it is possible for a knowledge-acquisition experience to encompass use of all four functions, it is also possible for information to be transferred when only one, two, or three of the four primary learning skills are applied. In some instances, there is no choice. People who lack or are deficient in primary senses such as sight or hearing can compensate by applying the capabilities they have more intensely. One universal characteristic of a learning process is that the student controls the application and degree to which knowledge is registered through variable use of sensory-based skills, whether they are applied individually or in combination.

For example, a student learning arithmetic will typically be exposed to a spoken description of how to perform a multiplication problem. As part of the same learning process, the student will also receive visual stimuli through a textbook, by watching a teacher solve problems on the board, or both. Then, the same student will apply the sense of touch to complete written exercises that replicate the work done by the teacher and/or observed in print. In addition, speech reinforcement opportunities may be introduced through class recitations.

Learning takes place. But there is no way to know for certain the extent to which use of each of the four sensory tools contributes to the student's understanding of the principles and methods and/or the retention of the lessons in memory. The point, rather, is that a rounded experience involving use of all four sensory functions does promote the acquisition and mastery of knowledge.

Note the interaction in this example. The student has controlled acquisition of knowledge through use of sensory-based skills, even though there is no way for a teacher or tutor to know which skills were most vital in the learning process. In this arithmetic experience, use of all three prime senses is required and use of speech in class recitations also may be added. But this doesn't necessarily mean that all of these traits are equally important or that they are used in a specific sequence or relationship. To the contrary, each individual student uses his or her own sensory skills in unique combinations. Thus, as long as the classroom experience involves application of multiple skills, the student is free to learn in a personal pattern that is completely individual.

INDIVIDUALITY IN LEARNING

The above is a simplified description limited to the effects of external stimuli on a highly complex process called learning. Learning doesn't happen until the senses deliver their acquired information to the brain, where extensive processing takes place. A large part of why learning is so individual results from the totally different capacities and memory content within each person's brain. Factors that affect learning include:

> Intellectual capacities vary widely. Involved here are a number of elements that encompass intelligence, attitude, and focus of attention at the given moment when a stimulus is presented.

> Each person "bounces" newly acquired information or ideas off an existing knowledge base, which is an accumulation of retained impressions from a lifetime of experience and intellectual exposures.

> Based on acuity of senses and formed habits, each individual has a different approach to or style of learning.

Problems arise when a teaching methodology abridges opportunities to apply sensory-based learning by limiting exposures and opportunities available to students—and by setting standards that **assume all students can master the same content in** *the same way, at the same time,* a blatant impossibility. This kind of obstruction is particularly common in prevailing methods of language instruction. While standard arithmetic lessons apply the three main sensory skills and often add recitation practice, language instruction generally lacks this kind of balance. This shortcoming is critical because *language is the avenue traveled in all student learning experiences and opportunities.*

FOR EXAMPLE: PHONICS AND FUNCTIONAL ILLITERACY

To demonstrate, consider a hypothetical but typical experience in reading instruction. The teacher introduces a lesson by stressing phonic sounds for portions of words, then demonstrates by reading words built from these phonic components. The lesson may consist of words only or may include sentences and stories that use the target vocabulary. Students may be told to study the lesson at home; or they may go directly into oral recitations in class, with students taking turns reading the lesson materials for a minute or so each.

Recitation time, the key exercise that adds a "doing" dimension to typical reading instruction, is limited by the size of the class. Thus, if there are 20 students at a lesson, there probably will not be time for everyone to have a turn at each class reading session, and those who do read may be limited to one or a few sentences. Again, the time constraint is a major culprit. Students and teachers alike are prisoners of class schedules and hours available in the school day.

Compare the elements of this experience with the arithmetic example. Participation in a reading lesson requires hearing and seeing, speaking only occasionally, with the possibility that there will be no "doing" type experience at all. Allowing that learning results from and is reinforced through practice, the limitations of established reading instruction methods are obvious and costly in terms of their contribution to the functional illiteracy that can evolve. Students who do not practice reading on their own, possibly at home, simply do not have an adequate opportunity to master their language.

Is there any wonder, then, that a significant number of young adults in America—in some schools as many as 30- or 40-plus percent—test out as functional illiterates? This generally is accepted to mean that their reading comprehension capabilities are insufficient to enable them to cope with the required financial and social responsibilities of society at large or to support the learning requirements of today's technological workplace.

This functional illiteracy stems only in small part from lack of reading recitation time. A far deeper problem results in large measure from the very existence of a curriculum that separates reading from the rest of language communication. Adding further to the problem is the teaching-oriented methodology used in reading instruction.

Sadly, low achievement levels in reading would seem to indicate that the teaching approach that has dominated the American education system has done irreparable damage to the potential of too many students. Affected are the abilities to communicate and to absorb knowledge and skills through use of language. One reason is that communication is a rounded, multifaceted process. Facility as a communicator requires extensive practice in a series of skills—reading, writing, listening, and speaking, with reading and writing proficiencies and the ability to decode symbols or graphic images closely linked.

When reading is isolated as a separate instructional subject, the probability of attaining communication proficiency is inhibited greatly. In elementary-level reading instruction as presently constituted in many schools, training typically concentrates on syllabic enunciation of phonetic word segments and pronunciation of words. This is not necessarily bad. The ability to decipher and pronounce words is an important initial skill on the way to becoming a proficient reader. This means that phonics can be a valid starting point, just as spelling is a prerequisite to proficiency in writing. But phonics is not anything like a final objective.

However, under many phonics programs, students do not progress from this beginning to the ability to derive meaning from and interpret what they read. There is little or no emphasis in typical phonics-based programs on analysis or response to message content of the material that is read. Thus, a student might well earn an A grade in reading and still not understand the meaning of the words that are enunciated. The student may have little or no ability to read and understand text in an academic content area, as happens when students who don't understand word problems in math are diagnosed as needing help in arithmetic. The academic fragmentation practiced commonly in many schools ignores the reality that language communication **requires** multiple, coordinated skills that **must** include capabilities for transmitting and receiving information and ideas via verbal channels.

In an effort to deal with the limitations of a purely phonics approach to reading instruction, some educators devised and espoused a method known as **whole language.** Instruction through whole language techniques is based upon word recognition, with the meanings of words introduced as sight-recognition capabilities increase. One source of problems has come with a widespread belief that these methods are mutually exclusive, that a class instructed in whole language doesn't need or shouldn't have lessons dealing with phonics.

The reality, we at ICLE believe, is that kids need all the help they can get. Our stipulation is that the purpose of language and the ultimate test of instructional programs lies in the ability of students to achieve communication through reading and writing. Further, our experience indicates that coordination of instruction in reading and writing—as well as in listening and speaking—enhances total language communication skills.

A TOOL FOR PLANNING AND MONITORING LEARNING PROGRESS

A person entering the workplace is expected to be able to communicate with peers and supervisors, to follow instructions, and react to encountered conditions. Therefore, rounded, balanced communication capabilities must become a target for learning-oriented curricula. Task forces overseeing educational change must **both** set high expectations and assess progress to assure that all students have a fair chance of meeting those expectations.

Toward this end, the Relational Model provides an ideal management tool. To make this point, consider that Bloom's Taxonomy has, for years, been useful in rating progress in reading alone. It's relatively simple to classify a student as a level 3 or level 5 reader with confidence that colleagues within the system can interpret such ratings readily. When expectations broaden to encompass overall communication capabilities, the Bloom's scale becomes inadequate. However, the Relational Model does provide a method for integrating and displaying multidimensional knowledge and skill levels that cut across disciplines and indicate a level of understanding that encompasses practical applications of knowledge. The model also provides a medium for recognizing creativity through the level 6 Innovation dimension.

To illustrate, Figure 2-8 presents a graph that could be used for reports on both expectations for language communications achievements for all students and accomplishments for specific individuals. This graph represents the kind of capabilities employers will be seeking from now on, capabilities that are beyond the reach of students when reading is isolated as a separate discipline.

MONITORING ACHIEVEMENT

Given availability of a mechanism to set learning goals and to report on achievements, the next logical question is: How do we assess student progress within a learning-oriented school environment?

One answer: We don't cling indefinitely to narrowly focused multiple-choice tests that measure a student's ability to collect facts rather than requiring a display of comprehension and interpretive skills. The multiple-choice test has been the standard—and a major limitation—in education for at least 60 years. And where has it gotten us? Answer: We have created an environment in which students develop cunning in analyzing and determining what responses are expected on multiple-choice questions. A potential for even greater damage exists when children are conditioned, probably unwittingly, to believe that **there is only one correct answer to each question.** As graduates

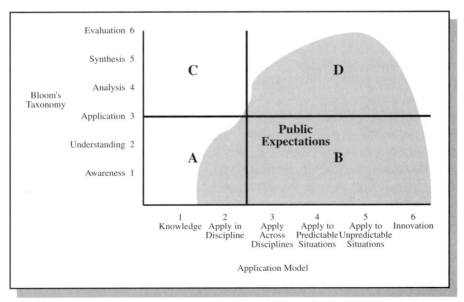

FIGURE 2-8. THE RELATIONAL MODEL HAS THE DIMENSIONAL REACH TO REPRESENT LEARNING ACQUISITION THROUGH READING AND WRITING ASSIGNMENTS THAT ENCOMPASS MULTIPLE DISCIPLINES, AS WELL AS A MEASURE OF CREATIVITY.

enter a world of diversity and innovation, they need all the flexibility and adaptability they can muster.

The ease of preparing and mechanically grading multiple-choice tests has created a major ambiguity in American education: American students are, hands down, the most tested in the world. However, they are also the least evaluated in terms of relationships between academic activities and the applied proficiencies they are expected to acquire in preparation for adulthood.

Most tested … and least evaluated? Look at the "most tested" facet first. What do tests do for American students and educators? A number of descriptors come to mind: stress, cramming, belligerence, intergenerational friction, heartbreak. Those few (and many more could certainly be added) convey the idea. Also try: indictment.

How can American kids be both most tested and least evaluated? It isn't easy. But American education has succeeded with the seemingly impossible, separating the keeping of score from the performance being rated.

If student evaluation is unsatisfactory, what's the purpose of all the testing? The answer, sadly, is that testing does a number of things for American education, achieving purposes other than evaluation or guidance in restructuring curricula for greater effectiveness. The following three are most significant.

1. ***Testing provides a mechanism for selecting and sorting students.*** At an early age, the great majority of American students take a battery of tests that will usually set a course that will guide the rest of their lives—all from a series of pencil strokes on special answer sheets. Within education, test scores function much like a switching yard for a railroad. Is this analogy extreme? Answer for yourself. American schools now accommodate some 28 to 30 million K-12 students. The millions who enter for the first time or transfer from one school to another in any given year come to their schools as strangers. Since it is impossible for administrators and testers to get to know and evaluate each student individually, it is inevitable that classroom placements be based on some objective measurement tool. Far too often for many observers, however, these cursorily evaluated students are placed in academic programs that guide substantial portions of their educational careers.

2. ***Tests are used for auditing school quality and perfor-***

mance for accountability purposes. Assumption: If all or most of the kids in a given school test below an anticipated norm, there must be something wrong with the school as an organization and with the teachers and administrators who run it. There are ample supplies of tar and feathers to cover one and all. Since some students and schools do well on standardized tests, those who do less well are automatically judged less deserving.

3. ***Tests can be used to evaluate and improve instruction and curricula.*** Standardized tests are monuments to the status quo. The culture of standardized testing defies responsiveness to educational challenges or changing needs. Processing and grading of test sheets is generally an off-premises operation with no reaction or feedback provided to schools other than raw, uninterpreted grades. Individuals have no way of knowing which questions they answered correctly or incorrectly. For classes or schools as a whole, the grade reports deal in averages, providing little or no guidance on where curriculum modification or remedial instruction could benefit students. Clearly, some other, more responsive approach to measuring and evaluating student achievements on a timely enough basis to guide revision of teaching/learning processes would be handy. That method, which can and should coexist with standardized testing, is interactive qualitative assessment.

OVERLAPPING NEEDS

A point of clarification: This is not the opening shot of a campaign to do away with standardized, multiple-choice testing. That would be like throwing out the baby with the bath water. Standardized academic tests do have an established and ongoing value within American education. It's just that they fall short of meeting total, fairly balanced needs for measuring achievement levels, particularly in a school committed to a learning orientation.

Standardized multiple-choice tests are generally accepted as indices of how well students can be expected to perform in colleges. If this assumption is true, why is it that only 42 percent of students graduate from the four-year colleges that accept them as freshmen, primarily on the basis of their test scores? At the same time, however, it seems fair to recognize that multiple-choice tests cannot be held solely responsible. Part of the college dropout problem may result from lowered admission standards.

In addition, college-entry requirements have been reduced significantly and frequently in recent years as financially strapped schools seek to fill empty seats generated by zealous building programs that created surplus capacities. (The number of seats open to college freshmen has increased by some 800 percent since the end of World War II.)

Quantitative, multiple-choice testing was adequate and satisfactory for a system that stressed the same basics featured throughout its decline over the past several decades. Those multiple-choice tests are still essential because they are relied on as the main basis for evaluations and decisions by college admissions officers and governmental funding agencies. Another potential negative is that standardized, multiple-choice tests that require one correct answer to each question contribute to an environment of *form over substance.* The constraints of having prepare for and pass tests can also encourage faculties to *teach a syllabus rather than students.* Students must become and remain the focus of all educational activities.

Realization that there is more to student potential than test scores has led many admissions officials at prestigious colleges to broaden the measures they apply to incoming freshmen.

THE NEED FOR QUALITATIVE ASSESSMENT

Other assessment methods are needed when a school makes a transition to a learning orientation aimed at preparing students for the adult roles they will ultimately have to assume. To evaluate the ability of students to apply their acquired knowledge, qualitative, analytical, performance-based assessment methods are necessary. These assessments should be administered as part of a school's learning program and should be a direct extension of instruction. In this way, results can be known to students and educators immediately so that remediation or curriculum adjustment decisions can be reached while there is still time for students to benefit.

Within a program aimed at promoting learning, some form of testing that permits students to demonstrate their progress in multidisciplinary areas that conform to the expectations of the Relational Model should be part of any program aimed at stimulating student learning. Methods for implementing a learning orientation in the classroom and for progressive, qualitative assessment, are revisited and reviewed in depth in Chapter 11.

The intent here has been to implant an awareness and to build recognition for a need that marks what might become a major frontier of American education in the first part of the twenty-first century.

The chapter that follows discusses some processes by which people utilize and apply knowledge—how students put together the performances represented on graphs of the Relational Model.

Chapter 3
Assimilating Knowledge

Properly honed, knowledge becomes a sharp, productive, and readily marketable tool. The ability to apply knowledge practically and efficiently is a high-demand skill in an information-dependent society. The ICLE Relational Model recognizes and evaluates the knowledge-application relationship. This model has achieved wide acceptance and extensive use among educators committed to employability of their graduates as well as from business and government leaders who will depend on these students' future capabilities.

Several years of experience have established the model as a natural, valuable tool in the design and implementation of enhanced, socially responsive curricula. The model's primary value lies in its ability to project a graphic image that relates the degree of knowledge to the ability required to complete a given task.

CHALLENGING SUCCESS

Educationally, the Relational Model has provided a positive method for setting standards for curriculum content and student performance. Many thousands of educators have accepted the validity of the model and shaped their curricula and teaching strategies accordingly. With experience, however, questions have begun to appear:

❑ How does a curriculum design assure that a student who completes a given course of study will be able to internalize the acquired knowledge and use it to perform at the anticipated application level?

❏ In other words, where and how is the connection made between knowledge and performance?

❏ What criteria can be used to establish targeted application levels of a task or body of knowledge?

❏ What kind of pedagogy can help students bridge the gap between knowledge and performance?

Analysis of these questions leads to some obvious conclusions:

1. The connection between knowledge and performance is obvious because defined tasks couldn't be completed without requisite knowledge.

2. It doesn't follow automatically that a student who acquires knowledge will be able to apply it effectively or use that knowledge in real-world types of performances.

3. Pedagogically, it would be useful to define principles and methods to help students understand the power of lessons they have learned and be able to make the intellectual connections for use of knowledge in performance situations.

This line of thinking, which incidentally applies the principles behind the design of the Relational Model, has led to a conclusion that, pedagogically at least, there is a logical link that needs to be formed between acquisition and application of knowledge. As shown in Figure 3-1, we've elected to call this link *Process.*

Identification of the role of an intellectually based process as a connection between acquisition and application of knowledge led quickly to some new questions:

❏ Why is it important that students be able to connect knowledge and actions, or applications?

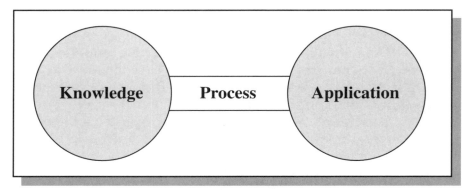

Figure 3-1. The connection between Knowledge and its Application is formed through use of a Process that uses intellectual logic.

❏   What are the elements of this process?
❏   How does it work?
❏   Does one process fit all needs or do teachers and students
        have to learn to use different or modified processes for dif-
        ferent situations?

MAPPING A ROUTE

Thinking about the first question in the group above led to some
obvious conclusions about the value of the Relational Model. A
tool like the model is needed because education is finally accommodating to the world of its clients and students, a world
undergoing constant, dynamic change. Bloom's Taxonomy de-
buted into a relatively stable environment. At that time, schools
could be content with acquisition by their students of a fixed
body of knowledge. In that world, students were judged by their
ability to absorb and respond to the relatively static presentation methods of the day. Knowledge stood on its own without
having to be applied or related to anything else. Mark the end of
a long-running chapter in that ongoing story!

Then came computers. Then, with their help, came international and multinational organizations and markets. Nothing
stood still. Change ruled. Suddenly, it mattered—mattered drastically—whether American kids could read and deal effectively
with numbers, scientific progress, and the growing ubiquity of
computers and their technological siblings. It certainly mattered
then if they lacked skills or experience to apply the knowledge
with which they entered the job market.

So, the answer to the first of the rhetorical questions above
is that the Relational Model is a way of establishing and demonstrating that a student can, in fact, apply knowledge to decisions and actions.

PROCESSES EVOLVE

The next two questions deal with the nature and functions of a
process. By its nature, a **process,** any process, acquires source
materials, handles or modifies them, and produces a product or
result that is different from, and also greater than, the sum of
its parts. To achieve this transition, a process applies a series of
steps. For example, the chapter that follows introduces a six-
step process for management of educational change, which involves a series of group-participation activities.

But processes also take place internally within the minds
of people faced with tasks or challenges. These processes are

intellectual in nature and can vary infinitely with the learning and thought patterns of individuals. Within the current context, for example, students apply processes to acquire and retain knowledge, solve problems, reach decisions, or demonstrate skills.

In committing to a learning-oriented environment, educators must be aware of both the need for and nature of processes that students should learn about and be able to call upon in acquiring and applying knowledge. The linkage between knowledge and its application is not automatic. In between are skills students must acquire, hopefully with coaching from committed faculty. One of these must involve learning to learn.

STUDYING AS AN ART

A well established study method of proven effectiveness was introduced during the 1950s under the designation **SQ3R.** This name stands for the steps in the process, **Survey, Question, Read, Recap,** and **Review.** Back when the technique was devised for high school and college students, it was intended for use with reading or research assignments. Assume, for example, that a student has been assigned to study a chapter in a textbook or cover a designated unit of published material.

The **survey** step involves an overview of the assignment to identify the general nature of its content and the way the material is segmented and/or organized. For example, the student should observe all headings and subheadings within the assigned document.

In the **question** step, the student relates the assignment to his or her existing knowledge base and thinks about how the new material will add to or alter his or her knowledge or opinions. Then the student devises informal questions for which he or she anticipates answers from the study assignment.

Keeping the questions in mind, the student **reads** the assignment.

Following the reading, the student writes a brief **recap** of the learning experience, including notes on specific, newly acquired information and also any associations or deductions that have been triggered in relating the new information to existing knowledge. In this sense, **relate** could be a fourth **r** of the knowledge-acquisition process.

The recap becomes a record of the learning experience. When the information has to be **reviewed** for further work, or for a test, the student can reinforce knowledge through a re-examination of the notes rather than requiring a complete re-reading of the source material.

Does this process or set of activities sound familiar? Almost surely it is a much earlier incarnation of the methods being applied today in thousands of middle and high schools for the building of student portfolios. For those who might need encouragement or reinforcement, this observation may serve to justify the accumulation of a portfolio. Or, perhaps more to the point, the written recaps of study experiences might provide a constructive way to guide students in the accumulation and maintenance of a portfolio to help them achieve maximum performance.

Notice use in the previous sentence of the word **guide.** The references above and the discussions in the rest of this chapter use terms such as **process, framework,** or **algorithm** to describe pedagogical methods that promote learning and application of knowledge. It is also intended that, in promoting learning, these methods will help teachers to shed some of the constraints of traditional instructional techniques. Therefore, a caveat: **Don't be tempted to use the techniques described here as molds rather than models.** An effective learning environment should promote flexibility of thought and method for both teacher and student. The idea is to guide students while they are permitted to seek their own pathways to knowledge. Don't be tempted, particularly if you have survived under a rigid teaching-oriented structure for a number of years, to treat these suggestions as mandates.

Bear in mind also that models or guidelines have to be adapted to individual or developmentally based student situations. Specifically, the processes covered here are designed to promote the acquisition of knowledge. Be aware that it is up to a facilitating, coaching teacher to understand that knowledge acquisition is transient in nature. To become imbedded in a person's body of knowledge, new material must be recalled and used, with some regularity. Even if knowledge acquisition is rendered more efficient through a learning approach, people still forget. **Knowledge not used may be lost.** Thus, it is up to a resourceful teacher to structure requirements for students to recall and apply lessons so they will be retained and will contribute to the students' continuing growth.

Also be aware that student development is ongoing. As related or new material in a given discipline is covered, be aware that the students will be more sophisticated as they mature.

Instructional plans and activities should mature and gain sophistication accordingly. The best indication that a teacher has succeeded may occur as students come up with ideas or interpretations that are not part of the instructional materials put before them. Just as our culture encourages achievement levels in which children surpass parents, teachers also should take pride in the intellectual growth of their charges. For this to happen, students should be made aware of their own knowledge acquisition and application functions and led through processes that extend their ability to apply what they know or learn.

APPLYING KNOWLEDGE

Knowledge, of course, comes from many sources; academic learning is just one small stimulant. Far more knowledge is encountered and absorbed in the course of everyday experiences. This is *informal learning,* an area under intense study in some quarters, with possible future implications for educators. A child doesn't study a book or listen to a lecture to learn that it's not a good idea to touch a hot stove or step into a street without looking to see if cars are coming. The lessons of burns or near-accidents are firmly impressed in memory and serve as guides to be applied in experiences that follow.

Things become more complicated when it comes to blending multiple knowledge elements into a finding or course of action, or when a person recognizes a gap in existing knowledge and has to figure out how to fill it. This, basically, is what happens in making the transition from knowledge to application within a relational experience. The process that applies to this kind of need calls for a series of steps that go beyond the study technique described earlier in this chapter.

To illustrate, consider the kind of challenge that might be presented to a high school class that deals with career and lifestyle planning:

> *After completing an interview and a performance test in word processing, you are offered a position as a word processing operator at a bank in a town located 75 miles from your present home. The job pays $11.50 per hour, which seems like a good starting wage. To take the job, you will have to move to a location near your work. You are interested in the position. But, before you accept the job, you need to find out what it will cost to live in the new location and determine if you would earn enough to be able to support yourself if you decide to accept the bank's offer. How will you go about de-*

ciding what you need to know, gathering the information you require, and reaching a decision?

Note that this assignment meets some key characteristics that identify an effective performance-based assessment exercise: The student does not have all of the needed information from past instruction or experience. Before the problem can be attacked at all, the student will have to identify information gaps and take steps to fill them. Also, the problem is open-ended in that there is no one correct answer. Rather, multiple, varying results are possible and the challenge put to the student is to explain the reasoning that leads to the selected answer.

The process that fits this kind of situation follows five steps, several of which are **recursive,** subject to repetition or iteration until all needed information is in hand and all relevant factors have been considered. The process steps:

1. Identify the task or problem. *[Should I take the job I've been offered?]*
2. Recall or retrieve personal knowledge about the task or problem. In effect, ask: What do I know about the situation? *[The job is in word processing. I completed the qualifying test before the bank made the offer. I can do the work and would find it interesting.]*
3. Identify new information needed to deal with the problem. Ask: What information do I need before I can make a decision? *[What real, take-home pay can I expect? How much rent will I have to pay? What would my living expenses be?]*
4. Combine new information with existing knowledge. What questions do I have to answer so I can reach a decision? To come up with answers, I may have to combine stuff I already knew with information I've just collected. *[Is the pay enough to cover my expenses and leave a little for recreation? If so, what will it be like to live in the new town? Will I be comfortable? Happy? What other problems might I run into if I move? What are the future prospects on this job? Will the rate of advancement satisfy me? Will I eventually be able to afford a car of my own? If the living costs seem high, can I save money by looking for a roommate or a rooming house? How will I feel about leaving my friends and family and moving to a new community?]*
4A. Repeat steps 2 through 4 as often as necessary to be sure you understand the consequences of the commitment you are asked to make. If necessary, seek more information—

from bank officials in this situation. When you think you have an answer, check it out with friends and family if you feel more comfortable seeking advice. Repeated review of this type is **recursive processing.**

5. Confirm your understanding of the situation, then communicate your decision.

This, basically, is an approach that can help students to make the connection between knowledge and application in learning-oriented situations. Depending on how far the teacher or counselor wants a student to go as a problem solver, trouble shooter, and decision maker, some variations of the above process may apply. Under real-world conditions, widely varying conflicts and obstacles may present themselves. Unknowns may not be so easy to identify and missing information may be more elusive. Some variations of applicable processes are described below.

APPLYING KNOWLEDGE—PROBLEM SOLVING

Everyone, students included, anticipates, faces, and solves problems every day, possibly on an hourly basis. Most of these problems are so minor that they are handled routinely, without any focused thought, identification, or evaluation. For example, there's a problem of what to wear today. Evaluations and reactions are routine. *Will it be cold or rainy? Will I be running a lot or will I need to look my best for an assembly?* These situations are so routine that they rarely merit any special study or serious thought. But they nonetheless offer a good example of how everyone has to anticipate and respond to everyday events. These examples also represent simple applications of experience-based knowledge.

Other problem-solution situations involve the setting of priorities for a person's time. *Do I do my algebra homework first or study for the history test? I've been invited to two parties. Which invitation do I accept? Which elective should I choose for next semester? Do I want to go to college or should I look for a job after high school?*

The variations can be virtually infinite. But all problems have one characteristic in common: They are initiated from an external source, originating outside the control of the affected individual. In most cases, at least those in which application of a logical process is needed, some action by the person faced with the problem is either necessary or desirable.

Job-related problem solving is a key example of the use of

the application of knowledge in the varying degrees represented by the Relational Model. This also holds true for performance-based, or integral, assessment exercises applied to learning-oriented courses. These assessments replicate challenges encountered and solutions devised in real life.

To illustrate, a fourth- or fifth-grade math class may be assigned to develop a route for an auto trip from a given point of origin to a destination. The students may be told that they have to arrive at the destination by a given time for a special event. The problem also may stipulate that the family wants to see certain sights along the way if possible. Using road maps, students are to identify alternate routes, give the distance for each, then determine the most desirable route and time of departure, figuring out whether time will permit side trips or stopovers for the identified sights.

As described in a later chapter dealing with math instruction, this kind of problem provides a good opportunity to guide students in the formulation of problem-solving algorithms, a skill with lifelong potential value, particularly later in their school experiences when they encounter application or programming of computers. In the travel instance, students would identify the answers they are required to derive, in this instance, the time of departure first and the feasible route second. Then they switch their attention to the given elements, in this instance the requisite time of arrival. In between, they consider alternate routes and consequences of each, settling on the solution that best meets their given objectives and priorities.

In business, employees face similar problems in manufacturing or customer-service situations. A manufacturing company, for example, must monitor supplies of parts or materials needed to build given products. The idea is to get the most production from the lowest feasible investment in inventories. If inventories are too large, costs of the goods—and the time it takes to bring them from a supply area to a manufacturing location—are too high. If supplies are not available when they are needed, the entire operation may be shut down. Each considered condition is a problem and each action a solution.

APPLYING KNOWLEDGE—TROUBLE SHOOTING

Problems like those described above are relatively routine. In most cases, the person can identify a requirement to make a decision or avoid a problem, then act routinely. A different kind of problem-solution process is encountered in **trouble shoot-**

ing, where something goes wrong, unexpectedly and often inconveniently or dangerously.

The challenge in trouble shooting is to *pinpoint* the problem, avoiding the temptation to guess at what's wrong and make the wrong fix. In the current climate, almost infinite possibilities exist to pose trouble shooting problems based on computer utilization. Typically, this kind of problem might begin with an assumption that the student turns on the computer at the beginning of a lab session and nothing happens. In devising this kind of trouble-shooting case, you can be as wild or far-fetched as you like and you still won't come close to the ridiculous encounters the industry experiences almost daily. It may even help to cite a story like the following, which really happened.

A customer called the service number for a company that markets computers by mail and reported that nothing happened when he turned his system on. The support person started by asking if the system was plugged in, the typical opening question. The answer: it was. Then the service person asked the customer to check the back of the machine to locate a circuit breaker and make sure it was set.

"I can't see back there," the customer reported. "It's too dark."

"Turn on a light, then," the service rep suggested.

"I can't," the customer advised, "we've had a total power failure here."

As the story was relayed, the service rep advised the customer to put the parts of the computer back in the boxes in which they arrived and return the whole thing to the manufacturer. The logic: There was no way the company could handle all of the troubles an individual like that was apt to report.

Seriously, now: In dealing with trouble shooting, there are many examples to be cited. The computer that won't boot is one. Another might be a car that won't start. Still another might be communication over the phone with a doctor about a physical pain or ailment.

The common trait for all trouble shooting problems and the process for dealing with them is that something unexpected has happened; there's been a change. Assume that the problem has occurred within the context of an ongoing operation or with a device that's used regularly. The algorithm for dealing with this kind of problem is straightforward and highly profitable for students to learn.

1. What actually happened? *[The computer didn't start up when*

I turned on the switch.]
2. Where did the problem occur? *[At the switch.]*
3. What's different about the current situation from your normal expectation? *[The screen didn't light up.]*
4. Is everything else normal? Did the disk drive operate normally? *[Yes.]*
5. Check the wire behind the monitor and make sure it's connected to the computer. *[Whoops! The cord was loose.]*

Again, the lesson is in identifying a need and tracing an algorithm. Understand what's supposed to happen, then trace conditions and functions from the source to the end point. Thus, if a light goes out, check the bulb before you change the fuse, etc. These examples may seem simple. But helping students to understand cause-and-effect logic represents one of the best investments in the future for both student and teacher. Effective problem-analysis skills will endear any worker to future employers and will go a long way toward qualifying the individual as a true lifelong learner.

APPLYING KNOWLEDGE—DECISION MAKING

Problem solving and decision making are mentioned in the same breath so often that many people connect the two as part of the same basic skill. Students properly trained in the processes for application of knowledge should know the difference and be able to match the appropriate process with any given challenge.

A **problem** results from an event or source external to the individual or his/her control. A **decision** responds to something the person wants to do or make happen. From another viewpoint, solving a problem is something the person **needs** to do. Making a decision represents something he or she **wants** to do. This implies different levels of requirement or urgency. Another important differential: **In making a decision, one of your options, always, is to do nothing.** If you are the originator of the idea, you can always elect to do without the object of your desire. Another differentiation: **Problems have solutions, decisions have consequences.** For instance, if the decision is whether or not to buy something, the consequence is an expense.

Serious Business

In dealing with students and decisions, a good point to impress upon them is: **Your skills as a decision maker will be criti-**

cal in guiding you through the rest of your life. They will play a vital part in determining the success and/or happiness you attain.

One way to prove this point is to find or, possibly with the help of community resource people, present cases involving career decisions. Point out that consequences of career choices can be enduring. The first career students choose on completing their education can influence their lives for a number of years, and may even limit their ability to change careers later in life. Yet it is also true that each individual may be faced with four to seven career changes during the course of a normal working lifespan. In other words, this is serious stuff and the more skilled a person is at decision making the more likely he or she will be to achieve success and/or satisfaction.

A typical algorithm that may be helpful in building an appreciation of decision making skills:

1. Prepare a decision statement that describes what you want to achieve. *[What's the best career choice for me?]*
2. What are my strengths and weaknesses? *[I like dealing with people. I have a good imagination. I don't enjoy working with my hands. I do okay at math but I don't enjoy it and could not see myself in a job where I had to use math to make a living.]*
3. What options should I consider and what are expectations and requirements of each? *[Doctor, attorney, psychologist, teacher.]*
4. The list can be infinite. But it is best to limit consideration to one or a few at a time. Each student should be required to research each seriously targeted possibility in depth, identifying both the positive and negative elements of each profession or career. For each option, stress the importance of exploring and considering seriously *both* the positive and negative consequences of each course. *[Doctors benefit humanity; but they may face emergency calls and extreme unpleasantness and disappointment in working with sick people. A teacher may find it satisfying to help children learn. But there can also be tension and organizational requirements that are difficult or discouraging.]*
5. Consider the positive and negative consequences you have identified for each option. Be ready to identify and describe these consequences and rate their importance to you. *[A medical education takes at least eight years and can involve major expense. Doctors may face annual costs of $100,000*

or more for malpractice insurance. Also consider supply and demand. Is the target occupation overpopulated at present or might it be in the near future?]

6. Research and report on what you would have to do to pre-pare for each profession or career you are considering. *[What's the prospect of college admission in a field being considered? What kind of student loans might be required and what will repayment mean to your future?]*

7. Narrow the field as much as you can and either commit or keep your options open by electing coursework that will qualify you to pursue the fields that remain interesting.

THE IMPORTANCE OF PROCESS TO STUDENTS

As stated up front in this chapter, students are apt to come up with infinite variations of thought processes for absorbing and applying knowledge. The process approaches described above are not intended as rigid guides, nor is it suggested that these are the only approaches or algorithms that might work. Rather, these examples should be thought starters and provide the ba-sis for presenting students with situations that will help them identify, personalize, and adapt approaches of their own.

Note also that a number of situational descriptions and methods include references to behaviors appropriate in busi-ness careers or jobs. The idea, of course, is that these examples emulate the directions in which today's students are headed. At the same time, though, it is necessary for the facilitating teacher to make these materials relevant at the level of maturity and sophistication of each group of students. There is no intent here to impose business ideas and methods that are above the needs or capabilities of any given group of students. Rather, the idea is to provide thought starters and guidelines for promoting learn-ing experiences that correspond with the levels and needs of students.

For students, methodology is not critical. Awareness is. A lifelong learner is a person who can solve problems and make decisions as obstacles are encountered or opportunities are pre-sented. The effective educator's job is to establish the aware-ness and learning opportunities for students to develop their own, totally individual sets of lifeskills.

Part 2

Managing and Monitoring Change

Chapter 4
Managing Educational Change: Project Initiation and Definition

A merican education, one observer has noted, is not really about education. It's a political system laboring to justify spending the $200 BILLION or so allocated to provide storage and a modicum of care for some 25 or 30 million children.

GETTING ORGANIZED

Consider, for example, that, for almost 200 years, there were comparatively few laws and rules mandating that American kids learn anything in school. Yes, attendance was mandated— strictly. But attendance laws had little or nothing to do with learning. Their chief role was to keep kids out of the sweat-shops and factories that wanted to exploit child labor. Thus, if a youngster didn't show up, a truant officer would be dispatched to drag him or her into school. Until the mid-1970s, however, few states had laws stipulating courses of study, anticipated levels of achievement, and validation of learning through stan-dardized testing.

The spate of laws mandating learning represented a major change which, in turn, mandated modification of the ways in which schools do business. The shock has not yet worn off com-pletely. Many in American education are still grappling with the need to pull the system together so the business of imparting knowledge and skills can be transacted like a real business should.

Shortly after laws mandating instructional content began to proliferate, the *Nation at Risk* report hit the educational fan. In a sudden frenzy, the educational system reverted toward institutionalizing a status quo that had existed in the nineteenth century. Even the vastly popular name, *Back to Basics*, was retrogressive, forcing schools back into the patterns that had brought about the very failure that was being lamented. American education then needed several more years to get that nostalgic binge out of its system before serious organizational efforts got under way in the late 1980s and early 1990s.

AN INHERITED ATTITUDE PROBLEM

Significantly, much of the motivation toward restructuring and upgrading American education resulted from comparisons of test scores that showed performance levels of American students far behind those of Japan, Singapore, Germany, and, in some subject areas, a dozen or so other countries. Concurrently, American manufacturers found themselves losing shares of markets they once dominated to companies from other countries. These new competitors organized themselves more efficiently and achieved higher levels of product quality. This being America, where nobody loves a loser, these developments led to an immediate, intensive search for co-scapegoats. As one result of this search, part of the blame for manufacturers' setbacks was assigned to schools that turned out graduates not ready to compete in worldwide markets.

In the process, companies with the most to lose also took stock of their own operations, analyzing their now-apparent weaknesses. Among other faults, attention focused on the **strategies**—management policies, beliefs, and goals—pursued by the affected companies. Hold the term *strategy* in mind. Many schools are in the process of inheriting and adapting this hot-button area of management as a requisite for making American education more responsive to its communities and more effective in development of workers who measure up in internationally competitive markets.

Under close analytical review, it becomes apparent that the strategies for American businesses, like those for schools, had reflected thinking held over from days when the United States was isolated from the rest of the world by oceans and even more impregnable intellectual barriers. For some seven decades, American industry built its major strategies around principles derived from developments in 1908, when Henry Ford set up his assembly line. The Ford production system fixated on low-cost productivity by breaking the auto-building job down into components so small that cars could be built by unskilled workers. This proved a perfect match for the American education system of the day, which was turning out a plethora of un-skilled, semi-literate young adults.

Ford's strategy read the market of the day perfectly. Cars were new and in high demand. The public would buy whatever he could produce, as long as the things ran and the price was affordable. His strategy, through the assembly line, was to in-crease supply in the face of an apparently insatiable demand. One example of Ford's strategy could be seen in the color of his cars. Many people asked for vehicles painted in varying colors. His response was that customers could have any color they wanted "as long as it's black."

Through the years, colors and physical designs of cars changed. Engines became quieter, more powerful, and self-startable (eliminating the hand crank and thus expanding the potential driving population explosively). Interior designs be-came more comfortable. But the strategy of most huge compa-nies continued to regard market demand as a given; they fo-cused on engineering and manufacturing efficiencies. Customer demand was largely assumed.

Then the large American auto, appliance, and radio-TV manufacturers found major shares of their markets slipping away to manufacturers from Germany and Japan who took the trouble to analyze what customers wanted as a basis for design, production, and distribution of their products. Once the mar-keting focus shifted to customers, the production emphasis also changed to an obsession with *quality.* Ironically, the method-ologies that brought superior quality to mass-produced Japa-nese products were invented by an American. The then-revolu-tionary ideas of W. Edwards "Ed" Deming, originator of statisti-cal quality control and other manufacturing enhancements, were resoundingly rejected by American companies. So, he took them to Japan, where manufacturers eager for approaches that would help them break into the American market, welcomed Deming and made him a national hero. Ultimately the focus for strate-gies of large businesses all over the world fixated on customer satisfaction, leading to slogans like "zero defects," and greatly expanded product warranties.

As referenced in the first chapter, management emphasis in the oversight of business transactions has now shifted from the internal, monitoring-type functions of the late 1970s and early 1980s to a concentration on customer satisfaction as re-flected in quality of service. The automotive industry offers one vivid example. But think also of the changed attitudes and struc-ture in retailing. Monolithic department stores have lost ground to boutiques featuring style and customer-service break-throughs. Even Wal-Mart, the country's largest retail chain, employs greeters who stand just inside the entrance to every store with a broad smile and an offer to be of service.

Today, the critical key to business success calls for operation under a strategy that identifies the customers to be served, the products to be provided, and the *level and quality of service* to be rendered. Note this last point: ***Quality is not an absolute but rather a matter of degree of commitment.*** For example, General Motors makes different representations about the quality levels of its Chevrolet and Cadillac cars. Similarly, Toyota and Lexus cars are marketed under different representations.

STRATEGY IN EDUCATION

In many ways, America's industrial and educational strategies have evolved approximately in parallel. Initially, for example, the commitment of schools was largely that they simply existed and were ready to fulfill the basic function of enrolling and providing daytime accommodations that kept youngsters off the labor market. Beyond that, the extent of education was largely a matter of chance, centering around individual transaction patterns established between *a* teacher and *a* student, working principally in a ***one on one*** relationship.

Through the years and in response to evolutionary forces, schools began to assume an operating rationale similar to Ford's factories. Each school was set up as an assembly line that operated on a strict, time-based schedule calling for movement of products (students) in sequence from grade to grade. Echoing Ford's "any color as long as it's black" philosophy, students were subjected to "one size fits all" instructional routines. Too commonly, our better, brighter students misbehaved or failed out of boredom while those who needed more time and guidance were permitted to drift into the abyss of functional illiteracy. In disheartening numbers, too many in this last group were destined to become dropouts.

As was true for industry, the need for and logical direction of change are obvious for education. The goal upon which educational strategy must be based is universal: ***American schools must prepare students for participation as citizens in a free society and also for entry into the workplace as productive, efficient contributors.*** Further, these results must be achieved to the satisfaction of identified customers: Community leaders must be satisfied with the learning content and skill levels with which students enter the workplace while parents must be pleased with what happens at school sites.

To achieve these ends, we must recognize that the rate of change impacting the world's societies today is such that knowledge itself undergoes rapid obsolescence. The rate of informational obsolescence is typically expressed in terms of **half-life,** or the length of time in which half of the knowledge a person has mastered becomes obsolete or inapplicable. Today, the useful, job-applicable half-life of a high school or even a college graduate usually falls into the range of three to five years. For incidental knowledge of the type that qualifies a person as a conscientious, voting citizen, the half-life, unfortunately, can be a lot shorter, possibly even measured in months rather than years.

Such conditions lead to dramatic lessons about knowledge-forming strategies. As a leading example, to remain viable in the workplace, each individual must commit to and undergo a process of **lifelong learning.** Since, the full lifetime of an individual obviously extends beyond the scope of traditional school and college education, schools must recognize this condition within the society to be inhabited by their graduates. To meet the challenges of the current and future workplace, students must, over and beyond specific participation in prescribed classes, **learn to learn.**

This may seem simple. But the picture changes rapidly when you accept the principle that each child learns by a different process and at a different rate. Thus, education has many millions of parents and other adult customers who expect individual treatment of and service patterns for up to 30 million charges served by the system at any given time. Standards and goals are relatively uniform. But each student may have to travel a different route, under a different schedule, to get to a successful result. The changes needed to achieve these ends are nontrivial. On graduation, then, most of these students join a working population of some 120 million that is still expanding, and still must practice lifelong learning as a condition of economic survival.

IMPLEMENTING A STRATEGY

These few elements provide a conceptual outline for the mammoth expectations that should be incorporated in each school's strategy. But identifying a strategy represents only the simple part of preparing a school or district to undertake essential changes. Actually implementing a strategy and having results show up in the behavior and capabilities of students is something else entirely. Changing the structure and the so-called culture of a sizable organization such as an operational company or a school system can become a massive undertaking.

In the case of a school, the job involves challenging the assumptions held by and redefining the jobs of all participants, students and adults alike. The comfort zones in which many teachers and administrators have functioned for decades have to be disrupted, a feat that ranges somewhere between the ultradifficult and the virtually impossible, depending on the situation. In other words, a complete turnaround has to be undertaken. Inexperienced people may expect the job to present a degree of difficulty on the order of reversing directions for a rowboat. But they soon discover the job is more like turning an aircraft carrier. Patience, as well as diligence, are needed.

Experience in business and in scores of school districts has established that it takes an organized, step-by-step approach to plan for and implement meaningful change. This has to be understood early in the game for any educational change: It is not possible simply to identify goals and proceed to implementation. Billions of dollars worth of failures attest to this truism. What needs to happen is that responsible management in each district must commit to a structured, step-by-step *process* for defining, planning, preparing people for change, and implementing the new programs.

NATURE OF EDUCATIONAL CHANGE

Note the emphasis above on the word *process.* When school change is contemplated, citizen activism inevitably sets in. People inexperienced with the complexities of education as a system, parents often in the forefront among them, tend to indulge in immediate leaps, saying, in effect: "You're right. Our kids have to be able to read better. Let's go." Then, when they can't see results a month later, they heap further grief on the system and its professional staff. Often, they're ready to try entirely different solutions, right away.

Business managers and public officials will usually be more experienced in the complexities associated with major organizational change. They are apt to be more patient and understanding about the need for a process that establishes a step-by-step progression. This can be a big advantage, since, as indicated in the first chapter, members of these groups will emerge as primary customers of the education system, people who will establish the level and degree of satisfaction that will determine standards for the entire program for system change.

The point is, when a change-oriented program is undertaken, a diverse group of constituents must be assembled. The adults who associate themselves with the project will arrive with different levels of understanding and sophistication. Some will pursue an immediate call to action before solutions are defined, establishing the kind of pressure that can hobble or even doom the program. It is critical that the initiators of the project help all interested constituencies to understand that this kind of change doesn't happen overnight. The strategy that usually serves best in relating expectations to realities is to keep all concerned parties fully informed, regularly. Progress will inevitably seem to happen slower than many key people would like. Regular reporting on activities, goals, and incremental progress is essential to keep enthusiasm and public support on track. The constituents should feel satisfaction in knowing that something is happening.

A further caveat: Defining needed change requires separate skills and a set of activities completely different from day-to-day operation of a school or district. The separate processes are, therefore, covered in different chapters within this book. This chapter concentrates on a process for investigating and defining change. Then, later presentations outline management strategies and processes that take over once targeted changes have been defined.

The International Center for Leadership in Education (ICLE) has devised and successfully used a six-step process for defining and initiating major changes in curriculum content and student achievement. These process steps, which are identified and described below, are the same as those introduced in a predecessor book in this series, *Education Is NOT a Spectator Sport.* However, the content and emphasis in this book differ somewhat from the presentations in the earlier work. The earlier book concentrates on identifying, defining, reviewing, and adopting curricula with content modified to reflect the demands of the modern workplace. In the presentations that follow, similar content definition activities are summarized, then discussions are added to indicate the organizational and structural changes that should be considered to support introduction of the new, more rigorous, more relevant content within a learning-oriented environment.

The six steps and their objectives are as follows;

Step 1. Create Awareness.

The public must be made aware of the deficiencies that exist in American education generally, and in their local school or district specifically. The requisite level of understanding, particularly among parents, is not a given. Recent surveys show an unacceptable level of complacency about school performance among American parents. Most parents are willing to believe that there is, in fact, a crisis in American education—someplace else. Those other schools may be in trouble, the general attitude holds, but we're lucky, we have good schools in our neighborhood. After all, we moved here on the strength of assurances from the Realtor that the local schools are superior.

Information must be disseminated to shake off complacency and to establish a will for change. Part of the awareness to be created in this first phase of a change program is the clear identification of the system's customers. In turn, the ultimate employers of a school's graduates and the parents responsible for making educational choices must be accorded strong input to help determine what a school is to become and what content is to be included in its curriculum. These inputs serve to help define the capabilities and skills to be acquired by the students who will become the primary products delivered by the system.

Accepting and assimilating these contributions may require vastly different attitudes among the adults employed by the school system. For many years, it has been common for school employees to assume a proprietorship over schools and their activities, keeping other adults out of the picture. This position is in process of undergoing significant, rapid change. Among the happier findings encountered during ICLE Management of Change projects is the willingness, often eagerness, of teachers to endorse and support realistic descriptions of existing problems and needs for change. In every section of the country, teachers have willingly enrolled in continuing education programs to prepare themselves to introduce workplace technologies into schools and their curricula. Teachers did not always have reputations as participants in programs for change. However, when the chips have been down, their professionalism has generally shown through.

Step 2. Focus on Adult Roles.

Educational goals must be focused on the capabilities students will need and the roles they must be able to play as adults. These adult roles must define the objectives for a successful education, replacing the emphasis traditionally placed on course titles, grades, and test scores. Among adult roles defined as part of educational upgrading programs are citizen, worker, life-long learner, consumer, effective family member, and wise user of personal health care and leisure time.

The idea is to concentrate particularly on the results toward which education is aimed. At this level, the focus is on defining skills and capabilities in practical terms. To illustrate, a traditional curriculum might specify courses in English. A revised set of standards, by contrast, should emphasize development of capabilities such as following orally delivered instructions; reading, interpreting, and acting on directions for the assembly or operation of equipment; writing reports on task performance and completion; or making oral presentations to groups. This is part of the transition from a student who is taught to one who is challenged to learn. When students are taught, their normal behavior is passive. Learning is active and demanding, with students responsible for their own performance.

Step 3. Identify Necessary Skills, Knowledge, and Behavior.

Participants in the process that manages change must include prospective employers of graduates from local schools, who are the primary customers for educational products (graduating students). These constituents must play a key role in identifying both the general knowledge and the practical skills that students should possess as they proceed to either jobs or college. The finally identified curriculum content must also, of course, encompass the important, gatekeeping role of standardized achievement tests critical to college admission decisions. It is also critical that teachers play an active, contributing role in these determinations, recognizing that nothing can be achieved without their involvement and commitment.

Core academic subjects should be re-specified for administration on a multidisciplinary basis as necessary to provide practical bases for skillbuilding. One frequently implemented combination involves history or social studies in conjunction with English. This provides practical experience in mastery of the writing and reading elements of language within the bounds of content on history, government, geography, or other element of the core content, often through team teaching or block scheduling. Although it is early in the process to deal with specifics of class content and schedules, discussions should be held that establish a framework for acceptance of the kinds of structural changes the school will have to undergo as it shifts to a learning emphasis.

This third step is also a good point to do some rethinking of the school's mission and role in its community. During these deliberations, the task force would do well to apply the practices associated with brainstorming sessions in business organizations. Also worth considering is a process approach sometimes carried out through written exchanges and identified as a **Delphi.**

The idea is to promote open-mindedness, to accentuate the positive. All reasonable suggestions, regardless of how extreme they may seem to some members of the group, are accepted, listed, and held for future review—without current discussion or judgment. Through the years, as schools have faced increasing charges of failing to meet community needs and as school and district officials have become more open to recommendations for change, ideas once considered impossible have become realities. Where education is concerned, these are times for open-mindedness. Some examples of suggested and/or actual changes include:

❏ Abandon lockstep teaching and promotion schedules. Promote on the basis of achievement rather than age.

❏ Recognize that students learn at different rates and through different means. Do not expect all students to acquire knowledge equally under a uniform, inflexible schedule. Students who learn at slower rates should be given opportunities to progress at their own pace. Students who learn more rapidly should not be held back but should be encouraged to move ahead into special, enriching experiences.

❏ Look closely at existing classroom management methods. Determine whether your school is attempting to teach diverse students under traditional lecture-type methods or whether methods are in place to promote learning. Consider a learning orientation as an essential outcome of any project for educational review and/or change.

❏ Lengthen the school year. Recommendations being heard with regularity include increasing student attendance from 180 to 200 days. Teacher presence should be extended to to 220 days, providing on-job time for continuing education and preparation for new, more rigorous curricula.

❏ Lengthen the school day. Many schools are actually adding one period or more to the school day and using the extra time for enrichment, vocational instruction, or tutoring of students who need extra help to meet learning standards.

❏ Consider the needs of modern families with two working parents or with full responsibilities assumed by single parents. Many schools open as early as 6 a.m. and stay open as late as 8 p.m. to provide care that helps keep families together functionally.

❏ Start learning experiences at lower ages. There is extensive evidence that children do better when they start learning at younger ages, as low as three or four. (In North Carolina, four-year-olds are admitted on a regular basis under a "smart start" program championed by Gov. James Hunt.) Helped particularly are children from economically disadvantaged homes.

❏ Include elements of character building, social "enabling skills," and acceptable standards of behavior in the curriculum. The aim: Reduce the negative influences encountered through the mass media and in most neighborhoods, including substance abuse, gang activities, and youthful crime.

As indicated, during this step of the management-of-change process, the idea is to be open minded. Consider everything and reject nothing. Sort and weed out the suggestions in later, separate deliberations.

Step 4. Identify Negotiables and Non-negotiables.

In every community, there are operational services and elements—calendar, curriculum, organizational structure, staffing patterns, tax base, and other factors—that community members or school personnel are unable or unwilling to change or accept. Surmounting such obstacles requires special negotiating and compromising skills.

During this step, participants begin to identify which of the elements suggested in the previous step have potential for improving the school's end products, its graduates, and can enhance services to identified customers. In the past, such deliberations have frequently broken down in the rancor of opposing viewpoints. Most typically, problems arise when adversaries focus primarily on contentious points, the elements of difference between them. When honest differences arise over an issue of school operation, ICLE consultants recommend strongly that the parties avoid concentrating on their disagreements. Instead, a better approach is to probe for points where agreement can be reached, then build mutually acceptable policies and programs around those agreements.

One area in which this approach has been fruitful has been for schools considering introduction of character education programs. Almost inevitably, the very mention of character education causes educational constituencies to choose up sides. One faction sees a danger that character education will serve as a platform to reintroduce religion back into curricula. Another group sees a danger that its antagonists will want to use a character education program as an opening to sneak in programs on sex education. To make educational reform work, it is best to move all such contentious items off the table and concentrate on points where opinions and attitudes converge. In character education, for example, virtually everyone can agree on the value of stressing honesty, truthfulness, teamwork, or other traits of universal value. These points of convergence provide excellent bases for a highly desirable curriculum.

As another example, it is more productive to concentrate on student achievement outcomes than curriculum-related administrative details. For example, almost everyone involved in educational change admits readily that it is essential to improve student writing capabilities. The urgency of the need can, however, be buried over acrimony about how teachers are to be paid for the time it will take to review and critique student writing and to monitor achievement. Experience has shown it is best to identify desired results first, then worry about implementation only after the job has been defined. It is not fruitful, when a team is working to achieve change, to base arguments on past standards or even the present status quo.

Other factors that come up for consideration can include tax rates, length of the school day and year, discipline, curriculum content, recreational or athletic programs, food service, transportation, and also teacher certification and tenure. In these deliberations, a lack of flexibility by any group of participants can hamper the entire effort. Such disputed or immutable items are best treated as non-negotiables and left for later resolution while working teams consider the positive elements of their job.

Step 5. Develop a Plan.

Note that this step occurs next to last in an overall program to implement change. Note, too, that the plan referred to here involves preparation for long-range organizational and strategic considerations. This planning should not be either mingled or confused with the kind of planning associated with ongoing, year-by-year management of school operations. The contexts for the two types of plans are entirely different. This process step centers on what constituents want their schools to become rather than on how they are to function. In other words, emphasis should be on elements of organizational and instructional structure rather than details of day-to-day operation.

Within the context of the six-step process, planning effectiveness is enhanced when negotiables and non-negotiables have been determined and dealt with in advance. When context focus is established in advance, the involved parties are more likely to leave the status quo behind and concentrate on the future. Too often, community groups seeking educational change permit their enthusiasm to govern their actions; they plunge impatiently into planning without pausing for the preparatory steps that set the stage. This can leave them enmeshed in current difficulties from which they are trying to distance themselves, following a course known as rear-view management. It is important to recognize that a program for change can't go forward until participants let go of the past.

Further, it is important to recognize that change is a constant of modern education, an ongoing requirement. Experience has shown that it is profitable for a district to review and possibly modify its plans for major, curriculum-altering change on an annual basis. Revisions should reflect progress in introduction of new curriculum or policy elements over the past year and new requirements identified through experience. Again, teacher inputs and commitments are critical because no change can be implemented in classrooms without faculty agreement and support. Thus, one of the critical planning needs involves provision for advanced education and training of teachers.

It is worth stressing that these reviews focus on major changes that impact curriculum content, educational strategy, or organizational structure and that ongoing, day-to-day operations should not be affected. Specific elements and options related to the planning function are covered in depth later in this work.

Step 6. Implement Needed Reforms.

This step calls for activation of changes for which commitments have previously been secured. Note that implementation is treated as an end result of a systematic process. This is the point at which changes become visible within ongoing, day-to-day operations. Implementation of major system changes will often be implemented over a multi-year schedule. In effect, the school or district changes gradually, ultimately becoming a different organization when full implementation is complete.

This approach represents a marked difference from the many educational reforms of the past that have jumped immediately to introduction of changes, too often without adequate consideration of objectives or plans. When implementation happens, distinctions should be made between programs that introduce major changes in organizational structures and those that simply modify day-to-day procedures.

Again, discussion of specifics and presentation of practical examples occurs later in this work.

WORKING THE PROCESS

Educational reform, under the process described above, begins with determinations of who is to be made aware and of what. It can be accepted as a given, in light of years of carping by the print and broadcast media on falling test scores and any other negatives they can find, that most adults, in most places, will be aware that American education is underperforming.

As noted above, however, there will be differences between general awareness that education is in trouble nationally and recognition that the specific community where a given person lives has schools that are not functioning up to their potential. A prerequisite for improvement of school performance involves recognition that conditions in local schools require improvement and that the entire community shares a vested interest in upgrading capabilities and performance.

For many years, school officials themselves compounded this problem by putting out grossly misleading information about student achievements. By selecting small segments of test score results, they were able to report to state legislatures that children in their specific state or region were performing above national norms.

As one recent example, test scores for a half million students in 41 countries developed under TIMSS (Third International Mathematics and Science Study) in 1995 showed United States students placing twenty-eighth in math and seventeenth in science. To transpose this picture to display a positive image, scores and results from TIMSS were extracted for students in a relatively small suburban area north of Chicago where public schools were known to be among the best in the country. Selected scores for students in this target area put them in fourth place in math among the 41 participating nations, second in science.

These data were then widely heralded as proof that the United States was actually delivering students with world-class performance potential. The reports on this supposed success failed to mention that the high-performing population came from schools with a total enrollment of some 37,000, as compared with the overall population of some 25 to 30 million in American schools.

Offering this group as a source of potential pride may be justified. But it would seem to be a stretch to postulate that all American students can achieve this level of performance. Rather, in district-by-district and school-by-school deliberations, it would seem that responsible policymakers had better set realistic goals for acceptable levels of achievement, then measure performance against standards that responsible leaders have set and agreed to.

OVERCOMING COMPLACENCY

Once constituents of a given school or district are convinced that things aren't really rosy and that change is essential, an initial, important question to be faced is: How large is the gap between current customer dissatisfaction with educational transactions and the results that would satisfy customers and other constituents? The answer must be as objective as possible.

Sources of information and evaluations may vary, depending on the positions or roles of the questioners. A change alert may be sounded through the announcement of results from standardized test scores that hit new lows. Another possible source of alarm may be loss of accreditation. Or maybe irate parents have been storming the schoolhouse. Law enforcement statistics on juvenile crime or substance abuse may also sound alarms.

A sure-fire place to look for indicators is in the local workplace. Involve prospective employers of future graduates and ask them how local, entry-level applicants qualify or fail to qualify when they seek jobs in a market that is becoming increasingly technological universally. It is important to get prospective employers to identify problems and define needs. Then, as a followup, community-committed business leaders should be encouraged to participate in programs aimed at upgrading student capabilities through school-to-work partnerships, collaborations, or other efforts that guide students from school to productive jobs.

Things need not necessarily be at a crisis stage. Maybe an alert individual or group is convinced that the kids of their community deserve a better quality education than they're getting. Maybe, for example, parents find that diplomas from the local high school don't impress admissions officials at top-level colleges, causing their children to settle for second or third choices in colleges. Regardless of source, the common denominator that starts a call for change is an awareness by an individual or action group that school performance falls short of what the community has a right to expect and that something has to be done.

Whatever the stimulus, the job is to define the situation, identify what's wrong, and describe what has to be fixed. At this point, *a political campaign has to be launched.* In other words, a platform has to be established and people need to be invited to climb aboard.

The challenge involves communication. People who should be concerned about the current condition of education must be identified and a call to do something must be issued. Channels of communication can involve appealing to local media—newspapers and radio or TV stations—to take an interest in the problem and spread the word. This can be done by calling a news conference and issuing a statement, then presenting convincing evidence to make the public aware of their shared problem.

Over and above the media contacts, the initiators of the improvement effort should spread the word through civic organizations with a stake in the quality of local schools. Speakers should be made available for consciousness-raising programs that are offered for presentation at meetings. In every news release or public speech, the theme must be a call to action.

In devising appeals for action, sponsors should focus on the situation and needs of students. Descriptions of requirements should emphasize such factors as changes in society and the workplace that may have outpaced local educational programs. One of the easiest ideas about which to convince any American community is that children represent society's future. Hundreds of billions of dollars are being invested in programs that should assure productive, secure lifestyles for tomorrow's adults. It takes continuing adjustments of attitudes and commitments by the entire community to redeem and acquire the benefits of these massive investments.

The awareness-raising initial activity in the process for educational change should culminate in a call to action, possibly a meeting at which shortfalls, needs, and potential solutions are aired publicly. Ideally, this session will produce a group of volunteers for a task force (which might also be called a business-school partnership, a joint planning committee, or other designation that indicates communitywide cooperation). Regardless of name, the volunteers should commit to carry the program forward through development and implementation. That task force should include elected officials, teachers, parents, educational administrators, and business leaders. A final constituency that should be included, though it is easy to overlook, is students. Mature, thoughtful students can contribute point-of-contact perspectives and important insights on the need for and projected benefits from proposed changes.

DEFINING ADULTHOOD REALISTICALLY AND PRACTICALLY

As the work proceeds into the next step in the change process—Focus on Adult Roles—everyone on the task force or partnership should participate and contribute. The objective in this step is to define the roles that students will be expected to assume when they leave school. Note that the adult roles to be defined apply to all students, regardless of whether they are headed directly to work or on to college.

In particular, changed curricula must overcome the inappropriate but longstanding prejudice holding that students entering the workforce after high school don't need as rigorous an academic background as those headed for college. Between the late 1940s and the early 1990s, high school curricula tended to focus on college preparation as the logical end result of a secondary education. Technology and international competition have pretty much dispensed with such notions. As illustrated in Figure 4-1, there has been a steady shift in requirements for students going on to college and those proceeding directly into the workplace. A few years ago, standards and challenges of the workplace became more demanding in areas of knowledge and skills than those for college entrance. This may reflect an assumption that college-bound students have time to continue to develop career choices and workplace skills. At any rate, the time for assuming that direct vocational preparation curricula can be less stringent academically than college preparation sequences is long gone. Plans for change must most certainly take this situation into account.

The definitions and descriptions developed at this stage become the basis for curriculum revisions and/or special academic or vocational programs or other learning transactions aimed at guiding students into adult roles. Measures for reorienting the school toward learning, identified above and in Chapter 1, should be considered seriously at this point.

As adult-role-definition activities are introduced, it becomes

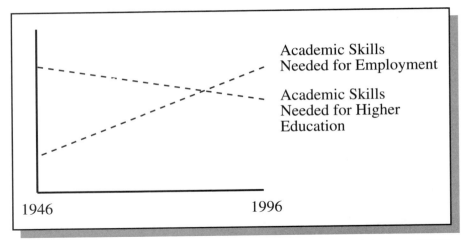

Academic Skills
Needed for Employment

Academic Skills
Needed for Higher
Education

1946   1996

FIGURE 4-1. THIS CHART ILLUSTRATES THE TREND TOWARD INCREASED RIGOR FACED BY STUDENTS HEADED TOWARD THE WORKPLACE ON GRADUATION FROM HIGH SCHOOL.

crucial that the working group do whatever is necessary to keep the public informed. There must be thorough informational coverage throughout the community about the outcomes of any meetings that are held and appointments that are made. Specific statements of vision or objectives must be developed, their content circulated, and their consequences explained.

In particular, these statements should call attention to potential loss or damage from failure to make recommended changes. These statements should reflect the consequences in loss of career potential that might be suffered by students or the penalty paid by the local economy because of the inadequate preparation for adulthood should the recommended changes not be made.

Benefits from changes seen as freeing the school from traditional constraints of time should be emphasized particularly. Questions to be addressed might be:

❑   How can students and the community benefit from a longer school year and/or an extended school day?

❑   Why will the students perform better under a block scheduling structure than they do in a series of separate periods that deal with limited content?

❑   Why do teachers need more time to prepare for the challenges of the new curriculum and to enter continuing education programs aimed at upgrading their skills?

❑   What use will be made of workplace mentoring and work-experience assistance and how will students gain?

ENHANCING ACHIEVABILITY BY LIMITING SCOPE

Throughout the process, the task force must never lose sight of the need to focus strongly on future adult roles of today's students.

The end product of this activity should be a fairly simple—but well considered—list of *five to seven areas of competencies* to be developed further and ultimately implemented. Note the designation about number of items to be recommended. In any program that sets out to alter human behavior, there must be reasonable limits based on the number of alternatives or objectives human beings can consider and deal with at any given time.

It is a longstanding psychological principle that the number of elements people are capable of remembering and dealing with is "seven, plus or minus two." In other words, the number of guidelines to be followed should be limited to between five and nine. This principle has been adopted by developers of business and organizational systems as a kind of practical cap on the extent of change that should be undertaken as part of a single program. To illustrate, North Carolina settled on six statewide competencies: *communicating, using numbers and data, problem solving, processing information, working in teams,* and *using technology.*

This limitation of five to seven is recommended even though the authors recognize that any probing examination of a community's education is likely to find more than seven ingredients that could profit from change. That kind of finding is to be expected. Any and all areas of potential improvement should be noted and recorded in some kind of working queue for eventual implementation. The point for this second process activity is that it is essential to prioritize identified opportunities and to select the five to seven that are deemed most critical and that can reasonably be achieved. These items then become part of the change program's working framework.

GETTING SPECIFIC ABOUT SKILLS AND CAPABILITIES

The third step in the process for change calls for identifying necessary skills, knowledge, and behaviors related to each of the adult roles identified in the previous step. Also considered should be methodologies and organizational structures designed to assure that students are challenged by a learning orientation and that the schedules for the school year and school day are modified as necessary and feasible to help achieve the new goals.

Again, it is good practice to limit the scope of change activities to between five and seven items, that is, five to seven expectations for each of the five to seven targeted areas.

Although each school or district task force should identify its own particular needs, experience in districts across the country has identified a number of common requirements. For example, speaking and listening skills have been identified as essentials for communication in the workplace, home, and society. In addition, reading for acquisition of information is used extensively in all adult roles with the possible exception of leisure time activities. Also well established is the principle that additional practice in writing is essential to improve communication skills.

A recent ICLE report cited a "Career Preparation Validation Study" by the New York State Education Department that generated a number of important recommendations about requisite adult skills. The ICLE report listed the following skills related to curriculum content in English and language arts:

❏ As requisites for entry-level employment, the study suggested building competencies in *Reading for Information* and *Reading for Critical Analysis and Evaluation.* Another related skill, *Reading for Personal Response* was found to be personally valuable.

❏ Job prospects can be enhanced for students who develop skills in *Writing for Information.* Also valuable for job performance, though to a lesser extent is skill in *Writing for Critical Analysis.* Two other desirable personal skills, even though they are used less frequently on a job, are *Writing for Personal Expression* and *Writing for Social Interaction.*

❏ The New York validation study also stressed that many workers need and all adults can benefit from skills in effective listening. Two listed topics were *Listening/Speaking for Information and Understanding* and *Listening/Speaking for Critical Analysis and Evaluation.*

In retrospect, it would appear that further qualification and simplification might be indicated on the basis of experience since the report was issued. For example, it is true that the three identified reading skill areas have separate and significant importance in career building. It is highly desirable that students be able to demonstrate these three capabilities. However, this doesn't mean the three designations have to be incorporated as three separate course areas within a school curriculum. The same is true for the four designated types of writing listed above and for the two separate listening/speaking skills.

Desired outcomes do not have to correspond on a one-for-one basis with course designations. To achieve the identified reading, writing, and listening/speaking competencies, it would be feasible to incorporate a series of activities and exercises under a general heading of Communicating With Language. Such a course sequence would coordinate skillbuilding in reading, writing, listening, and speaking, and also encompass the grammar and structural elements of language. Further, all this can be done in a multidisciplinary course that deals with both English and technology (or science, or history).

Mathematics-related skills identified in the same study include capabilities in Basic Operations, Logic, Probability, and Measurement. Interestingly, Algebra and Geometry were found to be less relevant for entry-level workers, even though they are prerequisites for college-bound students.

The New York study recommended that curricula aimed at workplace-bound students expand coverage of basic topics such as interpersonal skills, thinking skills, human relations, information systems, and personal skills. Existing curricula were found deficient in these areas.

KNOWING WHAT CAN AND CAN'T BE DONE

As the change program heads into its fourth process step—Identify Negotiables and Non-negotiables—it becomes necessary to think further about and prioritize the content areas and skills, as well as modifications in organizational structures, that should be targeted. As indicated above, the leaders of the change-oriented program should bear in mind that it will probably be impossible to implement all desirable changes at once. Feasibilities and human capacities have to be factored in and priorities must be established. Everything is attainable eventually. But a series of phase-ins may be necessary to get it all done. That's where the consideration of negotiables and non-negotiables comes in.

For guidance in evaluating and prioritizing content- and skill-area potentials, as well as structural adjustments, experience has evolved a series of questions that can guide the decision makers. These include the following:

❑ What is the point of departure for prospective changes? (Define the present situation.)

❑ Is the school or district committed to adopting a learning orientation or will it be necessary for internal political rea-

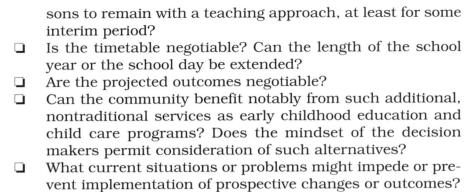

sons to remain with a teaching approach, at least for some interim period?

❑   Is the timetable negotiable? Can the length of the school year or the school day be extended?

❑   Are the projected outcomes negotiable?

❑   Can the community benefit notably from such additional, nontraditional services as early childhood education and child care programs? Does the mindset of the decision makers permit consideration of such alternatives?

❑   What current situations or problems might impede or prevent implementation of prospective changes or outcomes?

Answers to the questions posed during this step require serious, collective soul searching by the transition group. For example, consideration of the first of the above questions often leads to discussions and decisions involving a topic that doesn't come up in deliberations centered on content and skills—discipline. Yet discipline is an essential in building an effective environment for learning.

DISTRACTIONS AND DISCIPLINE

Under the best of circumstances, prospects for achievement of academic rigor and relevance lie somewhere between the difficult and the impossible. Educators must face up to situations that, today, are rarely acted upon and even more rarely dealt with effectively. That issue: Substance abuse is rampant in virtually every community and can undermine or obstruct real intellectual progress if the basic problems are not confronted.

The full extent of substance abuse problems in American schools was unveiled in a presentation before the 1997 ICLE Model Schools Conference by Dr. Gary M. Field, Superintendent of the Zion-Benton Township High School District 126, in Zion, Illinois. Dr. Fields stressed: "We can never reach the level of academic achievement we desire as long as we have so many serious issues of a personal nature compromising our children … one common denominator … our schools … must address is alcohol, tobacco, and other drugs. …

"Nationally, we know that typical schools and communities have approximately one out of three secondary students coming to school each day compromised by a chemical. This includes their own use or the negative impact upon them by substance abuse of someone in their family. On the elementary level, we know that approximately 25 percent of our students are children of alcoholics or children of substance abusers."

Dr. Fields outlined the need to involve parents and the entire community in confronting and dealing effectively with such complex problems. Similar stocktaking and planning should be included in the work of every task force that seeks improvement of academic achievement. Solutions may depend on the makeup and spirit of individual communities. Universally, however, it should be agreed that constructive discipline that supports a learning environment requires implementation of measures for dealing with substance and other material-abuse problems. In this area, business members of the task force can recount experiences that establish the necessity and profitability of decisive actions that eliminate waste, enhance productivity, and add to the well-being of workers.

Discipline problems, of course, also involve a wide range of aberrant behavior demonstrated by students, often through either neglect or encouragement by parents. The ICLE report cited above also has some important observations about discipline programs in schools:

> We have long known that a classroom in which there is respect for others and good discipline leads to productive students. Unfortunately, the discipline problem facing American classroom teachers has accelerated during the past several years. While parents and the general public agree that schools should require well-disciplined students who respect authority, an immediate outcry occurs as soon as one child has been disciplined. Parents have proved to be both the group most often calling for this issue to be addressed and the ones quickest to express outrage when their children are personally involved.

> Lack of discipline in American schools has increased for a number of reasons. . . . We have attempted in many American schools to regulate this problem through reducing class sizes. . . . We are treating a symptom, not a cause. Japan, whose students consistently score higher than U.S. students on international tests, has the second highest class size in the industrialized world—42 to 1 in high schools and 34 to 1 in elementary schools. The nation with the smallest class size, the United States, has among the poorest test scores and among the most disruptive students.

> As a nation, we must decide whether respecting others and self-discipline are indeed qualities we want our young people to possess.

The fourth step, which deals with the need for discipline and also sets priorities for changes in content and skill goals, becomes a point of demarcation in a program for educational change. Among other reasons, this is because most schools and districts don't bother with the first four steps; they launch immediately into detailed planning, the fifth step, then rush into implementation of insufficiently considered remedies. School or district leaders define problems and proceed immediately with plans for change, throwing solutions at problems they have not positively identified.

Since there is never an absence of problems to be dealt with, this approach has been called the "plan of the year" system for school management. A typical scenario often goes something like this: A state legislature or federal agency allocates money for a specific program. The local administrator at the district or school level looks at operations and finds a program that is meeting with apparent success. That program is renamed to conform to the specifications for the newly allocated funds, the money is sucked into the system, and all parties declare victory.

TRANSITION TIME

Completion of the fourth step in the process marks a critical point of demarcation for efforts to bring about educational change. Up to this point, efforts have concentrated on evaluating existing achievement levels and defining how they are to be altered. Now, in the two remaining activities, the task force gets down to firm commitment and action. The planning phase which follows commits the school and its constituents to action, to achieve specified changes to be implemented in the final phase.

This, therefore, is a good point for a warning: Planning for and implementing change often become highly detailed, sometimes rancorous activities that present special challenges that are different from those encountered in the initial, foundational steps. Also, the makeup of the working task force changes, since these final steps place responsibilities on the system's professionals, teachers and administrators, who deal with the everyday realities of running a school. This means, in turn, that the quality of the final results delivered depends heavily on the clarity of the goals and specifications evolved during the four preparatory stages.

Therefore, this is seen as a good point to take a breather and demonstrate the kind of effort that goes into preparation for educational change with some actual case illustrations. The preparatory phases of change programs for two districts—Polk County Schools, North Carolina, and Roseville Joint Union High School District, California—are described in the chapter that follows. Then, Chapter 6 covers the remaining elements of the change process, followed, in turn, by further case illustrations from the two districts.

The idea, of course, is to establish that the principles of the ICLE Management of Change process are practical and workable.

Chapter 5
Making Change Happen: Analysis and Progress Review

A basic design principle, known to all architects, centers on functionality of space and facilities occupied by humans. A cardinal sin in the design and construction of facilities that people occupy or in systems that guide work performance is to put *form over function.* Appearance is important, but less so than the need for efficient, effective operations that deliver quality results.

MONUMENTS TO FORM AHEAD OF PERFORMANCE

Recall that one of the steps in the ICLE educational change process calls for identification of potential changes considered to be negotiable and non-negotiable. Educators are old hands at living within systems that place form ahead of substance. In this field, we understand the principle that things are done the way they are because that's the way they've always been. But does this qualify as a non-negotiable reason to resist change?

For an example of how ridiculous tradition can become, look no further than the school year. School facilities sit idle between 25 and 33 percent of the time because the kids were needed, 200 years ago, to help with planting, cultivating, and harvesting the crops of a nation that was 90-plus percent agrarian.

It's part of human nature to resist change, then to offer indefensible explanations for clinging to the antiquated or obsolete, such as: "That's the way things are around here. After all, this isn't New York or Chicago." Don't misconstrue the meaning of this citation. Regionalism is America and America is regionalization—in lifestyles, customs, and the working patterns and transactions by which people earn their livelihoods. But it's also true that people share common human traits wherever they happen to live.

RECOGNIZING THE OBVIOUS

When it comes to applying the form over function design concept to the redesign and/or modification of an educational system, another factor comes into play, one relating to the principles of identifying and satisfying customers. Constituents involved in a program for educational change need to recognize that ***American education is now functioning in a buyers' market.*** If the trend is not yet clear in your area, you'd best not wait around to be convinced, get off the tracks you've been standing on or you might be hit by the next train that comes along. Clear messages that are being written all over schoolhouse walls may be worth reading.

❑ In urban areas, enrollments in private and church-operated schools are multiplying explosively.

❑ The population of students being educated at home is estimated at between a half million and a million and a quarter. A major subindustry has grown around small firms that provide curriculum planning, progress monitoring, and tutoring assistance to home-schooling families.

❑ Private companies are contracting for the operation of public schools.

❑ Schools are becoming part of the workplace. Companies are creating schools in their own facilities, making it possible for workers to bring children with them, to visit during breaks in the work day, and to gain a sense of security that contributes greatly to employee loyalty.

❑ The charter school movement has taken hold and is growing rapidly in every corner of the country. Though charter schools tend to be considered a form of public education, many of these facilities have been organized in response to frustration with the hidebound rules that haunt public education.

In this increasingly market-conscious era, public-school responses to consumer demands have tended to follow the "squeaky-wheel" philosophy of management: The squeaky wheel gets the oil, the others run on neglect.

QUALITY IS UNIVERSAL

School constituencies are different. Traditions differ between regions. Intellectual interests are almost infinite, and also infinitely variable. All these things are true. But it is also true that we are all human and that there are universal elements in our shared cultural background. Among these, Americans have always been strivers. As a nation, we have devised ways to innovate, to be productive, and to achieve quality—elements we all understand, respect, and seek in our transactions with the educational system.

The two cases cited in the discussions that follow demonstrate that widely different principles of quality education are appropriate in places of economic, cultural, and regional diversity. Certainly, the backgrounds, economic bases, and historic traditions of areas in predominantly rural southwest North Carolina and central California represent American diversity in its extremities.

> **Polk County Schools** serve a rural area in southwestern North Carolina. During the late '80s, county officials, in response to a statewide trend to merge districts on a countywide basis, merged the former Tryon city and Polk County districts into one. Though encouraged by the state, the local citizens clearly took this as an opportunity to enhance educational quality. Logistically, the merger proved sound both economically and in terms of quality enhancement. The total county population was only about 16,000 and combined school enrollments were just over 2,000. It became clear that change and quality enhancement would benefit through formation of a single district that could be managed and equipped to provide higher quality, more relevant education.

> The **Roseville Joint Union High School District** lies in the rolling foothills of California's Gold Country, an area that has evolved over the past 20 years into a kind of exurban adjunct to the Silicon Valley, home of the personal computer revolution. Inhabitants (and taxpayers) in the area include companies like Hewlett-Packard, Intel, Xerox, and IBM. The city of Roseville is also next door to and subject to second guessing inspection from Sacramento, California's capital. District leadership foresaw the need for and moved toward modernizing their schools early in the 1990s.

Before ongoing programs for change were initiated, one of these districts qualified as a rural system with limited resources. The other enjoyed a more successful, middle-range reputation. The differences will be apparent from the descriptions that follow.

MERGER WITH MERIT—POLK COUNTY

In Polk County, the separate Tryon City and County Schools were each too small and generally underfunded to provide the caliber of education that increasingly upscale residents wanted to see. In 1989, none of the six schools in the two districts was accredited. Absent commitment from residents, none of the local teaching positions was supported by local funding and budgets for the purchase of educational materials stood at less than $1 per student, per academic year. District officials launched a program that has catapulted Polk County Schools to a position near the top of the heap in a number of categories of state standings.

The district's program for change was initiated by preparing and widely disseminating a public statement that identified the system's problems and needs—in detail. In essence, the community as a whole was guided toward recognition of the need for Polk County Schools to produce graduates who could compete and succeed in the world at large. The challenge was laid down to elevate Polk County Schools to a position among the best in the state.

ORGANIZING FOR ACTION

Local media responded and spread the word, attracting almost 400 people to an open meeting to kick off a major program for educational improvement. This level of participation within a 2,000 student, 179-teacher district was large enough and loud enough to stimulate the required level of action. Attendees enthusiastically supported formation of a 25-member "commission" charged with carrying the program forward. Within a few weeks, this commission drafted and approved an initial "vision statement" that proclaimed:

> The mission of the Polk County Schools is to prepare students to be literate, informed, responsible, and productive members of a global society who believe learning is a lifelong process.

A vision or goal statement is the logical starting point for any school reform undertaking. Its purpose is to establish a consensus for targeted results and a commitment to the actions needed to achieve those results. Within the Polk County statement, it is obvious that thought and discussion were applied to selection of the descriptors of graduates. They are to be **literate, informed, responsible,** and **productive.** These related adjectives serve to establish a framework of where the creators of the statement want to go. Note also that the statement establishes four target results, well within the comprehensibility and tracking capabilities of the campaign that followed. The reference to a **global society** also seems significant for planners located in a rural corner of North Carolina.

Finally, note the closing reference to **learning** [as] **a lifelong process.** This highlights an important element that should be considered by planners of any effort to restructure and improve public education. That is, the ultimate skill that education should impart is the ability to learn, coupled with a commitment and understanding that the need to learn never stops. A school is successful if its students learn to learn.

As another important startup element, the working commission that launched the Polk County program listed the basic beliefs that were to serve as the foundation for all work to follow. These beliefs are as follows:

1. Human potential varies and can be fulfilled.
2. Recognition of superior performance inspires others.
3. Diversity is a source of learning and can be valuable.
4. Potential is developed best when the community is committed to lifelong learning.
5. All people have worth.
6. We live in and are affected by a global society.
7. Democracy works best when citizens are literate, informed, and responsible.

Again, note that the list, which could conceivably have been virtually infinite, contains seven items. This approach of incremental development has been referred to as working in "chewable bites."

To fulfill the promises implied by the vision and beliefs statements, the leaders of the Polk County education commission called for a program that would focus on an individual learning approach to education. The initial focus of the reorganization was to be a concentration on targeted achievements for the community's high school graduates. The project description that accompanied the statement of beliefs stipulated further that a task force of committed adults would guide the effort and that all teachers in the district would play active roles in decision making and implementation.

PREVIEWING RESULTS

This is a good point to jump ahead of the story by demonstrating that commitments of this type do pay off. In Polk County today, all schools are fully accredited. Test scores for Polk County students are at or near the top for the state of North Carolina. Polk County moved up to the seventeenth position statewide in per-pupil funding. Some 53 percent of teachers in the county now hold advanced degrees, an achievement that ranks them fourth in the state. A total of 23 new teachers have been hired to establish a teacher-to-student ratio of one to 13, making it possible to eliminate combination classes at the rural schools.

Facilitating these results required a major revamping of standards and procedures and a restructuring of educational transactions. The district implemented a series of tough-minded rules that ranged from modification of student grade reporting through stringent standards for responsibility, with close monitoring of achievements.

A significant factor at work here is that North Carolina, a right-to-work state, has no labor agreements with teachers' unions or organizations representing administrators. Thus, the superintendent could set some drastic rules. School administrators and teachers were held accountable for stipulated improvements in the test scores of their students. Staff turnover was high. But results were noteworthy, providing direct proof that a system of rewards based on results can be a major factor in educational improvement.

THE WHOLE COMMUNITY HELPED SET SIGHTS

To implement the step in the process calling for a focus on adult roles for which high school graduates were to be prepared, conferences were held to seek advice and input from influential adults within the community. Inputs were provided by parents, public officials, and business leaders, including but not limited to prospective employers of the graduates. The main output of this activity was a concise statement that identified five adult roles targeted for students, stipulating that:

Each student shall be prepared to assume the adult roles and responsibilities listed below in an ethical manner.

❑ **Personal Well-Being (Health)** An individual must maintain positive mental, emotional, and physical states in order to fulfill his or her other roles.

❑ **Lifelong Learner** An individual must strive to acquire new skills and knowledge in order to live in today's dynamic society.

❑ **Nurturer** An individual must support and nurture the emotional, mental, and physical well-being of others, including family members, in order to safeguard the well-being of the individual and society.

❑ **Citizen** An individual must understand and respond appropriately to the rules of society, respect the rights of others, be a responsible consumer, recognize and respect differing interests and cultures, and contribute positively to the community, state, nation, and world.

❑ **Worker** An individual has a responsibility to develop the skills and competencies that enable him or her to pursue a livelihood which provides self-fulfillment and financial resources for oneself and dependents and which serves society.

These defined roles helped establish the expectations of the educational reform program. Note again that the list is of manageable size. The statements covering roles and responsibilities, like the mission and belief statements produced previously, were disseminated widely.

DEFINING STUDENT COMPETENCIES

Acceptance of the definitions of adult roles moved the program into its third process step, "Identify Necessary Skills, Knowledge, and Behavior." To implement this next step, working groups—led by teachers—created a list of competencies to be achieved by high school graduates. In compiling this list, the working groups avoided any temptations or easy-way-out options that could have been based on subject content of existing curricula. Instead, entirely new, multidisciplinary skills were identified based on traits students would have to acquire to fulfill previously defined roles. The list of competencies evolved for Polk County follows:

Communication Skills Each student will master communication skills needed to:
Speak, listen to, read, and write clearly and effectively in English.

Comprehend written, spoken, and visual presentations in various media.

Determine information required for particular purposes and select the appropriate resources and tools to acquire, organize, and use that information for those purposes.

Speak, listen to, read, and write at least one language other than English.

Appreciation of the Arts Each student will acquire knowledge and understanding of the artistic and intellectual accomplishments of various cultures and develop the skills to express personal artistic talents. Areas include:

Ways to develop knowledge and appreciation of the arts.

Aesthetic judgments and the ability to apply them to works of art.

Using resources of museums, libraries, theaters, historic sites, and performing arts groups.

Producing or performing works in at least one major art form.

Materials, media, and history of major art forms.

Understanding the diversity of artistic heritages.

Thinking Skills Each student will develop the ability to:

Think logically, creatively, and critically.

Apply reasoning skills to issues and problems.

Mathematics/Science/Technology Each student will develop skills to:

Learn methods of inquiry and acquire knowledge.

Understand the scientific theories and principles underlying physical, biological, and information technologies.

Acquire and apply knowledge of the ecological consequences of choices to the environment.

Perform basic mathematical calculations.

Apply statistics and probability.

Acquire technical skills, including keyboarding, computer applications, and other vocational competencies.

Personal and Career Development Each student will acquire knowledge, skills, and attitudes which enable development of:

Self-esteem.

Time management.

Responsible consumer behavior, satisfying interpersonal relationships, and appropriate sexual behavior.

Physical, mental, and emotional health.

Understanding of the ill-effects of alcohol, tobacco, and other drugs.

The ability to make self-assessment of career prospects.

Career skills, including work attitudes and habits, teamwork, and work ethic.

Study skills.

Social Science/Civil Behavior Each student will acquire knowledge of political, economic, and social institutions and procedures in this country and other countries. Included are:

Knowledge of American political, economic, and social processes and policies at national, state, and local levels.

Knowledge of political, economic, and social institutions and procedures in various nations; ability to compare the operation of such institutions; and understanding of the international interrelationships of political, economic, social, cultural, and environmental systems.

Each student will respect and practice basic civil values and acquire the skills, knowledge, understanding, and attitudes necessary to participate in democratic government. Included are:

Appreciation and acceptance of the values of justice, honesty, self-discipline, due process, equality, and majority rule with respect for minority rights as civil values upon which a democratic government is based.

Respect for self, others, and property as integral to a self-government society.

Ability to apply democratic processes and reason to resolve societal problems and disputes.

The statements above, added to the earlier definition of adult roles, offer a good example of the value of the step-by-step approach to educational change. Frameworks of thought and planning are created in incremental steps, then enlarged during succeeding activities. In effect, the listing of skills to be mastered identifies academic requirements for curriculum coverage of the adult roles.

Another advantage is that the succeeding lists of roles, skills, and others to follow provide rough drafts that can be polished or refined in ongoing activities to help hone in on curriculum content and learning activities. At the outset, as noted above, the planning team in Polk County freed itself from dependence on current course listings. Focus is on the student and his or her eventual success as a successful, adjusted adult rather than on past, largely failed concepts.

To illustrate, note that the first set of competencies listed, which is common to all learning processes, avoids preoccupation with currently emphasized instruction in reading, writing, grammar, and language usage. Emphasis is on the value of acquired knowledge and skills through the ability to interact with others. It is significant, then, that the next set of skills deals with culture and humanities while the third covers generic thought processes.

CONSTRUCTIVE CHALLENGES BECOME ESSENTIAL

Within this reference framework, it is worth noting that constructive criticism can help either to adapt competency lists like the above, to alter or update them on the basis of experience, or to edit draft documents to provide more specific guidance for the development of specific curricula.

An initial, overall, observation, for instance, might deal with the ambitious scope of the list of competencies. To achieve all of the competencies identified, the district would have to restructure all course and instructional activities, at all high school grades and in a massive single effort. This degree of change would involve all course descriptions, lesson plans, test and assessment programs, and development of study materials or texts (since these listed criteria differ from any that exist).

Further, a study of the outlines themselves indicates a number of areas where the logical design and learning sequences might profit from review and revision. For example, consider the communication skills listed. It might help to incorporate descriptions of the levels of skills targeted, possibly in conjunction with identification of audiences to be addressed or sources of messages that must be comprehended. As an example, it might be useful to relate skills in speech and writing to audiences such as future customers, employers, or personal acquaintances. Similarly, it might be helpful to specify that the student should be able to understand oral instructions for job performance.

As another example of how critical review can help such documents, consider the skills listed for appreciation of the arts. The reference to accomplishments of "various cultures" is broad and vague, particularly since the arts to be appreciated are not identified specifically. Note also that the category involves appreciation while the listed skills call for "producing or perform-ing works."

These are small points and there is no intent to be hyper-critical. Rather, the idea is to stress that documents created during a series of stages represent works in progress. At this point in the process, it is not necessary to establish hard-and-fast commitments. The idea is to invite revision and improve-ment, not to resist change the way many longstanding educa-tional structures do. Iteration through a series of steps pro-vides an opportunity at each point in the process for construc-tive criticism, analysis, and adjustment as necessary. Also, de-velopment of written documents provides a basis for dissemi-nation while comments by participants help to establish the kind of consensus without which a program of this type cannot be implemented effectively.

MONITORING BEHAVIOR

Note that the third process step also stipulates definition of ac-ceptable behavior. Polk County did an effective job of pioneering in this area, establishing a basis for discipline and control over deportment necessary to assure rounded performance by stu-dents. Over and above traditional academic grades for tradi-tional academic courses that remained in the curriculum and for which standards and requirements were not compromised, Polk County Schools established a series of behavior-based ar-eas for grading, including Performance Objectives, Behavior, Attendance, Assignments, Motivation, and Group Work. The ac-companying table (Figure 5-1) outlines these criteria and the bases for grade assignments.

Creation and review of this table provide an excellent ex-ample of the kind of rethinking that can take place through realistic evaluation of proposals that sound good initially but have other ramifications. (Coincidentally, this is the kind of achievement the authors had in mind in adding the sixth level, Innovation, to the Application Axis of the Relational Model.) This plan for multidimensional grading was reviewed and accepted readily in a series of meetings held in the rural parts of Polk County. Then, when the plan came up for review at a commu-nity meeting in the county seat, entirely new dimensions of con-cern were voiced.

Among town-resident parents, many families expected their children to go on to college. Parents of college-bound students objected strenuously that the multidimensional approach to

	C	B	A
Performance Objectives	Demonstrates command of all knowledge and skills identified in the performance objectives.	Can use knowledge and skills learned to solve daily problems and complete everyday tasks of a citizen, worker, lifelong learner, nurturer, and user of good health care.	Can use knowledge and skills learned to solve complex problems and complete challenging tasks encountered by citizens, workers, lifelong learners, nurturers, and users of good health care.
Behavior	Respects the rights of others and exhibits self-control.	Is thoughtful of others, is cooperative, and respects individual differences.	Serves as an example to others and helps others modify their behavior by serving as a model and exerting peer pressure.
Attendance	Meets the standard established by the Board Policy.	Consistant pattern of being in class and on time.	Has no class absences and is never tardy.
Assignments	All assignments are completed with high degree of accuracy.	All Assignments are completed on time and correctly.	Completes additional assignments on their own.
Motivation	Follows directions of teacher in a timely manner.	Is actively involved in the learning process and does not need close supervision of teacher.	Helps others, does more than assigned tasks, and serves as a model for others.
Group Work	Is non-disruptive to the group and does a fair share of work.	Helps others to complete tasks and is commited to the group's success.	Provides leadership to the group to complete tasks in a timely and effestive manner.

Table VII. Criteria for Grading in Polk County, North Carolina

FIGURE 5-1. BEHAVIORAL GRADES INTRODUCED AT POLK COUNTY AND THEIR CRITERIA.

grading could dilute student Grade Point Average (GPA) scores and class ranking that would have been achieved based entirely on academic marks. GPA, it was stressed, was a major basis for college admissions.

After considerable negotiation, a decision was reached that academic grades would count for 50 percent (instead of one-fifth) of the overall student evaluation. Thus, through direct community involvement, the district broadened its base for performance evaluation while also satisfying its academically oriented constituents.

This particular compromise makes everyone involved a winner. The multidimensional grading system is designed specifically to reward diligent work habits and personal reliability, factors that are important to student successes both as workers and as college students. In college, it was stressed in explanations to parents, work habits and diligence are the major keys to success. College dropouts, parents were shown, tend to result from lack of student self-discipline. To dramatize the exposure, parents were advised that, of all students entering four-year college programs nationwide, only 42 percent graduate. At two-year colleges, the graduation ratio averages 23 percent nationally.

ENCOURAGING INNOVATION

The fourth process step is identification of negotiables and non-negotiables. Examples of these criteria are given in the previous chapter. These highlight the benefits of the incremental approach, establishing that it's necessary to complete the work in the first three steps before the fourth step can be carried out. This is because everything that impacts adult roles becomes non-negotiable as the process is carried forward. Thus, the grading system and other elements described above carried the Polk County program to readiness for outlining of curricula and plans for implementation, covered in the chapter that follows.

The developments described above occurred chiefly in 1991 and 1992 and called for a four-year implementation cycle. Programs implemented since then are summarized in Chapter 15, which identifies Polk County as a poster district demonstrating model achievement from commitments and programs for educational change.

A WESTERN VANTAGE

The Management of Change process, proponents assert, is flexible enough to fit the circumstances of virtually any American district or school. One way to test this thesis is to compare opposites, using as prime examples Polk County Schools in North Carolina and the Roseville Joint Union High School District in California. The geography and demographics of these districts are obviously diverse, about as different as two systems can be.

Regional dissimilarities mark only the beginning, symbolizing multiple diversities that identify and represent the majority of American communities and regions. Polk County is predominantly rural. So are parts of Placer County, California, which houses, among other trophies, Sutter's Mill, where the Gold Rush started. However, Roseville is markedly downslope from the Gold Country, an area of gently rolling foothills that give way to flat plains of the Sacramento Valley. Blessed with resources that include plentiful water and favorable climate, the Roseville area became a haven for high-tech overflow from the nearby Silicon Valley and also from nearby Sacramento.

Then there's population density. Polk County enrolls some 2,000 students over the full K-12 spread. Roseville serves 9-12 students only; but there are some 5,400 of them. Prior to undertaking major change, Polk County's schools were close to hitting bottom academically. Change resulted following a loud, resounding wakeup call. Roseville's academics were considered good. But the district's constituents wanted to do better, particularly in equipping schools and students to deal with the impending realities of the twenty-first century.

Back in 1991, in an early response to the national *Goals: 2000* program, the administration proposed and took tentative first steps toward implementation of this institutional set of dreams. Roseville's 1991 effort was entitled *Strategic Plan for Quality Education.* But progress stalled. In a recent district presentation on its program, the problem is identified this way: "In 1993, the district began to intensify its efforts by implementing a program of Total Quality Education based upon the principles of Dr. W. Edwards Deming. In mid-year 1993-94, however, it was apparent that this new approach was meeting with strong resistance from teachers and staff because it was viewed as 'just another program,' with little chance of making any real difference in the lives of students and teachers."

SELLING THE NEED FOR CHANGE

Clearly, it was time to get serious—and to convince the district's constituents that something was really going to happen. In an area where a significant part of the population earns its livelihood through expertise in systems development, Superintendent Robert Tomasini moved to cash in on capabilities of the dominant local industry. The district contracted with an experienced systems development consultant, Don Prentice, to help oversee implementation of the ICLE six-step change process.

Tomasini explains: "The fundamental decision in this new approach was [to work] through implementation of ongoing dialogue processes with all constituent stakeholders, or customers. We call this the Design Team Process. The district's future vision is also based upon a strong commitment to transforming the fundamental working relationships among all the people in our organization. This commitment includes significant trans-formations in the organizational structure, processes (includ-ing technology), and culture. We call this the Continuous Im-provement Process (CIP). Together, they form the compass that guides the district's transformational change journey."

RATIONALE FOR CHANGE

In launching its program for change, the Roseville team adopted a formal statement identified as the *Rationale for Change*. This statement stipulated:

The Roseville Joint Union High School District is strongly committed to a Continuous Improvement Process. Continuous Improvement means that we must build upon what we are already doing very well and change those things that must be changed in order to meet the challenging standards for our information-based, technological, global economy and society. Rationale:

- ❏ Our school standards must be aligned with world-class stan-dards of the twenty-first century.
- ❏ The knowledge, skills, and behaviors we teach our students must meet rigorous performance standards that are relevant to the world in which we live.
- ❏ We must create and use new processes and practices that allow our schools to catch up and keep up with the constant changes in our economy and society.
- ❏ We must change so that we can better teach our students life-long learning skills, adaptation skills, people-interaction skills, a strong work ethic, and strong personal ethics.
- ❏ We must change our educational system by opening it up to create and use a variety of processes that allow us to con-duct on-going dialogues with all constituent groups: students, parents, business/community groups, higher education rep-resentatives, and educational leaders.

THE DESIGN TEAM CONCEPT

Given the management-technology makeup of the community, the six-step process at Roseville acquired a specially flavored set of terms and descriptors. In light of the composite personal-ity of the district's constituency, the methods and terms pro-vided workable rallying cries and rationales. In the first step, aimed at creating an awareness of current situations and future opportunities, the district assembled a Design Team (working groups were always teams, never committees) that included students, parents, teachers, staff, businesspeople, community groups, and representatives of higher education. Among other responsibilities, the group was charged with developing a set of adult requirements that became part of the district's graduation goals. These were incorporated in a descriptive statement dubbed Essential Knowledge and Skills (EKS).

Within the Design Team structure, Action Teams were formed to deal with separate EKS areas. Examples included the Organizational Culture Team and the Organizational Infrastructure team, which collaborated to devise ways to restructure both the organizational scheme and the new working relationships needed to guide attitude and commitment adjustments among faculty and staff members. These and other elements of the Design Team process are diagrammed in Figure 5-2.

IDENTIFYING ESSENTIAL KNOWLEDGE AND SKILLS

The combined Design Team set the tone and established goals for the entire restructuring project by issuing a document entitled *Statements of Essential Knowledge and Skills*. Eight separate areas were encompassed, beginning with Basic Skills:

❏ Basic Skills: Reads, writes, performs arithmetic and mathematical operations, listens and speaks, uses visual skills and technology.

Descriptive listings were added for each of the identified skills. To demonstrate the analytical thought that went into EKSs, consider the statements covering reading and writing.

❏ Reading — Locates, understands, and interprets written information in literature, manuals, graphs, maps, schedules, textbooks, on-line computer services, and other sources.

❏ Writing — Communicates ideas, information, and messages by creating documents such as letters, essays, memos, e-mail messages, creative writing projects, directions, manuals, reports graphs, and flow charts.

Note that both these statements concentrate entirely on results, practical applications of acquired knowledge through student performance. Also implied by these statements is the development and use of communication skills within a context of multidisciplinary learning under the revised curriculum targeted

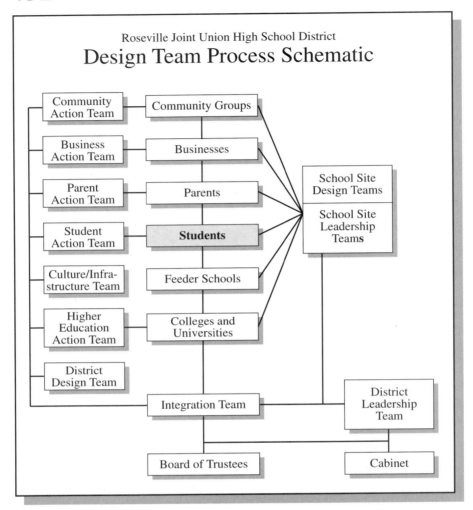

Roseville Joint Union High School District
Design Team Process Schematic

FIGURE 5-2. THIS SCHEMATIC IDENTIFIES THE ELEMENTS OF THE ROSEVILLE DESIGN TEAM APPROACH AND IDENTIFIES THE MAIN COMPONENTS.

within the Roseville transition. Further, it is clear that, to meet these achievement goals, students will have to master the elements of communication through reading and writing, including vocabulary, spelling, grammar, usage, as well as logic and continuity in writing or spoken presentations.

The next EKS component was Thinking Skills, stipulating that a graduating student "visualizes, interprets, thinks creatively, reasons, solves problems, and makes decisions." Interpretive Skills, one of the elements of Thinking Skills, requires: "Analyzes the images and messages from audio and visual sources to identify information, misinformation, facts, opinions, and real versus fictional portrayals." Under Creative Thinking

Skills, the student "Formulates new ideas and approaches to tasks, problems, and creative expression."

The EKS entry for Personal Development stipulates "Displays responsibility, self-respect, integrity, honesty, and perseverance."

Under the category for Resources, the EKS statement says "Identifies, organizes, plans, and allocates various resources." The identified resources listed include time, money, materials, and human resources.

EKS Interpersonal traits require that the student participates on a team, develops and demonstrates leadership, provides services to clients/customers, works with diversity, and understands human development.

Responding to the influences of its community, the EKS statement includes a set of goals entitled Information. The performance criteria are: "acquires and uses information, evaluates information, organizes and maintains information, and interprets and communicates information."

Also significant and responsive to its community, the EKS statement includes a separate category for Systems. This indicates that the student "Identifies, describes, and understands processes, roles, and interrelationships." Subcategories here stipulate "Understands Systems, Monitors and Corrects Performance," and "Designs or Improves Systems."

The final category is Technology. Performance criteria are "Selects and Applies Technology to Tasks," and "Maintains and Troubleshoots Equipment." Note the absence of preoccupation with software packages or Internet connectivity that are currently so prevalent among secondary schools. Roseville's teams have clearly concentrated on understanding the makeup and components of educational transactions that lead to advancement in the workplace.

APPLIED SYSTEMS THINKING

A major foundation for the Roseville program called for building a strong commitment to change among administrators, teachers, and other staff. This is the point at which the Continuous Improvement Process (CIP) was applied. Among the elements of CIP are establishing a "learning organization," promoting dialogue rather than discussion or debate in recognition of the need to arrive at consensus, avoiding having to deal with a series of separately defined bastions of opinion. The theory is that it is preferable to base decisions on consensus rather than majority votes, making it possible to operate through teamwork rather than committees.

Among the "tools" for CIP documented by the Roseville program is Applied Systems Thinking, defined as "Applied systems thinking is the context for CIP. It is a way of viewing and characterizing the decisions, communications processes, problems and issues that we face." A diagram representing the Applied Systems Approach is shown in Figure 5-3.

The view established under applied systems thinking encompasses a number of elements:

- ❏ Everything is connected to everything else.
- ❏ The whole is greater than the sum of its parts; the nature of any system cannot be inferred from knowing its particular parts.
- ❏ Understanding processes.
- ❏ Understanding that a system is a set of interconnected processes working toward a purpose.
- ❏ Understanding how processes connect people's roles and responsibilities.

Practical use of applied systems thinking, both for the adult design team and for students entering society and the work-

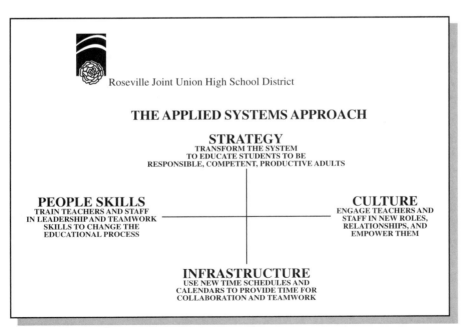

FIGURE 5-3. THIS DIAGRAM IDENTIFIES ELEMENTS OF THE APPLIED SYSTEMS APPROACH AND ILLUSTRATES THEIR RELATIONSHIP TO ONE ANOTHER.

place requires acquisition of a series of skill-based building blocks:

❏ Personal mastery: Continually clarifying and deepening our personal vision, the focus of our energies, our patiences and tenacity, and our ability to see reality objectively.

❏ Mental models: Understanding our deeply ingrained assumptions, generalizations, and mental pictures or images that influence how we understand the world and how we take action.

❏ Building a shared vision: A strong consensus on a shared picture of the future we wish to create.

❏ Team learning: Through dialogue. Creating a system where people learn to learn together and work to maximize their energy.

MISSION AND GUIDING PRINCIPLES

In its version of the educational change process note that Roseville, in response to existing beliefs and habits among its professional staff and permeating the community at large, tackled concepts for organization and infrastructure first. Then, in the third step of its process, the final increment before planning and implementation activities, the Design Team enunciated a Mission Statement and a set of Guiding Principles.

The mission statement:

❏ The Roseville Joint Union High School District will provide all students with a rigorous and relevant education design to give them the opportunity to acquire, apply, and practice the knowledge, skills, and behaviors needed to fulfill their adult roles and responsibilities in the twenty-first century.

The Guiding Principles:

1. Students are the center of everything we do. Our district will change and adapt to best serve our students.

2. Students will experience in school what they are likely to experience after graduation through work that requires them to solve problems and to apply learned skills and behaviors in real-life situations.

3. Students will be guided and supported by valued educational staff members who seek, develop, and implement successful practices and innovative ideas.

4. Students will be served through a process of continuous assessment and improvement that requires and values the ac-

tive participation and contributions of students, parents, staff, and other stakeholders.

5.   Students will be provided with a safe and supportive learning environment that involves the active participation of the educational staff, students, parents, and community members.

READY FOR ACTION

The narratives above cover the progress of two model districts in creating an environment to promote change and establish goals to be achieved. The succeeding steps, involving detailed functional planning and implementation, tend to require management training and skills that are often absent in university curricula directed toward teaching careers. So, the chapter that follows reviews some of this background and associated knowledge and skills in preparation for review of process completion, followed by reviews of results actually attained at Polk County and Roseville.

In closing this discussion, note that the major part of a change-oriented program lies in building the foundation for innovation. By contrast, the history of education is replete with cases where solutions have been introduced and implemented without benefit of problem identification or consideration of real needs.

Also worth noting is the spirit of consensus and commitment created in each district as a byproduct of group activities. In particular, it is worth stressing that, at the present state of American education, any change in curriculum content or targeted student achievements cannot happen without first establishing a spirit of cooperation by teachers and securing their commitment. Earlier chapters refer optimistically to a future time in education when teachers will become learning facilitators and classroom managers. If that is to happen, quasi-political practices like those described in this and the previous chapters must be in place.

On the other side, it's best to note that the process also contains some potential booby traps. One such hidden hazard results from the disregard for existing curriculum course listings implicit in concentration on multidisciplinary competencies. To illustrate, consider competencies such as logical thought, decision making, or problem solving. Who teaches them? Do the evolving courses show up as spin-offs from English? From social studies/history? From business? From math? From computer training? Whatever assignments are made, the appointed teachers are faced with restarting a major segment of their careers from scratch—with no firm guidelines or yardsticks against which to measure relative success.

Nobody says this kind of transition is going to be easy. Now, this is the point in the transition process where some of the real challenges come to light. Is it necessary to devise new tests? It would be difficult to administer a fully objective, computer-gradable test for courses involving judgmental and analytical end results. There's also the related question that applies to standardized, multiple-choice tests: ***Do we want American kids to go through their educational experience thinking that each question has only one answer?*** Shouldn't student assessment challenge students to conduct new research and to apply logic and judgment? Shouldn't students face assessment projects that do not have just one set answer? If so, what criteria apply to the mix between standardized testing, performance-based assessment, and grading? How does a teacher go about a changeover from a teaching to a learning environment, from the role of overseer to one of coordinator or facilitator?

This kind of consideration foretells the type of challenges that lie ahead. These involve acquiring and applying management methods, then converting statements of targeted student achievements into a workable curriculum, topics covered beginning with the following chapter.

Chapter 6
Managing Education as a Business

To get serious about what a school is going to look like and how it's going to operate at some future date, one workable—and frequently used—technique is for the key members of the task force responsible for change to leave the premises entirely. In effect, the planners are seeking a *virtual reality* that is unfettered by and different from traditions that can constrain imaginations and limit the possibilities considered.

RETREAT FOR ADVANCEMENT

A number of schools and districts have adopted a plan that calls for a two- or three-day retreat devoted entirely to formulating a new, improved vision of the school and the results it is to achieve. To establish an especially positive outlook for these sessions, the staff at one school (Caledonia High School, Caledonia, Michigan) has opted to call these sessions *advances* rather than retreats.

It's not easy to give up existing practices and prejudices and to cast an entire operation in a new image. For example, it's one thing to commit to creation of a learning environment and quite another to discard attitudes and actions that may be firmly implanted by one, two, or even three decades of teaching experience. But that's what it takes; commitments, relationships, and even teacher and staff identities have to be rethought.

Whether planning sessions are held locally or at a remote site, total concentration must focus on the changes to be implemented. The main concentration at the outset should be on the behavior that has to be instilled in students. Throughout their school experiences, most students have been cast in passive roles. That changes. In a learning environment, students are **active, not passive,** participants. Teachers who have been performers concentrating on delivering lectures to audiences must transform their efforts. The new emphasis is on ways to involve and motivate students so they absorb knowledge on their own and become active learners.

As key contributors to this transition, a role in which they are essential, teachers must also adjust their own sights and expectations. Environments in which all students are expected to progress at the same lock-step pace must give way to practices in which student individualities and divergences are not only allowed, but encouraged. Learning is individual, teaching is group-oriented.

PREREQUISITES FOR EDUCATIONAL CHANGE

The kind of transition demanded in education today presents its own, prerequisite requirements for professional constituents: **teachers must become planners, managers, and leaders capable of reinventing their own profession.** This transition is both major and basic. In the past, teachers' responsibilities and activities have focused chiefly on responsibilities and events within a single classroom. In the major transition involved in a changeover to a learning environment, each teacher must now learn to think and reach decisions in more global terms, including immersion in interdisciplinary instruction.

In the past, teaching responsibilities in many schools have been both defined and constrained by the content of an existing, narrow, often-outmoded syllabus. If the learning transition is to succeed, teachers must assume active roles in redefining education, then involve themselves actively in management functions that may be totally strange to them. Meeting this challenge requires an educational activity of its own. Teachers and other school personnel must be instructed and indoctrinated in the basics of managing a major organization with large budgets and extensive responsibilities for product delivery and customer satisfaction.

A good place to start planning the transition might be with a blank sheet of paper. Use it to design an effective and efficient school system, starting from scratch. Would any thinking person create a system that looks exactly like the one that exists today?

Try this on any group interested in education. It will get a laugh every time. The problem is that it's not funny. America finds itself today with an education system that has all the characteristics of a rudderless ship. Things happen by default. Effective and efficient management is, too often, the missing dimension.

START WITH THE PRESENT

What can be done? A good strategy in this situation is to take stock to see which parts are broken. Then, by concentrating on elements that need fixing, it may be possible to guide the vessel onto some constructive course.

Does this sound uncertain? Complex? Nearly impossible? Unpleasant at best? It certainly does. But, as the saying goes, somebody has to do it. Left as it is, education will not improve itself, by itself. Change requires planning, commitment, and supervised implementation of identified fixes. After that, the changes themselves have to be reviewed and monitored to determine when further fixes are indicated. In a time of continuous change, the process carries on into infinity. If enhanced educational results are to happen, a prerequisite ingredient that is largely missing must be added.

The absent ingredient in education, identified above, is management. This is not an indictment of school administrators. There are many talented, hard-working individuals among them. But they have an impossible job; it's hard to accomplish anything when you are working, figuratively, with your hands tied.

As presently structured, the American educational system limits school administrators to the literal meaning of their title. They are administrators, not managers. They hold a job that collectively is scoffed at as "clerk of the works." As a general rule, management, with its implication for devising and implementing change, is out of the question, unpermitted. Rather, the role of administrators is to keep things going as they have been for many years, protecting past practices and, in particular, the turfs of the adults with vested interests in the status quo.

In other words, nobody is piloting the ship. Nobody has responsibility. Nobody is accountable. If you do take that blank sheet of paper and lay out a new system, figure out who should take charge and how. A survey seeking a definitive description of management as it is currently practiced in American education might come up with this answer: *management is somebody else's job.* That description, almost unfailingly, draws at least a smile, sometimes a laugh. Unfortunately the joke is on all of us.

EXPENSIVE MISTAKES

But this situation isn't funny. Consider the stakes. Education, the unmanaged business, uses revenues—tax revenues—that are larger than the world's largest business entities. In 1995, the largest business in the United States, General Motors, had total revenues of $168.8 billion. The largest corporation in the world, Mitsubishi (of Japan) reported 1995 revenues of $184.3 billion.

American public education serving kindergarten through twelfth grade students, as an overall entity, experienced cash flow in excess of $200 billion. Now add expenditures for private schools, college, university, adult education, and training programs underwritten by businesses to overcome educational shortfalls. On this basis, total costs of education come to a serious multiple of revenues for even giants like General Motors. Like education, General Motors and Mitsubishi also are highly diversified. Services are rendered in thousands of different locations. But products of successful businesses are well defined and customers know what to expect. If education ever reaches that point, many existing problems will vanish.

Now consider the way education manages and accounts for its cash flow. There is no single executive or group of managers responsible for results delivered. All parts of the organization—at national, state, and local levels—operate, for practical purposes, with virtual autonomy and without direct operational responsibility and accountability among them.

THE CLASSROOM AS A FIEFDOM

In the classroom, the ultimate point where educational transactions happen, management responsibility and accountability are effectively absent as operational criteria—permanently truant. Each classroom is, effectively, an independent, isolated kind of fiefdom. Once a classroom door is closed, only one person in the entire world—the teacher—has any significant impact on the content presented to the captive students. As noted in the Federal report, the students are *prisoners of time* within a system of total captivity.

The content prescribed for any class at any time, by fiat from higher up, is, in most instances, narrowly defined and within a single discipline. Further, the teacher, without allocated time for professional study or lesson preparation, is apparently expected to teach the same constrained content this year as last year, the year before, and back through the decades.

Within these severely limited conditions and, absent real guidance, that teacher dominates, absolutely, the activities of the students and the information content to which they are exposed. In any other context, such conditions would attract outcries of human-rights violations. Yet, even within these limitations, an encounter between an eager student and a gifted teacher can become a life-enhancing, enriching experience. Compounded through a career-long exposure to a generation of students, a teacher's contribution to the dynamism and well-being of the community can result in massive benefits.

Now consider the consequences that could evolve from providing adequate teacher preparation and support within a learning-oriented environment. This potential makes many current realities even more tragic. Present methods constitute a highly ineffective and inefficient way to manage the completely random occurrences of contact between students and teachers. As the American education system is now constituted, the law of averages is against the student. Teaching is possibly the only—or at least the major and most tragic—example of an occupation in which on-job performance, once tenure is awarded, has virtually no effect upon either job security or career advancement.

Student achievement—the ultimate and only effective measure of the quality of the system's major outputs—is, in most instances, not considered. Student achievement is rarely considered in rating teacher performance or in determining future career opportunities, including promotability. Tenure remains a battleground on which some vital issues must be resolved before schools can deliver the caliber and competitive stature of services required by their constituencies. As this battle is joined, objectives must ultimately be clear: Student achievement must be accorded priority over the personal concerns of any and all employees assigned to serve students and other constituents. The *de facto* structure under which the educational system operates for the benefit of its adult employees must be altered.

In fairness, there are problems that make performance measurement difficult. Teachers have no control over which students are assigned to their classes. They have no say in what their students know at the beginning of a school year—or their learning potential. Neither do teachers generally have the kind of discipline options formerly available. The fact that physical punishment is no longer a societally accepted option under ordinary operating circumstances tends to be interpreted to mean that teachers have to accept whatever behavior students choose to display. Though that assumption isn't really true, it suffices to excuse intolerable conduct and to at least partially explain teacher feelings of helplessness and inability to improve substandard results.

In this respect, teachers themselves are victims within a system that greatly limits their options and opportunities. Teachers who feel they are functioning inadequately under existing constraints are severely limited in their ability to innovate or even vary slightly from business as usual. As things stand, teacher freedom is tightly constrained: They can go along with the status quo or risk becoming scapegoats.

To repeat an earlier caveat: No real improvements in educational rigor or relevance can be achieved unless and until teachers participate actively in the management of change. Thus, development of managerial skills in teachers becomes one of the major requisites for any program aimed at educational upgrades.

BASIC PRINCIPLES OF MANAGEMENT

Any organization too large for the top manager to oversee every detail related to delivery of products or services, particularly relationships with customers, must delegate operating responsibility. This need is present in the great majority of schools and districts. The only way management can happen within a school is through delegation of both responsibility and accompanying authority to carry out assigned tasks, then holding the designees accountable for results.

Operationally, a service organization is, effectively, a community of individuals each responsible for his or her performance—but also committed to a collaborative effort to achieve common goals. Thus, the people who operate a school are a team. As with a team in sports, it takes a series of activities—a process—to achieve winning coordination. The process for overall organizational management includes four steps, or phases:

1. Plan
2. Organize
3. Implement
4. Monitor and Adjust

Bear in mind that this entire process for management planning and control, including implementing change, is carried out separately from the ongoing operation of the school or district. Thus, the activities associated with changing a management system can—and, wherever possible, should—be separate from day-to-day operations. Planning, structuring, and even implementing a new curriculum element can be tried out—piloted—externally to day-to-day operations and phased in as tested, proven innovations with minimal impact for day-to-day functions. Changed methods are monitored after implementation and can be modified on the basis of experience.

ROLE AND NATURE OF ORGANIZATIONAL STRATEGY

As discussed in Chapter 4, enterprise management happens within a framework, or general set of guidelines, known as a **strategy.** A successful organization implements a sound strategy. Within this context, *a strategy is a set of policies, commitments, customs, and basic beliefs that, collectively, determine the constituencies an organization serves, the kinds of products or services provided to its customers, the resources utilized, and the quality of products or services.*

Every organization has a strategy. That strategy may be stated formally and reflect serious thought by the organization's leaders. Or it may have evolved informally, through impressions or interpretations based on incidental, possibly unintended, actions by the organization's people. A clear, formal statement of strategy is a better way to go, supporting much more effective management than the alternative, which is to let a strategy develop by default.

Consider the differences. If a strategy is planned, stated clearly, and disseminated to all parties who are to be involved in its implementation, it serves to guide decisions and actions at all levels and in every part of an organization. A clearly understood strategy becomes the basis for the culture of the entity. If a strategy evolves by default, the standing of an organization and the acceptance of its products or services is apt to be vague and subject to frivolous interpretation or change. One way or another, though, there will be a strategy that establishes a framework that defines an organization.

CHANGING ATTITUDES ABOUT STRATEGY IN SCHOOLS

For many years, a substantial part of the educational establishment—perhaps a majority—permitted strategies to evolve without benefit of any real forethought. Through the years, the *de facto* strategies that did exist responded to pressures created by taxpayer activist groups, state or federal regulations, or special grants or programs that conveyed their own funding. Strategies responding to such pressures were not likely to be responsive to factors such as quality of customer service or level of satisfaction. Under these conditions, each time a teacher faced a class or an administrative employee dealt with a parent, the interpretation of strategy could be altered. The surrounding world often changed without producing any reaction or adjustment from the school system.

In taking hold of the ongoing management of a school, the starting point is to identify and define the existing strategy. In other words, start with what exists. Then compare what exists with the statements of mission and lists of targeted objectives, as developed during the change process. These statements serve to enunciate the policies and guidelines that should direct the organization's future efforts. The new strategy then describes what the organization is expected to look like after the changes are implemented. A challenge, then, lies in modifying the culture and operating continuity of the organization to accommodate the new strategy.

Following this logic, establishing a strategy is an early and essential byproduct of the ICLE six-step process for managing change. A school district begins to establish a formal, implementable strategy when a statement of vision and basic beliefs is adopted formally following a procedure that includes drafting, reviewing, revision, and consensus acceptance.

In effect, a vision statement tells all constituents why a school or group of schools exists. Goals and purposes are clearly understood on reading an effective vision statement. Purposes and principles are defined further with a statement of beliefs that tells all parties what the organization stands for. Strategy is elaborated further with definition of adult roles targeted for students. Cumulatively, these documents tell the world why a school exists, what its leaders expect to achieve, which constituents are to be served, and the commitment that has been made in terms of content and quality of education to be delivered. In other words, all of the ingredients for strategy formation are inherent in the beginning stages of the six-step change process.

To visualize or symbolize a strategy for universal understanding, a pizza can be a helpful device. Begin with the crust, which provides a foundation that establishes an understanding of where the school stands at any given moment. Then add the cheese, sauces, and toppings by producing a vision statement and enunciating goals and purposes. The crust by itself isn't very appetizing. But the product becomes more savory each time a new ingredient is added, finally becoming irresistible when everything is blended together by the baking process to form an attractive result.

Within a program aimed at guiding a school or district through a major set of changes, a clear statement of strategy provides a necessary cohesion for all participants. Everyone involved acquires a sense of purpose and commitment, an effective source of motivation for sharing activities and results. In this sense, a strategy is a constant; it is timeless, continuous. It also is subject to review and change within the current context of change-oriented activities, making for a flexibility essential in a constantly changing, technology-driven environment. When a strategy no longer covers a clearly perceived, consensus-accepted need for a school or district, the strategy is amended, but only after due consideration to the implications of the revision. A vision statement, however, is not subject to pressures of cyclic revision schedules or deadlines.

THE PLANNING STEP IN THE CHANGE PROCESS

The planning step within the educational transition is, by contrast, time-frame related. That is, while the strategy is continuous and timeless, management planning is very much time-dependent and subject to schedules. Typical designations and timeframes for managerial planning are:

Strategic planning covers the long-range future of an organization, often described in terms of five to seven years beyond current status.

Tactical planning deals with an interim time frame and focuses on implementation of strategic plans, including preparation of physical plant and redefinition of organizational structures. Typical time frames for tactical plans are in the range of two to four years.

Operational planing covers ongoing operations, usually for the current year. An important part of every operational plan is the current-year budget. In schools, operational plans deal with staffing, teacher contracts, purchase of books and supplies, and other essential support functions.

Figure 6-1 represents the time frames for these three types of planning.

These three planning time frames, which are carried out at different organizational levels, must be integrated, or interlocking. Strategic planning forms a framework for tactical planning, which forms a framework for operational planning. These connections are illustrated by the U-turn patterns in Figure 6-1. For a more realistic example of these interrelationships, consider a school district that involves itself in the ICLE six-step change process.

Strategic plans based on community and research inputs establish and seek consensus on what the system should look like in the long-range future. The new look at adult roles becomes an important part of the strategic plan—but only one part among a number of others. For example, district administrators must look at the physical plant and its adequacy. Is the present student population housed and served adequately? Are additional facilities needed? What is the student-teacher ratio

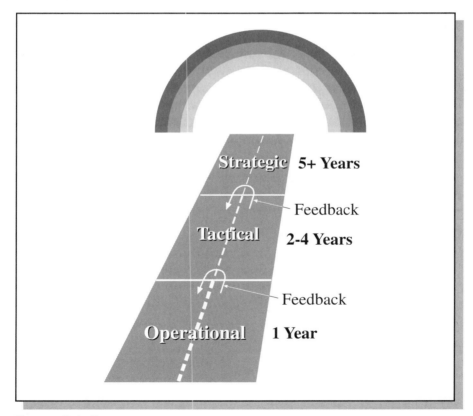

FIGURE 6-1. OPERATIONAL, TACTICAL, AND STRATEGIC PLANNING HAVE DIFFERENT, TIME-RELATED VIEWS OF AN ORGANIZATION'S OPERATIONS.

and is it effective? Do communication and computational facilities need upgrading?

Answers to these questions contribute to projections about facilities and staffing. Other inputs about facilities and staff come from monitoring construction permits within the district. For example, a plan to build a new factory can alert planners to look for the filing of permits to construct new housing. In turn, the projected extent and location of added housing can impact the future enrollments in the district's schools. Projecting long-range requirements can help prevent the too-familiar situation in which a district finds itself swamped with applications for enrollments and a shortage of classrooms for the new students.

Tactical plans then establish programs to monitor and implement strategic plans. For instance, as construction begins on a new housing project, tactical planners will match projected student populations against the district's facilities. Reassignments of school boundaries or even requirements for new construction must be identified and implemented before the kids show up to register. Staffing plans also must be forecast to cope with the operations anticipated during the tactical time frame. An important aspect of tactical planning is the projection of anticipated facilities, staffing, and supplies requirements into multi-year budget projections.

Within the context of instructional redesigns discussed in earlier chapters of this book, tactical planning also incorporates forecasts of when and at what costs modified curricula will be implemented. A major impact on multi-year budgets and instructional plans also should come from consideration of opportunities and requirements for applying technology in the classroom. The time has come when computer technology, including the availability of interactive instructional tools and information-network connections, must be incorporated in educational planning. Even though technologies change more rapidly than a typical tactical-planning time frame, planners must anticipate and provide for technology upgrades or find their schools and students hopelessly behind.

Operational plans follow up to implement strategic and tactical plans to meet the active needs of students, staff, and community. In other words, operational plans cover the short-term needs for running the school during the current year. Added details include specific classroom assignments for teachers and other staff, acquisition of books and supplies, and maintenance.

ASSEMBLING MANAGEMENT PLANS

Management plans generally are assembled from the future backward to the present. Strategic plans are developed first and used as a basis for tactical plans which, in turn, guide the preparation of current-year operational plans. This sequence and these relationships among plans also imply a hierarchical, or organization-level, connection between planning levels. Typically, strategic planning is done by top executives, tactical planning is implemented by middle managers, and operational planning is carried out by the people who run the school on a day-to-day basis.

Figure 6-2 shows this organizational relationship for management planning, using a pyramid that is widest at the bottom, narrower in the middle, and narrowest at the top. The pyramid structure reflects the fact that comparatively few people do strategic planning, with more involved as greater detail is required in tactical and operational stages. Also, the lower the

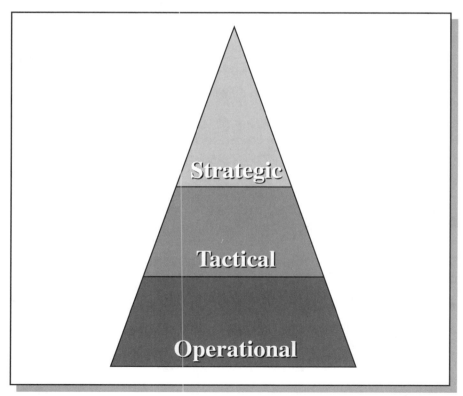

FIGURE 6-2. THE MANAGEMENT PLANNING PROCESS INVOLVES MORE PEOPLE AND ACQUIRES MORE DETAIL AS IT MOVES FROM TOP TO BOTTOM, FROM FUTURE TO PRESENT.

level, the greater the amount of detail, as current-year plans encompass classroom-by-classroom needs and achievement targets.

The pyramid structure that depicts management planning in Figure 6-2 represents only a first stage in a more complete and complex activity sequence. This diagram shows a top-down progression in which plans are elaborated as the work progresses from the upper to lower levels of an organization.

REVIEWING AND FINALIZING PLANS

The planning job should not end at this point. Managers at tactical and operational levels must have a chance to react to and comment on an organization's plans before they are adopted. Further, these comments must be considered seriously and factored into the final plans. In other words, plans formulated on a top-down basis must be reviewed and modified as necessary on a bottom-up basis.

Managers at all levels should accept, or "buy into" plans during the review and approval process. Plans are useless unless the people charged with implementing them agree that they are feasible and realistic. This is a basic characteristic of human nature, demonstrated by the truism: You can lead a horse to water, but you can't make it drink. You can set goals for people, but you can't force them to produce results that they feel to be impossible or unrealistic. The momentum for change starts with consensus among participants.

Thus, for example, you can load 40 students into a classroom. But, unless you make provisions for handling this workload and help staff prepare for the challenge, there's no way to predict whether or how much actual learning will occur. In reality, then, the degree of influence or impact of management plans is inverse to the level and number of people actively involved in preparation. The more general and far reaching the plan, the greater its influence and impact will be. This relationship is diagrammed in Figure 6-3.

It is also true that the people responsible for implementing a plan must be able to have some say in reviewing and evaluating, then modifying or restructuring that plan. Managers, regardless of level, must have a chance to pass on the feasibility of plans they are asked to implement. This is inherent in the system described here because the strategy provides a basis for guidance and evaluation at every level of planning. Any time plans and strategy disagree, resolution is necessary. Either the

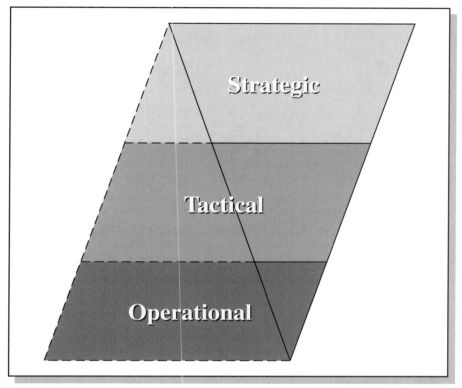

FIGURE 6-3. THE HIGHER THE LEVEL OF A SET OF PLANS, THE BROADER ITS IMPACT WILL BE ON ITS CONSTITUENTS.

plan or the strategy must be modified to avoid misleading or misdirecting an organization's constituents.

Accordingly, all plans, at all levels, must be reviewed and feedback must be sought from all parties with implementation responsibilities. This is part of the consensus-building prerequisite described earlier. People must understand and subscribe to their work assignments or both performance and quality are at risk. The relationships between the planning process, its impact, and the organization's strategy are diagrammed in Figure 6-4.

The essential process of plan review and revision typically takes place annually, ideally beginning several months before plans are actually activated. Drafts are circulated to everyone who will be involved in approval and implementation. Dissemination begins on a top-down basis, from the highest level down to individual schools and teachers and interested external constituents. Responses then should run from the bottom up and should be cumulative, with comments added at each level and

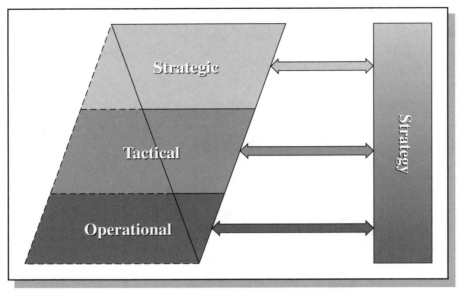

FIGURE 6-4. AS PART OF THE PLANNING PROCESS, ALL INVOLVED PARTIES MUST BE ABLE TO REACT TO INITIAL PLANS, OFFER COMMENTS, PARTICIPATE IN REVISIONS, AND ACCEPT ASSIGNMENTS THEY FEEL ARE ATTAINABLE.

the entire package moving back to the point where strategic planning originated.

DELEGATING IMPLEMENTATION RESPONSIBILITIES

To complete the planning phase of the management process when a major educational change is being implemented, this review-revision cycle may have to be repeated several times for the documents containing vision statements, basic beliefs, adult roles, and behavior descriptions. Within each iteration, personal judgments and expression of individual, possibly opposing, viewpoints should be anticipated, if not actually encouraged and, of course, resolved.

It is usually okay, for example, to establish curriculum content guidelines at a district level. Then, judgments about what content to include within each course and decisions about performance expectations from students can be left for standard setting in the individual schools. General guidelines from federal, state, or district departments are okay. But there has to be a point at which instructional guidance and learning are individualized for a given set of students and the teacher who facilitates their learning experience.

Major emotional trauma, and also loss of student achievement, can result from efforts to micromanage curriculum content—or even lesson plans—from the state or federal level. Intellectual chaos can result from programs that constrain the ability of teachers to adopt instructional programs to the needs of students.

For individual learning to happen, authority and responsibility for instructional delivery must be left with the classroom teacher. District and school managers can, with teacher concurrence, establish performance expectations. But when it comes to navigating a vehicle through the intellectual traffic of a classroom, each teacher should have final control over the route. A curriculum has to be translated into lesson plans and classroom strategies. This is the point at which teachers should be permitted to do their own things. But the right of individuality in the classroom should be earned and deserved. This level of independence should be awarded on the basis of performance for established teachers, and clearly understood commitments by newcomers.

The connection between authority or control over instructional content and methods, as well as responsibility for results, has been misunderstood, resisted, or both in negotiations between organizations representing teachers and educational entities. The management view tends to be that teachers want authority but refuse to accept responsibility. The teachers tend to hold that they really don't have authority as long as administrators retain control over assigning teachers to classes and assigning students without consulting the teachers.

As a management challenge, therefore, the authors believe that some form of consensus and compromise must be reached on the realization of expectations for student progress. This topic is revisited as this chapter progresses. The present discussion deals with the planning portion of management responsibilities, just the start in the challenge that educators must understand and accept.

ESTABLISHING AN ORGANIZATIONAL STRUCTURE

Strategies and plans are implemented by people through consensus and cooperation. Implementing a plan, in turn, requires an organization structured to facilitate consensus and cooperation. Right up to the present day, most educational organizations are structured in a way that blocks, rather than promotes, consensus and cooperation. Don't feel bad, though. Until the recent bandwagon for restructuring rolled through the corporate world, most business entities also were organized to assure that each segment or department was a natural enemy of every other segment or department.

The basic problem can be summarized in one word: hierarchy. Power, responsibility, and authority typically are vested in one or a few people whose positions are displayed at the pinnacle of a chart that presents all other jobs in the organization as subservient. Organizational charts are hierarchical, demonstrating a trickle-down relationship among job positions. Descriptions of relationships within organizations typically are prefixed with expressions such as "I work for" or "I report to."

A hierarchical representation of an organization structure imparts feelings of insignificance, presenting impressions that each individual is beneath someone at some higher level. A person situated at a middle or lower level on an organization chart is certainly not encouraged to assume initiative or to provide constructive criticism to plans or operating instructions that come from above. As an antidote, many large business enterprises have promoted team concepts and fostered the idea of organizations without boundaries.

American education also flirted with the same general principle during the early 1990s. The programs were known as "site-based management" or "site-based decision making." As the names imply, the idea was to move decision-making authority to individual schools, their administrations, and faculties. The trend was introduced in the same time frame as the federal *Goals 2000* initiative. Unfortunately, these ideas never really had a chance—they were moved directly from federal and state wish lists to implementation without any real opportunity to build consensus in local schools, as is being done under the ICLE Management of Change process.

Properly managed, team or task force learning activities can bring major benefits to schools. The principle, in education as well as in industry, is logical: Nobody is closer to the problems of a job than a person doing the work. Organization structures, therefore, should promote opinions and recommendations from the people actively involved in producing and/or delivering products or services. Then there should be assurance that constructive suggestions will be accepted and acted upon.

In manufacturing companies, recent experiences have shown that assembly line workers organized into teams can and do understand and apply principles of productivity and quality. Multidisciplinary teams have successfully promoted coordination between production workers, marketing people, engineers, designers, and management.

The experience in Roseville, California, covered briefly in the previous chapter, provides evidence that the same concepts can work in education. In Roseville, organizational considerations were dealt with early in the transformational process with appointment of a design team and other teams to coordinate different areas of projected change. The principle at work in this instance serves to give contributors a proprietary interest in new ideas and system modifications.

The kinds of working groups identified and described in the earlier discussion about Roseville's experiences embody the teamwork concepts that promote positive attitudes and support constructive change, with continuing attention to quality control. Thus, additional, detailed discussions should not be necessary at this point. It may be worthwhile, however, to think about how information on organization structures is communicated to an entity's constituents—most typically through an organization chart—and how meaningful ideas about team-oriented organizations can be communicated within an organization and among its constituents.

REPRESENTING TEAM STRUCTURES

Converting from a hierarchical to a team structure presents a challenge: How do you represent the new team approach graphically? After all, people have been used to looking at hierarchical organization charts for most of their working careers. Now, with new concepts being introduced, a natural way to show team-oriented differences is through a different kind of diagram, one that shows commitments and responsibilities that transcend traditional organizational boundaries.

One workable solution is to use an approach proven in a field that is being integrated increasingly into education—data communication among computer workstations and networks.

One configuration used frequently in computer communications systems is called the *star network.* In a star network, a series of small computers or terminals is linked into a hub, or networking computer that handles messages and controls access to a larger universe of communication devices. In applying the proven communication model to diagram an organization, a star network portrays a series of functions around a central hub that denotes the client, customer, constituent, or other entity that receives services or attention from the others.

By now, this principle should be familiar to the majority of the education community, since the Internet is, in effect, an almost infinite interlinking of star networks built around access points.

A fair question about the value of organizational diagrams might be: What's the difference? If people know their jobs and understand their relationships with colleagues, does the organizational diagram really matter? Possibly the most convincing analogy comes from sports. Helping collaborating professionals to understand their roles in an organization is akin to preparing a lineup and play diagrams for a football or basketball team. It definitely helps for collaborating workers to understand where they fit and what they are expected to do. The more clearly management can define roles and responsibilities, the more focused actual performances should be.

This approach was used to communicate the idea of a team organization during a consulting engagement by one of the authors in the fall of 1993. The assignment was to help Nograd County, Hungary, to devise a curriculum in mass media skills to be administered in a continuity encompassing high school and two years of college. Hungary was still emerging from the effects of more than 50 years of occupation by Germany and the Soviet Union, an era in which communication media were state owned and controlled. Independent media were still new and developing, making for a shortage of journalists trained to operate in an environment of press freedom.

Studies and design efforts focused primarily on fitting content covering media, journalism, and technical support into the existing academic curriculum, which was not to be varied or rearranged significantly. Near the end of the engagement, the county's director of education required an organization chart to help brief other officials on how the new curriculum would fit into established school system structures.

To demonstrate conceptual differences between organizational approaches, both a hierarchical and a star network diagram were delivered. Figure 6-5 shows the proposed approach to fitting the new activities into the longstanding hierarchical structure already in place in Hungary. Figure 6-6 shows the organization of the proposed new school with the student as a hub. This established a contrast of viewpoints, placing the student as the focus of activities as compared with a hierarchy in which the student was at the bottom.

Demonstrating how organizations are diagrammed through multiple, linked star networks, Figure 6-7 connects configurations that position the student, a teacher, and the school principal at hubs of interrelated star lineups. This diagram estab-

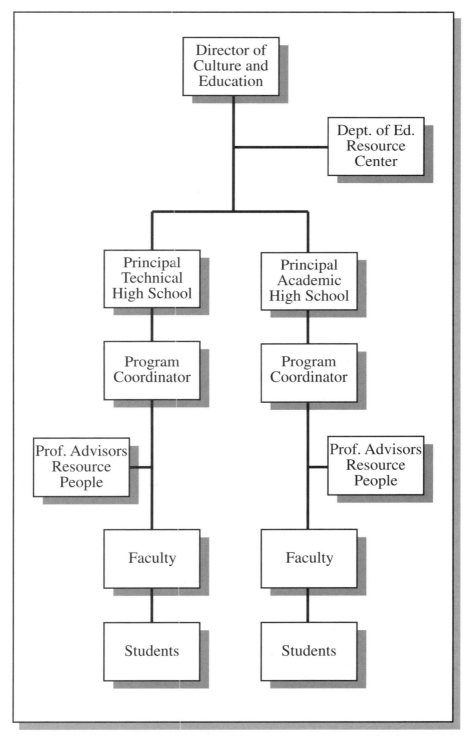

FIGURE 6-5. SCHOOL ORGANIZATION DEPICTED WITH A TYPICAL HIERARCHICAL CHART. STUDENTS ARE AT THE BOTTOM.

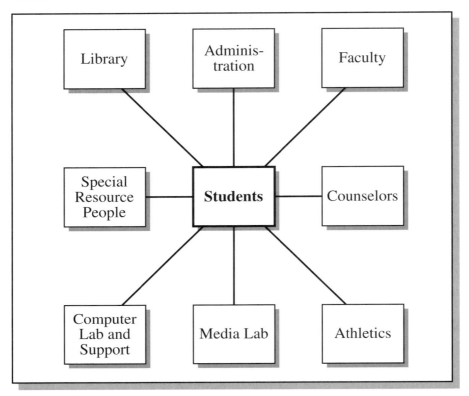

FIGURE 6-6. STAR NETWORK DIAGRAM SHOWING RESOURCES AND SERVICES FOCUSED UPON THE STUDENT. ELIMINATING HIERARCHICAL RELATIONSHIPS CAN HAVE THE EFFECT OF PROMOTING TEAMWORK.

lishes an overall organization composed of multiple teams, letting every person know where his or her support and contacts lie and showing connections with the rest of the organization.

Figure 6-8 is the star-network type of diagram used to demonstrate the transformed structure of the Roseville Union High School District. Figure 6-9 demonstrates how this same principle was applied to communicate the structure of the communications network of the Roseville district.

In considering star-based diagramming, think back to the earlier reference to the desirability of establishing accountability for results at the classroom level. Note, in this regard, that Figure 6-6 shows a direct responsibility relationship between teacher, support personnel, and students. By contrast, Figure 6-5 shows teachers responsible to school-level administrators, while students are at the very bottom of the organizational totem pole. Figure 6-7 then shows collaborating clusters set up on a functional basis. This works better, for example, than the hierarchical arrangement in which administrators are in direct-

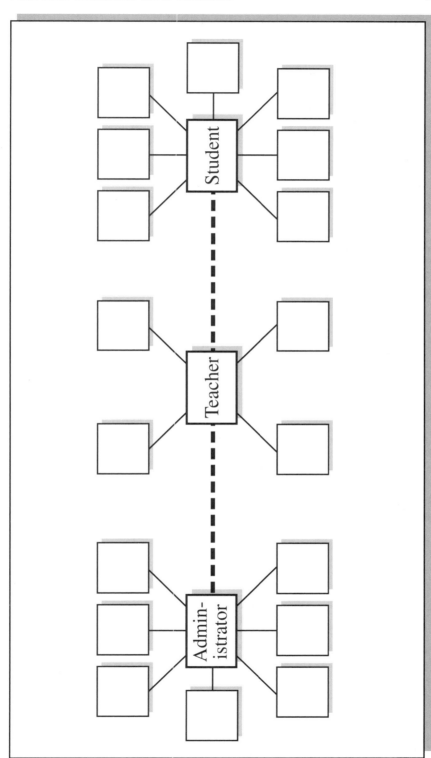

Figure 6-7. Overall organization structures that consist of multiple collaborating teams can be shown through interconnected star networks.

line reporting responsibility over classroom activities. Schools don't really work that way. Figures 6-8 and 6-9 then show how one American district has put the same principles to work to establish communication and understanding among all constituencies.

The star network is not recommended as either the only or best way to diagram organizations. Rather, the idea is that the more realistically relationships can be documented and dramatized, the better the understanding those diagrams will promote.

INTEGRATING CHANGES INTO THE ORGANIZATION

The organizational phase of a management program has three different dimensions. The first is to define the organizational structure and the responsibilities of the people involved. The

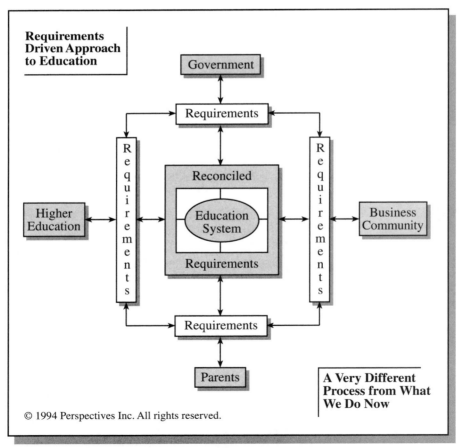

FIGURE 6-8. THIS DIAGRAM PRESENTS A STAR-NETWORK OVERVIEW OF THE TRANSFORMED ORGANIZATION OF THE ROSEVILLE JOINT UNION HIGH SCHOOL DISTRICT.

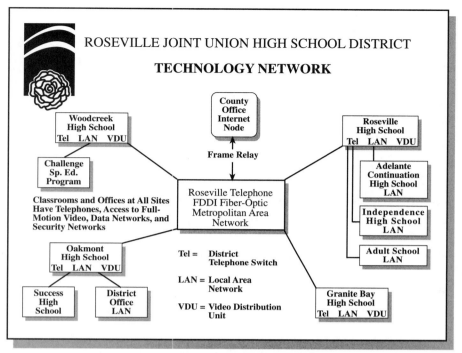

FIGURE 6-9. THIS DIAGRAM USES THE STAR PRINCIPLE TO DEMONSTRATE THE STRUCTURE OF THE COMMUNICATIONS NETWORK WITHIN THE ROSEVILLE JOINT UNION HIGH SCHOOL DISTRICT.

second is to inform and instruct the involved parties on their roles and responsibilities. The third dimension comes with implementation of the new organization structure.

Implementing the organization structure then ties in closely with the implementation of operational changes. There's an art in knowing when and how to introduce major change into the ongoing functions of an organization. The people must be prepared, the staff must be ready,. and the community must be briefed and supportive.

Until the changes are actually introduced, operations should go forward in continuity with the way things have worked in the past. Planning change and designing a new organization structure are, by nature, activities that are external to the ongoing, day-to-day, real-world operation of a school or district. Thus, when it comes to management responsibilities to implement a plan for change, new dimensions of responsibility and activity begin. Some people find themselves doing different jobs. Others are expected to change the way they do established jobs. Some people may be leaving; others may be added. Facilities may have to be rearranged, remodeled, or added.

Most difficult of all will be changes in expectations for students and teachers caught at midpoints in the existing educational curriculum. Learning achievement plans, which may go under the name of curriculum outlines or lesson plans, may have to be redrawn in their entirety. The process examples presented so far have included segregated statements describing core skills. Separate examples are given for skills involving reading, writing, and listening/speaking. This approach is fine for presenting subject descriptions. But a real student is not so easily broken into segmented classifications. Learning requires linking new with previously existing content. So, before new learning approaches can be implemented, curriculum or instructional plans have to provide for integration of objectives that have evolved within academic content areas that will remain as critical elements of the ongoing curriculum.

Breadth vs. Focus

In some important ways, the process for defining potential adult roles for students and incorporating targeted skills within curriculum content is at odds with the task of building the syllabus for an actual instructional plan. Recall, for example, that identification for potential curriculum topics is structured to encourage broadening of content coverage. The process followed, typically, involves a kind of brainstorming in which participants suggest content elements to be included. To avoid conflicts, a usual practice is to record all recommendations, then consider what to include and exclude in a separate, later activity.

Following this general route a few years ago, a task force concentrating on targeted student proficiencies came up with a list of language arts topics that occupied 14 pages under 11 separate categories. This kind of diversity early in the process is healthy, partly because, for teachers and other staff, it breaks the mold of outdated content and methods. The broad approach also introduces realities of language usage in the workplace.

Problems arise when teachers interpret these extensive lists as mandates. If they attempt to cover the complete content of such lists instructionally, their efforts are doomed. Only so much information can be imparted within the class times and student mental capacities that are available. In some instances, American curricula guides contain up to six times as many topics as their Japanese or German counterparts. When schools attempt to teach at this level of detail, students are spread too thin and their performances suffer. The tendency to encompass too much breadth has led to the comment that curricula in America tend to be "a mile wide and an inch deep."

A major challenge in finalizing curriculum design, then, is to reduce topical wish lists to proportions that can be scheduled within the allotted school day. For example, separate writing capabilities categories were established for *Writing for Personal Expression, Writing for Social Interaction, Writing for Information and Understanding,* and *Writing for Critical Analysis and Evaluation.* Literally dozens of separate proficiencies were established within this framework.

In practice, it is necessary to compress this kind of perspective into a rigorous, relevant learning structure. Accordingly, all of these writing-oriented knowledge/skill areas, coupled with seven others dealing with reading, speaking, and listening, were folded into a curriculum sequence called Communication Skills. In addition, communication skills were also incorporated into interdisciplinary curriculum units on social studies, science, and technology. The net effect was an academic experience modeled after the realities of the modern, high-tech workplace.

This approach expands learning horizons when students share the findings of different-but-related research projects. For example, consider a course in American history dealing with events between 1938 and 1946. It is virtually impossible to bring real depth into such a topic through traditional text-and-lecture instruction. However, the potential changes dramatically if teams of two to four students research and prepare reports on such topics as the Munich conference, the Russo-German non-aggression treaty, the outdated defense systems in France, the 1940 presidential elections and lend-lease policies in the United States, the Pearl Harbor attack, the Battle of Midway, the Normandy invasion and Battle of the Bulge, the bombing of Hiroshima and Nagasaki, and the Nuremberg trials. If each team prepares a written report and makes an oral presentation, the entire class experiences learning in far greater breadth and depth than could occur traditionally.

Such accumulation and refinement of academic content is only part of the job of planning for educational transition. A further, possibly greater, challenge centers around the need to implement the changes within a learning environment. Accordingly, the chapter that follows deals with characteristics and methods for structuring a learning experience. Also involved is a transition for teachers. They need to become facilitators and classroom managers rather than delivery mechanisms who lecture to passive, possibly inattentive, captives.

Part 3

Conducting Learning Transactions

Chapter 7
Creating a Learning Environment

*t*he relatively simple idea that schools should be dedicated to learning rather than teaching can lead to some significant, basic changes in education. There are vast gaps between talking about a learning transition and making it happen. Invariably, many questions arise that require meaningful interpretation as a basis for launching the far-reaching transitions involved. The presentations below anticipate and provide answers to a number of these questions.

What's the difference between teaching and learning?
They're different processes. In a teaching-oriented classroom, the students are passive. Interaction between the teacher and any individual student is minimal, often virtually nil. Contact and information transmission typically flows in one direction, from the teacher to whoever happens to be paying attention. There's no assurance that the transmitted message has been received and/or absorbed.

Learning, on the other hand, requires activity by students. Students participate. They interact with one another and with a teacher or aide who functions as a facilitator or coordinator rather than as a standup delivery mechanism. With a teacher providing guidance, the interaction is primarily among students who stimulate and support one another.

There's also a major difference in attitude and approach. In a learning-oriented classroom, targeted achievements are reviewed by all parties. Expected outcomes are understood in advance by the students responsible for meeting those goals.

Student achievements then measure the relative success of teachers as well as students.

How about an example of how activities and content are reoriented for learning rather than teaching?

Consider reading. This skill is primary. It's required for all learning that takes place, throughout the course of a student's academic experience—and on into the workplace. If reading is deficient, there can be little learning. The ability to continue learning, in turn, is the main job security for today's and tomorrow's workers.

Since the late 1940s or the early 1950s, true reading instruction in most American classrooms has been minimal. Emphasis has been on **recitation, not reading.** Recitation is different from reading, which demands a capability to understand written messages. This is an essential communication skill, one necessity for success in school, modern society, and the workplace. Instruction in a typical American school stresses decoding words by isolating sounds, then pronouncing them aloud. This, it is worth stressing, is recitation rather than reading. A further problem is that recitation wastes instructional time. In a class with 20 or more students, only one individual can recite at a given moment, leaving the rest in passive, spectator roles.

A learning approach would recognize that simple, repetitive recitation work can be overseen better by an effectively programmed computer than by reciting aloud in class. Another improvement might involve dividing a class into study teams, with students reciting their lessons to one another, rather than tying up the entire class. Even more significant, the small groups could also discuss the meanings of the words rather than being limited to their sounds.

To assure understanding and vocabulary mastery, students should write and/or keyboard-enter the words they are learning, achieving tactile reinforcement of lessons. Then they should write summaries or comments on the meaning of what they read, with members of the study team sharing reviews and comments on the work of group members.

Small study groups could also progress further, faster in content areas such as science, math, social studies, history, and geography, subjects in which reading plays a critical role.

Why is it important to change from teaching to learning?

Teaching, by its nature, assumes a fixed, or static, condition on the part of the student. The student is exposed to a lecture, generally supplemented with some kind of prescriptive study, such as a reading assignment or homework, all without any direct interaction between teacher and student. Completion of a learning transaction requires feedback. That is, the student needs to present evidence that information has been understood, absorbed, and internalized within the learner's body of knowledge. Emphasis is on *thinking* rather than on memorizing and recalling isolated facts.

In a teaching-oriented classroom, feedback comes chiefly through student recitation. Comparatively few students interact with the teacher because of time limitations in the typical class period. Even with written feedback such as homework, full evaluation and guiding response from the teacher is minimal because of constraints on the number of papers that can be read and corrected. In a learning environment, study and acquisition of knowledge require interaction that assures learning achievement on an immediate, real-time basis, as illustrated in presentations that follow later in this chapter.

As a process, then, teaching is limited to presenting a fixed, staple body of knowledge about a narrowly defined subject or discipline. Such presentations generally carry rigid time limits, partly because of the unrealistically broad content of typical American curricula. Under these circumstances, the ability to apply and use presented materials is also limited and, in turn, limits the depth of student knowledge.

For evidence, refer to the studies cited in Chapter 2. Relational Model diagrams created from scattergrams covering student achievement show large voids in capabilities for applying or interpreting academic content. This, of course, is in addition to low scores on competitive tests. Within a learning environment, application of knowledge is an essential part of the basic process.

Are lecture-type and blackboard presentations completely out in a learning-oriented classroom?

Absolutely not! In a constructive, learning environment, no presentation or communication techniques are ruled out. Lectures or illustrated presentations are still vital, critical to establishing the overall mission and purpose of a learning activity. To get students started in a learning program, the teacher has to brief the entire group on what they are about to do and why. Lecture presentations, blackboard notations, active demonstrations, or

TV and/or computer displays can and should be used. After such briefings, active question-and-answer feedback should be conducted to assure student comprehension. As long as such sessions are brief and specific, they play a vital role in setting the stage for the learning experience they introduce. An additional benefit can result from a teacher's use of a computer to display notes for student groups: The entries can be saved and printed for later study by students.

To illustrate, consider what happens when a football team is introduced to a new play or formation. One leader, say the head coach, describes the formation, player assignments, and signals to be called. Then the team goes into an active practice session to put the lessons to use. Different coaches work closely with linemen, receivers, backs, and defensive players. Effective play execution is the sum of a series of collaborating parts. The same principle applies within any learning experience. Teamwork in the classroom, in effect, models and prepares students for expectations they will meet in the workplace.

Why is real-time reaction and interaction important for learners?

Learning is a cumulative process. A lesson acquired today is added and related to each person's existing body of knowledge, which is accumulated continuously from birth onward. Within a structured school environment, the student is expected to acquire and master additional knowledge on a continuing, planned, modular (usually graded) basis. A student who does not learn in response to planned class or study activities risks falling behind his or her peers. When this happens, the student may be unable to recover, may underachieve permanently.

Interaction among students or between a student and a teacher serves to *verify* and *reinforce* specific lessons or content. Verification that learning has occurred, in turn, helps establish and/or build self-confidence in the student, adding motivation toward further learning. Iteration, or repetition, reinforces learning. Verification through interaction with fellow students or a teacher helps assure that the learned material is understood as it is assimilated.

Real-time responses also help to relate new to existing knowledge as students move along to succeeding lessons. Built-in responsiveness is also important for lessons designed to encourage creativity and/or innovation. Interaction with others enables students to verify their understanding and/or to test new theories within the context of knowledge being absorbed.

How can a teacher manage to coordinate and facilitate a learning environment and still cope with today's class sizes?

A teacher's time is critical to student achievement. This resource is used far more productively in a learning environment. When a teacher lectures to a full class of 25, 30, or more students as a group, there is no effective way to measure results. Students are under a constant strain to concentrate on presentations, to deal with classroom distractions, and to review and verify content understanding. This is because, in a teaching environment, student participation can be only minimal. For example, if there are 25 students attending a 45-minute instruction period, fewer than half are likely to be heard, and then only for perhaps a minute or two each.

When a classroom is set up for learning, the environment takes on new dimensions. As one effect, the arrangement of desks in rows generally comes to an end. Students are assigned to activity areas where they work in small groups of four to six and concentrate on specific challenges or tasks. Students interact, assuring continuous feedback and opportunity to challenge one another. Student study teams are jointly responsible for presentations on content and achievements.

When learning activities are assigned to study teams, the teacher is free to act as coordinator or facilitator rather than to serve as a delivery mechanism. The teacher, for example, can circulate among the several study teams within a class to monitor activities and verify achievements. In this way, a teacher deals with perhaps five or six students at a time. Each student team becomes a close, interactive community. In a team setting, problems in understanding content or group achievements are readily identified and understanding is verified.

Under the team approach, one member is assigned to report on each group's activities and progress to the whole class. Thus, students have an opportunity to share their comprehension of content, identify points that may not have been understood, and, with the aid of the teacher, build consensus on achievements. Where differences of opinion arise between individual students or groups, the learning approach provides an opportunity to understand and respect divergent viewpoints. An important benefit: Students learn there can be more than one answer to a question, a discovery that doesn't happen in an environment dedicated to progress measurement through standardized tests.

A valuable, nonacademic advantage to the learning approach is that students gain experience in functioning as team members, an important skill in the current workplace. By contrast, the kind of passivity promoted in a teaching environment diminishes opportunities for judgment and discourages initiative, traits that are negatives in today's workplace.

What are study teams and how do they operate?

The study team structure is basic to a transition from teaching to learning. A study team is a group of manageable size—typically four to six—that works together in learning assignments or exercises. Learning assignments carried out by teams largely replace teacher lectures. Learning is through active discovery rather than passive listening.

As every teacher knows from bitter experience, in a teaching environment, coordinating study and learning experiences for an entire class of 20 or more borders on the impossible. Real learning can't happen, especially since passive students can't really be counted on to master lecture-presented content.

A learning-oriented approach is becoming virtually essential as more and more computers are installed in classrooms. Computers are used interactively, with one student in control of each keyboard or other entry device. Interactive learning becomes instinctive. The teacher becomes a coach, rather than a drillmaster.

With some typical, traditional content, such as history and other subjects cited above, the time for passive student participation is long past. To absorb and internalize new content, students need opportunities to express their understanding of and to interpret the meaning of new content. This calls for discussion, perhaps debate, activities that just can't happen effectively in full, class-size groups. Questions and/or problems are open-ended, leaving students to apply judgment because there may not be a fixed solution. Under a learning approach, students assume responsibility for planning and completing their own study activities.

Under team study, one member of each group summarizes the findings, experiences, and feelings of the rest in a report to the class. As necessary, other members of the team can amend or supplement the report. The shared information can then be summarized or made more relevant by a facilitating teacher. The process is discovery-oriented and active. More learning happens than is possible when information is delivered by a single presenter.

How are student study team assignments made?

Very carefully! The teacher has to understand and respond to the makeup of the overall class group. To the extent possible, a teacher may want to build team assignments around existing friendships or rapport among students. If assignments are based on friendship, it's a little like what happens at a pick-up basketball game in a playground or schoolyard. Within any group, some members develop an affinity for others. They gravitate toward one another and "hang out" together, seemingly naturally. The same phenomenon happens in the lunchroom when people choose partners for meals or at snack time. Choosing up sides is a normal human tendency.

Almost always, one member of each such cohort group will become its natural leader, depending on the activity and the personality of the participants. For example, one student may be the natural captain of a basketball team. But others may gravitate to leadership in a study team on math, English, history, art, etc.

A teacher should observe student activities, should get to know the class members, and, wherever feasible, let nature take its course. Over time, and within an increased feeling for needs and capabilities, assignments can be made based on relative strengths and weaknesses. One strategy might be to team students who need extra help with a leader who possesses special knowledge or superior communication skills that promote information sharing. Regardless of how teams are formed, their very existence delivers more student feedback to inform and guide the teacher.

In general, it is a good idea to vary membership on study teams according to the rigor of the topic or the skills of individual members. When teams are involved in an assignment, the teacher should circulate to identify students who may need extra help, which can be arranged at separate points in the school day.

How long do team assignments last? All term? Single assignment? Should team memberships be rotated?

Length of assignments depends on the content being covered. In general, a team should stay together to see each assignment through. Consider a typical American history course. Suppose five separate study teams are established to review background and report on different aspects of the Mexican War. One group studies the situation of the American settlers who moved to the

Texas area on a promise of free land if they developed cotton farming, then were faced with a new law that raised taxes and deprived the group of some of their rights. Another team might examine attitudes of legislators in Washington eager to annex Texas to the United States. A third group might consider the concerns of a Mexican government under French domination that brought on the restrictive legislation. A fourth group might deal with the situations of farm families left behind when husbands/fathers/brothers left to fight the war. A fifth group might consider the situation of the Mexican soldiers suddenly thrown into a war. Reports by these separate teams provide potential for discussions of high interest levels and relevance.

When the class moves on to a subsequent topic, say arguments over slavery prior to the Civil War, the judgment of the teacher determines whether groupings are retained or changed. If rapport and team spirit are high and a sense of constructive competition among teams has developed, it might be desirable to carry forward the team assignments. On the other hand, if the teacher has a sense that a change might be constructive, that's the way to go.

How do you deal with disruptive student behavior within a team setting?

First, disruptive conduct is encountered less frequently within small groups where all individuals interact and share responsibility for their joint behavior. Further, disruptions and their associated problems are quicker and easier to spot in small working teams than in a class-sized group in which troublemakers tend to seek shelter in the back of the room or to locate themselves next to students they can dominate or control. Further, rigorous and relevant activities focus attention on learning and away from troublesome behavior.

When discordant behavior does occur, the students who are prevented from completing tasks to which they are committed have a stake in isolating the troublemaker. Serious students have an incentive to understand the need for discipline and to cooperate with the teacher.

Finally, each teacher should apply whatever rules and measures are necessary to maintain discipline. Discord that interrupts learning should not be tolerated. A teacher experiencing difficulty beyond his or her capacity to deal with it should seek help from the administration or should file appropriate grievances if help does not materialize. The need for discipline is non-negotiable.

An earlier chapter states that each student learns at an individual pace. How does a team approach square with standards that call for subject-by-subject, grade-by-grade, and skill-by-skill achievement?

This factor is critical to creating a learning-oriented environment. In guiding student progress, **time is critical to effective learning.** It is important to overcome the traditional attitude that expects all students to master the same content within the same time frame and under a lockstep schedule. When schedules are constant and inflexible, students become **prisoners of time.** A significant number of students can't do the assigned work in the allotted time. They fail, then are promoted anyway to conform to age/grade standards.

The team approach can help all students. Less-gifted individuals get more support through continuing interaction that can expose their needs for help. Thus, those who do not progress as expected can be identified quickly and provided special assistance through a program like PAR (Progress Assurance and Reinforcement), described in a later chapter. While some students receive review and reinforcement, those who learn more rapidly can be assigned to enrichment programs.

When time becomes variable and manageable, all students win. Promotions can be based on achievement rather than age.

If each student learns individually, doesn't a study team structure inhibit learning?

Absolutely not! A learning approach that includes study teams prepares students for the roles each must assume as a **team member** and **lifelong learner.** Teamwork is a vital requirement in the modern workplace, where persons of varying knowledge and skill levels must coordinate their activities. On virtually any modern-day job, each worker is expected to function as a team member. Study teams follow the same principles and methods as working teams in modern businesses.

Students going on to college will also encounter study teams if they enter such fields as law, medicine, or business management. Academic departments in all these disciplines encourage formation of study teams.

Teamwork also leads naturally to an adaptability required in a workplace where new developments in technology impose continuing change. In turn, workers must acquire the knowledge, skills, and attitudes necessary to make change an ally rather than an enemy. Lifelong learning is essential because of the rate at which new knowledge is generated. The body of knowledge acquired through formal study in school or college becomes obsolete quickly. Today, obsolescence of technological knowledge is a major management cost factor for the great majority of companies. In essence, study teams in school emulate ultimate experiences in real-world jobs.

Occasionally, parents who feel their students are brighter than most of the rest in their class complain that their children are held back if they are limited to the pace of other team members. The answer that applies for such questions is straightforward: A child working with a team that can move at a pace that suits its own joint comfort can impact the learning rate of a small group because, in a learning environment, the brighter children can set and move forward at their own pace. By comparison, if a bright student is one of 25 or more working under traditional teaching methods, the entire class is held back to the pace of the slowest student. Isn't the bright youngster better off accelerating with a few peers than if an entire class is being limited to the capacity of its slowest learners?

What academic subjects lend themselves to a learning approach? How about some examples? Exceptions?

Learning activities should dominate each student's educational experience. Learning happens any time a student is actively involved in acquisition of knowledge. Thus, learning can happen in a library, in front of a computer screen, in discussions or debates, or in any situation in which students conduct independent research, interact with one another as team members cooperate in study assignments, or simply go about their everyday lives.

Though passive attendance at lectures is generally not an effective learning experience, there can be important exceptions. Students, for example, may respond enthusiastically to a lecture from a celebrity or community resource person, particularly if special tools such as animation or graphics are used. Mentoring experiences, particularly with adults who establish valid role models, can also be extremely valuable.

For a primary example of benefits to be derived from an approach that applies learning to existing student knowledge, consider elementary reading. By the time a normal five- or six-year-old starts kindergarten or first grade, he or she is speaking and understanding anywhere from 2,000 to 4,000 words, more in some instances. **This existing knowledge should be the basis for building language skills.** Topical instructional content should encompass integrated learning of reading, writing, speaking, and listening.

But this ideal approach rarely happens. The child is exposed to an adult-selected vocabulary that ignores his or her existing knowledge. Further, in most classes, the child is taught pronunciation patterns that either replicate or unnecessarily complicate his or her learning experience. Then, the child's integrated knowledge base is fragmented with separate instruction in reading, writing, and other largely arbitrary subdivisions. To repeat: The methodology used for instruction in reading actually calls for recitation rather than comprehension of written messages.

Suppose, instead, the educational system were to give the child credit for knowledge already acquired. The student already knows, for example, how to relate oral vocabulary to images. Why not accept that status as a starting point in language education? Picture this: A computer presents an image and offers a keyboard-selected option on whether or not the student wants to learn to say and read the corresponding word. If the student opts to learn the word the computer presents and pronounces it. The student repeats the word aloud. The computer monitors for a match in sounds, requesting a repeat until the student says the words acceptably or the computer notes a possible need for student assistance. It also accepts the image and word for inclusion in a personalized reader that the computer will print for the student. The exercise is repeated with other words through a programmed cycle. When the lesson is concluded, the system prints out pages for a reader personalized specifically to add to the language knowledge of the individual student.

If the student has a native language other than English, the computer can pronounce the name of the image in two languages, Spanish and English for example. If the student is not literate in the foreign language, the reader is printed in English and exercises are structured to build English proficiency from scratch. If the student is literate in the foreign language, printouts can be in dual languages. The idea is to build on existing knowledge. Thus, if the student cannot read his or her native language, providing printouts would be counter to the assigned function of the school to build proficiency in English. In any case, effective English instruction begins immediately, with the opportunity open for PAR sessions later in the day, if necessary, to reinforce mastery of English vocabulary.

In a later exercise, the images can be displayed and students can be required either to enter matching words through the keyboard or to select them from a multiple-choice format. By using the power of computers in this way, language instruction becomes multidimensional, multisensory. Such instruction also is individual, permitting each student to progress at his or her own pace. This example is obviously simplified. But this kind of approach could greatly impact student achievement and also teacher productivity.

Now, suppose computers are not available for use in elementary language arts. Images could be reproduced on copying machines and students could be given models from which to print the corresponding words. A teacher or mentor can say the words and study groups can review and read aloud to one another, intensifying their practice opportunities while adding to teacher productivity. For written exercises, students can correct each other's papers, subject to spot checking by a teacher or aide.

No matter what content is being covered, and regardless of the subject, innovative planning can lead to a design that requires students to work actively at mastering the materials. The methodology is relatively simple and direct: Establish **shoulds,** or achievements students should reach. Then identify resources available for student use, including library books, periodicals, and textbooks. Break the overall topic or subject into interrelated segments that can be assigned to individuals or teams. Oversee team or individual study. Receive reports on completed work and assemble results to document progress and provide a basis for student satisfaction and qualitative grading.

Where do computers fit within a learning environment?

Just about everywhere! American education is reaching a critical point in the application of computers to promote student learning. So far, only a tiny fraction of the instructional potential of computers is being utilized. In some respects, computers are threatened with becoming just one more endangered species as an educational tool.

Education's track record in using promising new tools is on the dismal side. Throughout the twentieth century, new technologies have been introduced, accompanied by loud promises that they would stimulate educational progress. Enthusiasm by educators led to substantial investments in new hardware for each succeeding technology—phonograph records, 16 mm motion pictures, slide projectors, overhead projectors, sound/slide film projectors, 8 mm motion pictures, TV broadcasts, videocassette recorders, and compact discs. One after another, and at great expense in each instance, these innovations failed to fulfill anything like the promises made for them. There has been no really visible impact on student achievements. The reality has seen continuing stagnation in test scores and literacy.

Without special attention and due diligence, computers could go the same route. As a demonstration, ask anyone who campaigned for installation of many thousands of Apple II computers into classrooms and special labs how basic student performance has been enhanced. Through the 1980s, the predominant use of computers in high schools was for instruction in BASIC programming, which evolved into a skill with virtually no marketability. Impact upon academic skills and on overall student achievement levels has been far too small to represent a profitable return on the billions of dollars invested.

Recently, heavy emphasis has been placed on getting schools connected to the Internet. Priorities have been assigned by many authorities, from the White House on down. While the Internet can be extremely helpful for some student activities, people really familiar with education must recognize that mastery of core subjects deserves a higher priority. Nothing that happens on the Internet can help semi-literates master basic language, math, and science skills. Core education is the main area on which educational applications of computers should be focused.

Computers have been successful in some business and vocational-type applications. In comparatively few, special situations, students have used computers to enhance skills in drafting, publishing school newspapers and magazines, application of robotic equipment, and multimedia production. But computers still fall short when it comes to the major measure of their viability, instruction in core subjects such as elementary reading, English proficiency, math, science, technology, and real-world applications of computers.

So, to answer the question about where computers fit in a learning environment: *Computers must become tools to promote student learning in basic, core subjects.*

If computers are logical tools for learning, what needs to be done to assure that students master computers to a level demanded in a technologically dominated job market?
All students must become comfortable at computer keyboards, as well as with other methods for interacting with and controlling computers. One term used frequently to describe this challenge is education must prepare students to become *computer fluent.*

Using a computer must become as comfortable to future

information workers as driving a car is to workers in today's commuter society. In other words, the need is universal, applying to everyone from service workers in fast food restaurants to production workers in factories to office workers, managers, and executives. The same must apply to the learning-related activities of students. Beginning in the early elementary grades and continuing through high school graduation and college study, students must be as comfortable with computers as they are with textbooks—even with pencils and paper.

To achieve this level of comfortable mastery, keyboard familiarity should begin by fourth grade. Students should be exposed to exercises or lesson drills that require responses through keyboard or mouse. Among other interactive roles in education, the computer can be a tireless drillmaster. Computer-administered drill-and-practice exercises have been available to schools since the early 1980s. Their use—and relative success—have been limited. This is partly because the number of computers available has been insufficient to meet the potential needs of students who could use basic help in such areas as spelling, grammar, arithmetic, or geography. Complaints were also heard that routine drill-and-practice exercises were boring and ineffective. Partly as a result of perceived failures, these applications have languished, largely through lack of use or interest.

Since the early 1980s, the tragedy of functional illiteracy has expanded explosively. Since then also, many more computers have been installed in schools. Further increases in computer equipment populations should result from recent introduction of lower-cost computer workstations designed to operate within local networks.

Under these circumstances, the time probably has arrived to apply computers to achieve a degree of academic discipline that has been largely missing, particularly in lower elementary grades. These are the school years when students must acquire basic reading and math skills—or suffer lifelong handicaps through lack of the knowledge and skills needed for the majority of today's jobs. Today, a number of textbook publishers are providing suitable drill-and-practice materials as supplements to their basic products. Educational leaders can no longer afford the luxury of disregarding or looking down on such tools.

Once a goal of universal computer fluency is established, it follows that all students need to master keyboard entry by the touch method. With computers, keyboarding instruction is far easier and takes much less time than it did with typewriters. In part, this is because the computer itself can do the teaching.

When keyboarding was taught on typewriters, multiple semesters of instruction were mandated. With computers, an average student can master the rudiments of keyboarding in 20 hours or less.

Questions frequently arise about where to find time in already loaded schedules to add instruction on keyboarding. The answer is simple: Keyboarding is a communication-essential skill, a prerequisite all students must master. So, a promising approach might be to incorporate keyboarding into routine instruction. One approach could include keyboarding as part of English classes—along with instruction in language structure and usage. Rather than the traditional emphasis on fingering the keyboard with non-significant exercises, a new, proven method uses lessons built entirely with words, right from the beginning. As students advance, they enter actual content, such as rules about sentence structures, noun-verb agreement, tense, and so on. With this approach, students build both language and keyboarding skills concurrently, all within the time frame normally allocated to language courses.

Computers also can help attack the perennial problem of providing practice in writing. Part of the learning approach calls for multidisciplinary classes in which students get their writing practice by preparing reports for content areas such as history, geography, civics, literature, or science. When writing is done on computers, the student-produced text can be stored for reference, review, and comment by resource people who can help lighten the teaching load by critiquing writing and grading papers. Almost any community should be able to provide highly qualified volunteers who work in (or are retired from) journalism, public relations, advertising, or related fields to mentor students in areas of their special expertise. With computers, everything can be done on-line, meaning that assistance can be arranged from experts who don't even have to enter the school building.

With computers, school activities can emulate real-world work situations. In doing so, they enhance the future prospects of every participating student.

What's the best way to organize lessons to promote student learning experiences?

Overview the subject matter first, possibly through interaction among teachers from varying disciplines. Then segment the material to establish research and reporting assignments to be handled by study teams. The system usually works best when each student team has a slightly different topic for study from the others. Teams then compose and present reports that are used to share their findings with the entire class.

To illustrate, consider a class dealing with regional ecology. Team assignments can deal with soil and erosion, weather, plant forms, wildlife, etc. As they complete their assignments, groups may be either permitted or encouraged to, in effect, look over one another's shoulders to enlarge perspectives beyond their immediate focus. By sharing reports among teams, the entire group gains a scope of coverage that would be difficult if the entire class studied the complete field. Further, members of individual teams have opportunities to gain depths of knowledge that might not be possible under traditional teaching approaches.

How about testing and assessment? How are individual achievements documented?

Standardized, multiple-choice tests are still necessary because they provide an objective, uniform method of scoring the potential of students. Standardized testing can be necessary for college entry, where admissions officers rely heavily on test scores. Also, for a society in which students transfer between schools frequently, test scores provide a basis for implementing those moves and for placement of students at the new locations.

However, standardized multiple-choice tests have little or no value in shaping or adjusting active, in-process instruction methods or content. That's because grading is generally done off premises and results are reported too late to trigger instructional adjustments. Further, grade reports generally do not include indications of which questions are answered correctly or incorrectly, thus providing no guidance on where help may be needed.

Under a learning-oriented program, students complete written, graphic, or other tangible end products that summarize and demonstrate their progress. Student reports can be accumulated in a portfolio that is carried forward cumulatively through successive grades. The portfolios can become primary tools for monitoring student progress and as a basis for assessment and for coaching on potential improvements. Notes and written content of the folders also can be used as study tools prior to tests or special presentations that are part of the assessment process.

What are the shortcomings or traps of a learning approach that uses study teams?

As with any major change, the biggest potential pitfall lies in attempting to change too much, too soon. Implementing a transition to learning methods will be strange for teachers as well as students. It may be desirable, therefore, to make the change incrementally. That is, change one grade or one subject (or both) at a time.

Careful monitoring can spell the difference between success and failure. Students or teachers who find the new methods strange may need special coaching or support. It is important to get all participants to a level at which they are comfortable as quickly as possible. This, in turn, requires detailed advance planning and meticulous training in the new methods for both teachers and students.

A particularly difficult requirement centers around students who are in process within the system. For example, if a school shifts from a social-promotion policy to a standard based on achievement, some students who were socially promoted will need special help to get themselves up to new levels of performance. Special tutoring or intense instruction may be necessary. Even if the student has to move ahead at a slower rate, it is better to make small sacrifices early than to risk deficiencies on graduation.

What special in-service training and special preparation are needed for teachers committed to a learning-oriented transition?

As a prerequisite to any major change, all affected teachers must agree to participate. This kind of transition requires volunteers. This is no environment for the unwilling.

A complete briefing for teachers should be included in the initial phase of the Management of Change process. Then teachers should be part of the process that defines adult roles and specifies curriculum revisions. Teachers must then be trained fully in new instructional techniques before implementation begins.

If a transition to a learning-based environment is to succeed, teachers must lead the way.

How can community volunteers contribute to the success of a school implementing a learning-oriented approach?

Take full advantage of community resources. Adult mentors from local business and government organizations can add substantially to preparations for the workplace and for other problem solving and decision making situations.

Classroom appearances by community members who have special qualifications in content areas can help build interest among students. Practical advice from successful people should be sought and utilized actively.

At lower grade levels particularly, parents, retirees, or others anxious to be of service can help to facilitate sessions where learning teams undertake research or study assignments separately. If the material being covered is within the scope of the volunteers' knowledge, they may be able to resolve simple problems or offer constructive suggestions. Otherwise, they can certainly monitor what's happening and call situations that require assistance or problem resolution to the attention of the teacher.

How about parent participation?

A change as major as a curriculum transition requires full understanding and cooperation by all concerned parties. Under some conditions, parent permission may be needed for student enrollment in a new program. At the very least, informed parents should be a standard intent for any educational system.

Community meetings, informational publications, and special parent briefing sessions should be provided. As appropriate, outreach programs also should be conducted as a means of involving parents, some of whom may themselves be influential in the local business community.

Are so-called partnerships between businesses and schools potentially beneficial?

Absolutely, particularly when a school or district commits to implementation of a learning structure. Recall that the basic ICLE process for change emphasizes the importance of participation by business leaders, particularly those in line to become future employers of the school's students. Even if there is no other reason for seeking a partnership with business entities, it is vital that a learning-oriented curriculum reflect real-world expectations for entry-level workers and also ongoing working conditions for which students should be preparing. Appropriate levels of this kind of knowledge rarely, if ever, exist within typical school systems. Thus, if educators seek consensus with their community at large, partnering with businesses is vital.

How do school-business partnerships get started?

One way, particularly if you're just getting started, is to visit the local chamber of commerce. These organizations are dedicated both to community betterment and to involving their business-enterprise members in promoting civic pride and improvement. Many chambers have been instrumental in forming consortiums of business entities that are actively searching for ways to assist schools in their area.

A frequently cited alternative is to approach a parent employed by a prominent local business. Parents who are also business executives have a special stake in activities that can enhance the quality and value of education in local schools.

Still another approach is to target a specific local business you have read or heard about. Call for an appointment. Either invite an executive of the company to visit the school or offer to visit the company offices.

Regardless of which approach or combination of approaches is chosen, it is important to think about your school's expectations from such partnerships in advance. Be open minded, by all means. But also have goals and expectations ready to share with your potential partners. In each case, let prospective partners know what you expect to accomplish and what is expected of them. Be serious about partnering and its implications.

Can and do businesses impact education directly?

Absolutely, directly and with major positive impact. The thing to bear in mind is that each business is a citizen of the same community in which your school or district is located. Employees of these local business will have children of their own, giving them a direct, major stake in the quality of education you provide. Also, quality local schools can be a major factor in helping businesses to recruit top prospects to work for their companies. Assume that each company and its people want to help local schools if they are accorded a chance. You won't be wrong, at least hardly ever.

Guidance in providing information on job opportunities and requirements is obvious. Often, material help accompanies this advice. Many businesses provide financial support in the form of scholarships or direct support for specific instructional initiatives. Again, as the relationship develops, it is best to be specific in seeking financial or material support. Getting money or donations of equipment and supplies tends to involve problems if a school seeks open, unqualified donations. Businesspeople understand purposeful, fund-dedicated budgeting. To derive support in this arena, be as specific as possible.

Beyond these general considerations, school administrators and teachers really interested in building traversible school-to-work bridges seek direct support of students from knowledgeable workers. Bringing a working executive or engineer into the classroom as a visiting lecturer, for example, can help build workplace understanding and motivation among students. People making practical use of the content your faculty is covering in the classroom can underscore and support the practical value of instruction. Most businesses will approve some plan that encourages their employees to participate in school programs, often with full pay during these visits.

In special cases involving career education, it may even be possible to recruit experienced specialists to act as part-time instructors. An example of such relationships occurred when the Roseville (California) Joint Union High School District was able to arrange for a chef from the local Hilton Hotel to teach a class in culinary arts.

Another invaluable element of a partnership with business lies in finding mentors for students who have problems to solve or ambitions to realize. Direct contact with an adult role model delivers a value that needs no elaboration here.

Are there potential negatives from involving businesses in school management and instructional activities? If so, are they outweighed by positive results?

Negatives reflect the viewpoints of observers and are often derived from the attitudes or opinions of individuals. The major potential negative occurs within schools themselves. When a business partners with a school or district, change is almost always in the offing. And, any time major changes are proposed, the comfort zones of some people will be upset or invaded. Staff members and sometimes parents or even students may resist change. Since the participating business is the new element on the scene, it may be targeted for blame.

Negatives also can develop among persons with anti-business biases. There are people who see business organizations as inherently evil, responsible for pollution, exploitation, noise, or traffic jams. If these people are bitter enough, they will blind themselves to the potential benefits of the association. These benefits can include contributions of money, equipment, and/ or expertise that will help bring the real world to school and provide opportunities for students and teachers to visit the actual, active business organizations. An even stronger business-school connection can be established if arrangements are made for teachers to spend learning-working time at the facilities of sponsoring businesses. This is a highly effective way to bring real-world knowledgeability into your classrooms. Such interchanges also help build school-to-work bridges for your students.

Most schools that enter partnerships benefit from the association.

The questions and answers presented above deal primarily with the planning and policy-level aspects of a transition from a teaching to a learning environment in a typical school situation. The real challenge lies in implementing new and different practices through realistic solutions and applications. The chapters that follow deal with some major aspects of structural, organizational, and practical transitions to educational enhancement through community-based, community-supported programs.

Chapter 8
Breaking the Shackles of Time

O f all the shortages about which educators chronically com plain—with money primary among them and including everything else from public apathy to overwork—time may present the greatest detriment of all. For schools in general, time can be both despised taskmaster and a prime area of opportunity for improvement.

Most critical of all, time inhibits learning potential within the American education system as it is presently structured. The clock on a school wall currently functions much as a governor on an engine, limiting output and controlling progress. American schools, it has been said, would progress further if their inhabitants did less clock watching and shaped their lives more like kaleidoscopes than timepieces.

TIME AND TRADITION

Time, the old expression has it, marches on. One place this truism apparently doesn't apply is in American education. In terms of the regard for time, the outlook in too many American schools is still where it was some 300 years ago.

In the late eighteenth century, when 90-plus percent of the population were farmers, educational demands were rudimentary, minimal. If kids could read the Bible and an almanac and do simple arithmetic, their education was considered adequate and complete. Demands of society and the workplace were minimal. Literacy had little impact on a person's ability to earn a livelihood.

More important in those days, school schedules had to conform to farming seasons. Kids had to be home to help with the planting in late spring, the harvesting in late summer, and general chores and crop tending in between. The length of the school day was also relevant. School couldn't start until the cows were milked and had to end before they were brought in from the fields for the evening milking.

From the 1840s onward, farmers moved into explosively growing cities and became factory workers. Social and economic upheavals reached proportions that spawned the name *Industrial Revolution.* Everything in America went through drastic change, it seems, except the educational system. In retrospect, relegation of education to the backwaters of a world of industrial and economic advancement seems understandable, if not commendable. The extent and depth of educational achievement by the average American didn't matter all that much. The factory worker didn't have any greater need (or, generally, hunger) for learning than did the farmer or his children. The tasks of factory work during the nineteenth and early years of the twentieth century primarily involved brute force, endurance, or both. Requirements for reading, writing, or other educationally derived skills were absent or minimal. A person could spend an entire working life on an assembly line without being required to read or write. Math requirements were limited largely to dealing with denominations of coins and bills.

When a groundswell for educational enhancement finally surfaced, the motivation was focused largely on efforts to overcome social, economic, sanitary, and health-care ills. Knowledge was the platform from which Americans rose to modify the inequities and tribulations of existence in filthy, overcrowded, crime plagued, and illness ridden slums. Even with the best of intentions, however, educational progress was slow. For immigrants who poured in at the rate of a million a year, the dynamic pace of American development and the comparative improvements over conditions in the countries they had left generated a pall of complacency. This, coupled with the strangeness of many parents to the American political system, minimized the incentive for intellectual and academic upgrading of schools.

Time changed American society. But tradition inhibited the drive to upgrade American education. Only one major change occurred during the first quarter of the twentieth century: School attendance was made mandatory as a means of reducing or eliminating child labor, which had become a major social ill and political scandal.

TIME BECOMES A CONSTRAINT

Academic improvement became an issue some time after World War I. The move to improve schools responded, at least in part, to the impact of technology that had begun at the turn of the century. Consumers were fascinated by introduction of such new mass production wonders as the phonograph, the light bulb, and, most of all, the automobile. Higher levels of literacy and mechanical training were needed to deal with and harness these wonders.

In the countryside, general acceptance of automatic plowing, planting, harvesting, and crop processing equipment generated incentives to increase the literacy and academic competence of students. The Sears mail order catalogue, which became a staple of rural homes, may have done more than any other single development to stimulate a desire for reading skills.

Rapidly, commitments to increased academic achievements led to demands for still further intellectual content in school curricula. In cities particularly, hordes of immigrant parents were anxious to have their children learn to be Americans. They wanted their kids to acquire the skills they lacked and to earn a share of the good life that had attracted the family to a new land.

Respect for education grew rapidly. In turn, educators responded by adding content to curricula. The intent was partly to produce committed Americans and partly to prepare students for a workplace that was becoming increasingly sophisticated with the arrival of typewriters, punched card machines, adding machines, bookkeeping machines, and other forerunners of office automation.

However, despite all these stimuli and all the efforts to improve the intellectual levels of future Americans, educators made no effort to cast off their time-based bondage. Schools stood empty and useless for a quarter to a third of each year, honoring the schedule established to make kids available for planting and harvesting activities for which they were no longer needed. The school day remained artificially shortened during a time when the typical work week involved 10-to-12-hour days, honoring the original practice of restricting school attendance to the hours when the cows were out in the pasture.

During the twentieth century, time, expressed in terms of age, became a factor in defining what the American people were willing to recognize as a suitable educational career. Kids were required to be in school roughly between the ages of six and 16. The logic was clear: Below the age of six, the kids weren't of any real value in the workforce. After 16, they were needed badly enough so there was no use wasting more time in classrooms.

Education time frames, then, were defined by the social criterion for elimination of child labor. Schools were constrained in terms of the services they could make available in their communities. Citizens younger than six or older than 17 or 18 were generally unwanted or unwelcome within the time limits imposed on education.

DEALING WITH TIME AS ADVERSARY, CAN SCHOOLS OVERCOME?

It's part of our culture, the image of time as discontinuity and death. Recall all the pictures imposed on the public conscience to mark the end of one year and the beginning of another. The concluding year is an old man about to be discarded, obliterated. The full image also shows a new kid being enthroned to represent the year aborning.

Where does education fit? In a school or district with a flexible management committed to change in response to current realities, the passing of the old and the enshrinement of the new is a positive picture. But it's also oversimplified. Change is not really that abrupt. Transitions need to be planned and carried out through orderly processes.

In modern education, opportunities for enhancement can border on an infinity that has to be dealt with one dimension at a time. This discussion, therefore, will remain restricted to the transitions needed to convert the element of time from adversary to ally.

The School Year

Time cheats all schools and their constituencies when a district or school adheres to the 180-day year. The penalties for maintaining the status quo are so obvious that it should no longer be necessary to present the standard arguments about how students in countries like Japan, Russia, China, and Germany spend 20, 30, even 60 more days in school than kids in the U.S. It is true that students in most other countries do better than American kids in math and science, as demonstrated in the 1996 Third International Mathematics and Science Study (TIMSS). Of 41 tested countries, U.S. students scored twenty-eighth in math and seventeenth in science.

A number of observers have succumbed to the overwhelming temptation to correlate figures for school attendance days with the test scores and reach what seems like a reasoned conclusion that lengthening the school year will, automatically and directly, elevate test scores. Everything considered, however, *It Ain't Necessarily So.* The correlation is neither direct nor necessarily logical. Other factors can apply, such as the homogeneity of populations, the culture of the differing societies, and the existence of rigorous, feared tests that stratify the parameters of children's lives from age 13 on. One rarely cited circumstance is the existence of major subindustries in countries like Japan dedicated to tutoring students, privately and at great expense to parents, in preparation for the critical tests. These activities, in turn, reflect an almost demonic drive among parents to push their children toward passage of the test that represents an absolute threshold to future opportunity.

This is not to say that American kids will not benefit from a longer school year. Rather, the point is that the inexcusable wastefulness of the 36-week school year is so obvious that we shouldn't have to reach for international comparisons to shame ourselves into too apparent conclusions. To qualify this further, extension of the school year should result in additional, more rigorous, relevant, and culturally richer education for the attending students

If any additional grounds are needed for support of the extended school year, U.S. curricula themselves provide eloquent testimony. The TIMSS study, among other statistics, revealed that U.S. students are expected to absorb many more topical areas than foreign counterparts. For example, eighth-grade math students in the U.S. were expected to deal with 78 topics as compared with 17 in Japan and 23 in Germany. This is an example of why U.S. curricula have been characterized as **a mile wide and an inch deep.**

Not only does the extended school year make sense, but experience is showing that it works and works well.

THE INSTALLMENT-PLAN SCHEDULE

Suppose you could add 20 or 30 days to the school year. Wouldn't this make your semesters or whatever time increment you establish longer than the kids' attention spans? Ask any experienced teacher. Between eight and 10 weeks into your typical semester, kids suffer major burnout, evidenced by bored faces and lowered performance levels. So what would be accomplished by adding, say, two more weeks to each session?

The answer: Try some American ingenuity. An estimated 500-plus schools nationally, and at least 100 in North
Carolina, have added days to the school year without in-
curring either new costs or student boredom. The idea is to
deliver education in more chewable bites—and also to provide second chances for those who need extra help or enrichment for those who got it the first time.

In North Carolina, the year-round plan goes by the
name 45/15, meaning 45 days in nine-week sessions interspersed by three-week intersessions. The nine-week
quarters are short enough to minimize burnout, and also
to enable close monitoring of student progress. The three-
week intersessions provide opportunities for remediation
courses paid for with summer-session budgets or enrichment activities covered by fees from parents. Use of
intersession time for instruction can add up to 20 days to
students' school year. Summer vacations are shortened,
reducing the memory-lapse loss factor at the start of each
school year.

In areas where schools are overcrowded, the 45/15
schedules can be overlapped to increase student attendance
capacity by one-third without adding buildings.

Extended School Day

Perhaps American educators would be willing to allow special
dispensation for any children still needed at home for morning
and evening milking. For the rest, though, and for a number of
underserved population segments that could benefit from constructive use of school facilities, it is wasteful and inexcusable
to limit use of school facilities to six hours daily. After all, school
buildings are paid for by the entire, currently underserved public. These paid-for buildings could be available without significant extra cost for 24 hours daily. Round-the clock operation
might be extreme. But there certainly should be opportunities
to benefit current students and other population segments ranging from toddlers to senior citizens.

Consider how recent scandals have called attention to the
plight of parents who require quality child care, which is in ex-
ceedingly short supply in most communities. A number of American schools have already adopted extended-day programs for
pre-school children. Also consider our growing population of

active retirees who could benefit from outlets for productive use of their energies, skills, and available time. The potential is tremendous. At present, the potential for recruiting hundreds of thousands, possibly millions, of experienced, potential caregivers and tutors is going to waste.

Despite such peripheral benefits, the greatest potential advantage could accrue to presently enrolled students. A typical implementation of this commitment at the high school level calls for an **academic day** devoted to core courses and major sequences, typically completed before the lunch break. The **school day** then rounds out a seven- to eight-hour session. During the afternoon, students can be placed in electives or special classes that help them overcome deficiencies or provide reinforcement for learners who need extra time to complete standard courses. ICLE calls this afternoon program PAR, for Progress Assurance and Reinforcement.

In a number of districts—including Roseville, California, and Polk County, North Carolina—after-school tutorial centers are open on a "walk in" basis. Students who want help for any reason stop by and discuss their needs or wants with an attending teacher. Community volunteers also pitch in.

Extending the Day for Child Care

Another format adds care for preschool children and also provides extended-day activities for elementary-aged children. The schools offering these community services typically open at 7:30 am and remain open until parents pick up the kids, closing as late as 7 or 7:30 in the evening. Clearly, programs of this type help to blend schools closely into their communities as major service and cultural hubs.

A program that could serve as a model for extended use of school facilities is being implemented in Japan as a Lifelong Learning Center. A diversified facility accommodates preschoolers for child care, elementary and secondary enrollments, and a senior citizens center whose volunteers assist with preschool children and also read to and tutor school-age kids.

COMBINING SCHOOL AND CHILD CARE

In Wake County, North Carolina, a number of magnet schools situated in different neighborhoods are set up specifically to accommodate parents who need child care. Children may be dropped from 7 a.m. and may stay as late as 6 p.m. Certified personnel provide care before and after normal school hours. Parents using this extended-day service pay fees that are below commercial rates but are sufficient to cover costs.

Multi-age, Multi-grade Classes

If a school is ready to commit to learner individuality, the time-based constraint of lockstep instruction for grades and/or classes may no longer be viable. A number of districts are following age-independent, achievement-oriented programs for lower-level elementary and also for high school students.

OFF TO A FAST START

In Hernando County (Florida) Schools, classes are organized for students who would normally be in kindergarten through second grade. Age is disregarded so students can be grouped according to capability. Thus, first graders with special strengths in arithmetic might be grouped with second graders in math but remain at normal grade level for reading and/or writing.

A team of three teachers—who provide special instruction in math, reading, and language arts—stay with students for the full three years of K-2 experience. The children move between rooms for subject-specific work. The rooms themselves have six workstations each, making it possible to assign students to affinity groups for concentrated study experiences.

This is the kind of arrangement the staff at ICLE refers to in recommending that school activities be modeled more after a kaleidoscope than a clock.

At the high-school level, schools are beginning to value student proficiencies more than fixed notions about course sequences. Thus, for example, college-bound students may be expedited through core courses at the ninth and tenth grades so they can concentrate on advanced-placement work in their chosen fields during their last two years. One example lies in the Oakmont Health Academy in Roseville, California, described later in this chapter. Another can be seen in the high school vocational center in Mooresville, North Carolina, described in

Chapter 15. Students on this kind of track can arrive on a college campus with credits already earned for up to six courses.

In programs designed for school-to-work transition, students are able to spend significant portions of their eleventh and twelfth years being mentored by representatives of sponsoring companies or in actual work experiences on company premises.

The common denominator in these experiences is that class assignments are free of the bonds of time and are based on student strengths and achievement levels.

Multi-year Teacher Assignments

Everyone who works at or observes education appreciates the value of close, interactive relationships formed between students and teachers. Every teacher and a large percentage of parents have encountered situations in which students continue to visit with positive-influence teachers for years after they have been promoted to other grades. Many relationships continue to the adulthood of the students. Almost every adult remembers a favorite teacher with special warmth and thanks.

If student-teacher relationships can be so special, why subject them to artificial time limits? Experience is beginning to show that it can be profitable to keep elementary school classes under the same teacher for two or three years. At the high school level, schools are regularly assigning students to guidance-type classes that go well beyond the functions of a traditional home room. This plan has proved highly successful in Polk County, North Carolina. (See Chapter 15.) Students are advised regularly about decisions to be made in their academic programs and in choices of future careers or colleges. In effect, students in these small groups that meet briefly on a daily basis become cohorts who take a mutual interest in their collective or individual future prospects and support one another.

TIME FOR ACHIEVEMENT

A longer school year and extended school day, for all the logic behind them, invariably encounter big time resistance. Many of the kids will squawk at spending more time in school, objecting as though time were being added to a prison sentence. Teachers may present mixed reactions, including support from those who can use extra pay and objections from those who have already dedicated or sold their summers elsewhere. As real or imagined as such problems might be, they are the wrong place to start consideration of programs aimed at breaking the time barrier—the kids have to come first.

The main point here, to borrow another song title, is *Accentuate the Positive.* There are many ways in which school and community can benefit through liberation from the bondage of time. A few of these are reviewed below.

Multi-age, Multi-grade Classes Enhance Learning

When a school abandons the practice of social promotion, the ability to stimulate and monitor learning achievements for all students becomes critical. The commitment should be straight-forward: **Students must perform up to standards for each course, in every subject, before promotions can happen.**

It is a given that each student will learn through different information-absorption channels and at different rates. It should also be accepted that, within the instructional cycle, time is no longer fixed; time becomes a variable that is responsive to student capabilities, motivation, and diligence. Therefore, each student must be permitted to vary the rate at which obstacles are surmounted and goals are achieved.

In a traditional, time-restricted educational program, a class of cohorts is taught as a group and lockstepped through a syllabus in strictly enforced cadence. There's no provision for individuality under a system where all students share the same age brackets and grade assignments. But, put the same kids into a flexible, multi-age, multi-grade environment and they are free to function individually or to team up with others who share the same status and needs. Students who need more time can take it without holding back their faster-learning colleagues, who are now free to tackle enrichment assignments.

In an open, cooperative environment free of time constraints, students can help one another. The value of such peer tutoring is known and proven. Also known is that both tutored student and tutor benefit from these relationships. The student needing help benefits because he or she is more likely to comprehend communication from a peer and, with success, build a positive attitude about his or her achievements. The tutor benefits from the added perspective of the learner's experience. The old saying is that teaching is a great way to learn. Guiding somebody else's learning also adds to the understanding of the tutor.

Block Teaching and Multi-disciplinary Instruction

Of all the time-based tragedies endured by American education, the 40- to 45-minute class period may be the most constrictive. The "administrivia" of attendance taking, collecting homework or other assignments, and a few minutes spent greeting students shorten available time that is already insufficient. The time the students spend settling down and getting their books or notebooks open imposes further constraints on learning time. Almost invariably, students are gathering their things and preparing to leave before the prescribed presentation or discussion can be completed.

A typical, traditional high school day provides for seven instructional/activity periods. Everyone is poorly served under this status quo. The teacher facing pressures to improve test scores doesn't have enough time to prepare students to demonstrate proficiencies. Too often, results are frustrating and/or embarrassing, making it necessary to promote students to one more level for which they are inadequately prepared.

It's the kind of problem that everybody recognizes, resents, and becomes resigned to with increasing frustration. Again, time is the culprit, students the ultimate victims. Finally, new mandates for change and processes for implementation are beginning to break down these barriers along with the others. One aspect of current breakthroughs is block scheduling of instructional time. Classes are booked for extended, sometimes double, periods. Schools providing data for this book have described blocked periods ranging from 86 to 107 minutes.

Especially constructive use can be made of extended time blocks if curriculum content encompasses multiple topics taught by faculty teams. This approach makes it possible to coordinate multiple learning experiences and building of related skills. For example, math instruction can coincide with instruction in business, or in science. Business or history courses can be commingled with instruction in writing practice, language usage, and public speaking. Multidisciplinary scope can be particularly useful in career-related learning programs. Business majors can, for example, benefit from solving problems and generating correspondence in response to cases involving customer complaints or other management problems.

A word of caution is also in order about team teaching and multi-disciplinary courses: This kind of instructional format requires a great deal more attention to the organizing of classes and the planning of instruction than traditional formats. Let's face it. If teachers are not sufficiently prepared or if instructional content is not adequately challenging, 86 to 107 minutes in a single class can seem more like a penalty than an opportunity—to both students and teachers. Skills and personalities of the teaching-team members must blend. They must agree on what is to be accomplished and must be committed to each other and the students. The three chapters that follow touch further on the advantages and challenges of team teaching and block scheduling.

Accompanying examples attest to the constructive use of instructional time under the block approach, which have, in turn, made it possible to introduce the innovations described.

ACHIEVING MORE IN THE SAME TIME

The Roseville (California) Joint Union High School District uses a block scheduling design that they call a four-by-four college block. The school day consists of four 86-minute periods. The extended period beats the race with time by permitting students to complete, in one semester, a course that would take two semesters of normal-length periods. Thus, a student can complete eight courses per year instead of the limit of six annually when the schools were on six-period days.

Assistant Superintendent Alec I. Ostrom explains: "This method opens many new opportunities for our students. They complete most of their normal graduation requirements by the end of the tenth grade. To illustrate, students need 220 credits (at one credit for 10 class hours) to graduate. Under four-by-four, they can accumulate 320 credits, leaving most of the eleventh and twelfth grades available for special courses, including individual school-to-work courses or a career-oriented academy that incorporates actual job-site work assignments as part of their school careers."

Active participation and support by area business organizations play a major role in including extensive real-world experiences within school programs.

Investing Time, Buying Opportunities

It's one thing to agree that students learn individually, something else to make it work. But this breakthrough is really happening, largely as a result of creative attacks on time barriers. One dimension of this solution lies in extending the class day, providing an extra hour or two that can be allocated to meeting the special interests of students with recognized problems or ambitions.

The answer being implemented at a number of model districts involves extending, and usually partitioning, the school day into two specific sections. As mentioned earlier, part of the day, typically the time before lunch though the order can be reversed if necessary for staff utilization, is designated as the **academic day** and devoted exclusively to core courses. The remainder of the full, or **school day,** can be spent devoted to student individuality.

Gifted students can elect enrichment programs, including advanced-placement courses. In Roseville, California, for example, it is now possible for a student to enter college with as many as six advanced-placement credits. This is feasible because, under the block scheduling and multi-disciplinary programs in effect, a student can complete the equivalent of a year's work every semester. The student who takes full advantage of these offerings can potentially complete all graduation requirements by the end of the tenth grade. The advanced placement portion of the afternoon program has worked wonders in stimulating and maintaining interest of Roseville's best and brightest high schoolers.

The after-lunch program is also used constructively to assist those students who need extra assistance to assure that they will achieve up to established standards, course by course and year by year. This meets the district's commitment to rigor and relevance for all students, each supported on the basis of his or her personal needs.

A high-value return on the availability of review and catch-up programs during the extended school day occurs when students enter high school with academic achievement deficiencies. Most commonly, the shortages show up in English and math skills. The afternoon classes, as necessary, can take a two-pronged approach, covering current lessons so students can keep up, but also reviewing past and basic knowledge and skill areas. This kind of assistance provides a major confidence builder for students who might normally tend to be reticent in class because they are aware of their own slower rates of learning in specific subjects.

This type of special class also provides a major boost to students who speak a native language other than English. The extra practice at the end of the school day helps the students to keep up with regular classes, promoting a level of confidence that encourages them to stay in school rather than drop out as many have in the past.

These are the types of programs that ICLE now calls PAR, for Progress Assurance and Reinforcement. Some activity of this type is essential if a district is to meet goals of promoting on achievements rather than birthdays.

The principle of special instruction for students with unique needs has been proven for many years. Perhaps one of the best known and most successful examples of profitable catch-up instruction is the prep school operated by the U.S. Military Academy at West Point. Many years ago, this facility was set up to provide a year of special preparation for promising students with unavoidable academic deficiencies. Included were noncommissioned officers with known military capabilities who had been out of school too long to be able to handle the rigorous entrance exams. A year in the prep program has led to West Point admission and distinguished careers as officers for many candidates.

School-to-Work Success

A number of schools and districts are now making particularly dramatic use of extended-day classes for fast-track school-to-work programs. At their most effective, the programs are set up with people and support commitments from local businesses, including direct interaction between future employers, students, and teachers.

Under one approach, these offerings can be set up as individual courses based on student career interests. As examples, the Roseville district has one course in *Advanced Culinary Techniques* taught by a chef from the local Hilton Hotel and another course in auto mechanics handled by a mechanic with experience as a training instructor for a major automobile manufacturer. Both are held in 86-minute sessions, providing enough time and opportunity for students to preview conditions and opportunities in a field of potential career interest. The extended-period, block-scheduling format is essential for both these courses because it would be impractical to offer them in traditional, 40-minute time slots. Under some circumstances courses of this type can be repeated for additional credit, with students going on to advanced work in subsequent semesters.

An even greater level of career preparation is open through the academy approach, sometimes called a school-within-a-school. The difference is principally in the amount of study involved in career preparation. In the examples cited above, it has been possible to complete job-ready training in a single 86-

minute period daily. In the instance of the Health Academy described below, more extensive and intensive schedules were
necessary. An academy specializes its educational program to
match specific workplace practices and conditions. The students
typically are segregated from the rest of the student body in the
sponsoring school through assignment of their own facilities
and faculty members. Employees who work in the targeted in-
dustries or professions often assist in instruction and also mentor
the students, who typically spend working internships on site
in host companies or facilities.

Depending on the field, students can transition from a high
school academy directly into full-time jobs in their chosen fields,
can move into two-plus-two programs at community colleges,
or can go on to four-year colleges where they will pursue professions, taking advanced placement credits with them.

TO YOUR HEALTH

The Oakmont Health Careers Academy operates in Oakmont
High and is a showpiece of the partnership program be-
tween businesses and schools at the Roseville (California)
Joint Union High School District.

During the 1997-98 school year, the health academy
enrolled 132 tenth-through-twelfth grade students. The
study sequence at the academy qualifies students for one
of five jobs in the medical field: nursing assistant, front
office or unit secretary, back office or lab assistant, physical therapy aide, or service partner. Despite the fact that
they qualify for medical-field jobs on high school graduation, the majority of the academy students are college bound.
Some will choose articulated programs open to them at area
community colleges. Others will qualify for four-year schools
where they hope to pursue a variety of goals, including becoming doctors.

Students can apply to the health academy during the
ninth grade, where they concentrate on academic core subjects. During the three-year academy program, they complete a full academic curriculum adjusted to emphasize their
special career goals. The academy's full-time faculty includes
qualified medical specialists and also academic-subject
teachers who work closely with them.

Coordinator of the Oakmont Health Academy is Karen
L. Shores, a registered nurse also credentialed as a sec-

ondary teacher and administrator. She moved into the health academy field at another district where she had been employed originally as a school nurse. Three other qualified medical personnel are part of Shores's staff. In addition, there are academic specialists in English, social studies, math/science, and Spanish, an important skill for health care givers in the area.

The staff works as a close-knit team, integrating academic and professional content. For example, a world civilization course covers such health-related topics as population trends with emphasis on aging, governmental health care programs, or current situations in relation to diseases or health care problems. Within the same course structure, the English specialist on the team will review written assignments and mentor students who make oral presentations.

During the eleventh grade, students begin spending time at one of the two hospitals cooperating in the program. They start by "job shadowing" hospital professionals who may also serve as mentors. They progress during the eleventh and twelfth grades to positions as interns, functioning on their own under supervision rather than requiring a professional "shadow." Some students also land part-time jobs at the sponsoring hospitals, with the understanding that the positions will not interfere with their school work. Throughout, they accumulate a portfolio that documents their academic and work experiences, concluding their education with documents that can figure either in job or college-entrance applications.

Time for Professional Preparation

The kinds of transitions described above and in previous chapters require what amount to heroic levels of dedication and professionalism by teachers. In most circumstances and under today's conditions, participation in a major new program or curriculum change represents a sacrifice for the cooperating teachers. Even where incremental income is available, it generally does not even come close to compensating for the extra time and emotional investment that will be required. Teacher participation in every phase of a change-oriented program is essential. Teachers are the force that can make effective transitions happen. Without their participation no program that enhances student learning experiences can be really effective.

So, any program for change should, right from the beginning, include recognition and encouragement for teachers. Part of the incentive that draws teacher response should involve recognition that teachers are professionals who deserve professional working conditions. This means provisions should be made that encourage teachers to participate in staff development opportunities. Also, school schedules should be structured to assure adequate prep and grading time for each teacher. Further, teachers themselves should be involved in planning for and carrying out these professional-level programs.

SORTING THINGS OUT

The Oakmont Health Careers Academy in Roseville, California, operates under a four-period block schedule, with each class running 86 minutes. Activities vary widely, with some student sessions held in the two sponsoring hospitals and others in lab-type facilities within the school.

In addition to the direct, career-related courses taught by the Academy staff, students also require regular academic classes within the normal college-prep curriculum. To benefit both teachers and students, the schedule has been set up so that the academic courses are held during the fourth, final period each day.

This arrangement gives the Academy faculty a full period to review the progress of the students and to fine tune their instructional plans. This approach also is in keeping with the culture that has grown within the Academy, a caliber of teacher concern and student achievement that is both unique and heartening in its evidence of what American education can become. Each afternoon, the teachers confer on all students and all of their courses. Decisions are made about the assignment of students to shadow health care workers, or possibly to serve internships, in one of the participating hospitals. Students experiencing difficulties with a specific course or personal problems are identified. Their situations are analyzed and assistance measures are devised.

"In a situation like ours," says Karen L. Shores, "we become like an extended family. The students gravitate naturally into teams whose members help each other and study together for tests or special activities. Our teachers gravitate into guardian-like roles."

In part, Shores explains, the rapport at the Academy results from the continuity of relationships implicit in having the same students and teachers together for three years. Adding a community of interests in a career-oriented setting, the result is educational quality that could make any American community, parents, business leaders, and educators justly proud.

TIME'S SPECIAL DIMENSION

The altered perspective important to education is reflected in every community and throughout the world during this age of cyberscience. One important factor already identified is the phenomenon of half-life. No matter how much knowledge and how many skills a student may absorb in 12, 16, or even 19 years of education, half of everything will be obsolete or superseded within three to five years.

The impact of this element of time is that we all have to keep running flat out, as fast as we can, throughout our lives. And that's just to stand still at the level we achieve as we enter the workplace. That's a good reason for a change in educational emphasis from teaching to learning. Learning is something we all have to do for our entire lives.

Chapter 9
Everybody Learns:
Adjusting the System
to the Student

Recognizing that each student learns individually and at a different pace from all the others, how are achievement standards determined or measured?

One answer: With great skill and a considerable amount of patience. Also required is continuing application of systems principles. Each student and every human mind must be regarded as an integrated, interdependent, combination of intellect, senses, knowledge, and skills.

Another answer: Solutions must derive from a systematic application of inputs from the students themselves, combined with the teacher's knowledge, empathy, and sensitivities.

EVERY WHEEL IS A SQUEAKER

There's a classic expression about trouble shooting: **The squeaky wheel gets the oil.** This reflects a normal human tendency to deal with complaints and/or problems while permitting comparative neglect of the remainder of the system or equipment being monitored.

Either fortunately or unfortunately, depending on your viewpoint, that approach doesn't work in education where **every wheel is squeaky.** In any school setting, every student needs to be monitored continuously—exceptions or problems can arise just that quickly. The job is more easily managed if the school has created a learning environment in which students are treated as individuals. A learning approach provides an opportunity for open, ongoing review of student progress by the teacher.

An important skill in effective classroom management lies in knowing what achievements are expected, then comparing actual performance with those expectations. A learning approach makes this possible through continuous evaluations under qualitative, performance-based assessment methods, techniques that should be part of any learning-oriented program.

Every student should be evaluated continuously because it is easy to overlook student needs that are too easily ignored under traditional, teaching-oriented systems. These students, the ones at either the high or the low ends of the achievement spectrum, may be permitted to slide under a system that relies primarily on periodic multiple-choice tests.

Even if tests are devised and administered by a teacher, they usually are administered after a topic has been covered and the class is ready to move on. In such cases, and also when standardized tests are administered, feedback and evaluation generally come too late to be used in adjusting instruction or study routines to student needs.

Damage from such practices is inflicted on high-end students through loss of opportunities to move on to enrichment work. For low-end students, absence of status information may permit problems or remedial needs to go undetected.

ELIMINATING THE SQUEAKS

By contrast, consider what happens when performance-based, real-time assessment instruments are used. For one thing, students do not have either the fear or the frustration that comes with test-taking. They routinely report on their work status and summarize their learning activities and/or their deductions and conclusions. The teacher can tell more from such qualitative efforts than would ever be possible from a multiple-choice test or other traditional quantitative instrument. Students who have derived all the knowledge intended for a given segment can go on to some form of advanced study or enrichment activity. If a student is missing a key concept or failing to achieve up to expectations, special assistance can be provided in the elective portion of the school program through a PAR-like assistance. As appropriate, the student can be offered other study materials to clarify any lack of understanding. In other instances, special tutoring can be arranged.

Students benefit at either end of the spectrum. The bright student isn't bored by sitting around waiting for classmates to catch up. The student who falls behind, perhaps because of illness or problems of adequate understanding if English is a foreign language, can bring his or her achievements up to standard. In any case, frustrations are eliminated or reduced, potentially replaced by the pride of accomplishment.

Particularly in a team-taught, multi-disciplinary program, teachers have special opportunities to review student progress from different viewpoints and with separate sensitivities.

ENRICHMENT

For a dedicated educator, it borders on the criminal to have to discourage or squelch the interests of a student who is excited about a learning opportunity. This kind of tragedy can be avoided once the lecture-based pattern that demands concurrent attention of an entire class is broken. Students who have been motivated to forge ahead of the established activity schedule can be branched onto another, more challenging track.

For example, a student with applicable motivation and talent can be encouraged to use combined technologies to prepare a video presentation, an illustration, or a written report on a topic of interest. To illustrate, consider a course in history for students enrolled in a health-care major sequence. When the course covers World War II, one or a small group might elect special study of the impact and effects of the atomic bombs that led to the Japanese surrender.

In a school set up to promote learning, reference sources can be accessed through special services or on the Internet, which can make access to special libraries available. In a learning-oriented school equipped with current technological resources, teachers acquire unprecedented opportunities to stimulate and motivate gifted students. This kind of sensitive activity can make a direct contribution toward developing society's future leaders.

SUCCESS IS NOT AUTOMATIC

The mere presence of facilities and resources within a school may not necessarily be enough to motivate students to special efforts. Effective teachers, with high levels of administrative support, should build an awareness of opportunities and provide guidance to encourage examination and experimentation.

Such efforts must come from both students and staff, within a framework of systems-type thinking and analysis. Failure to establish an ambiance for learning within an environment well equipped with computers can lead to both loss of educational opportunities and waste of physical and financial resources. An example of misguided, inadequate application of equipment to creation of learning opportunities came to light in the course of a visit to a high school heavily committed to excellence and also to high-tech support of student learning. This school had a ratio of one desktop computer for every three students. All student-accessible units were linked to high-speed routers and high-capacity file servers that connected all schools in the district and also tied into the district office. These capabilities added up to an intranet with extensive potential for instructional support. At one specific high school, full supervision over the equipment, software, and student access to the system were assigned to a librarian who had received no special education or training about information systems management.

This site visit and the conditions under which computer support was provided drove home a vital lesson about curriculum enhancement generally and high-tech instructional support efforts specifically: Computer equipment alone doesn't assure student learning. Even with vast arrays of software support, results can range from inadequate to tragic *unless computer facilities and services are managed by staff with information system experience and expertise.*

That wasn't the case in this instance. The librarian who described this system was particularly proud that the district had arranged for a reference service that provided access to texts of some 550 international newspapers and hundreds of consumer magazines and scientific journals. Students were said to be making continuous and extensive use of this reference tool in connection with their class work.

Asked whether any special needs or problems had arisen in connection with use of publication references, the librarian explained that a number of students were having trouble getting the hang of computerized document searches. With the system used at this school, students were able to initiate searches of stored texts to identify items relevant to their research. Students could base text searches on a key word or words or a specific phrase that pinpointed document content.

To illustrate the kind of problems students were experiencing, the librarian explained that a number of students had tried to search for "mercy killing" as a content key. She explained that the system couldn't handle this kind of inquiry, that students had to learn to use "euthanasia" to direct their searches.

This example has two separate and important implications. First, it is clearly healthy that students have an interest in researching euthanasia-related events, laws, and news developments—and in using computers to add depth and breadth to the work they perform in school. Second, there's a lamentable side to the librarian's position. If the idea is to challenge students to use computer technology for research, closer understanding and coordination are going to have to be developed between faculty guidance and student eagerness. It is true that students need experience in developing information queries capable of pinpointing the subjects in which they are interested. But it is also true that sound systems thinking has to prevail in staff actions and information system management. In this instance it would seem fair to assume that search-engine software should be capable of relating and coordinating text reviews for terms that are virtual synonyms, such as "mercy killing" and "euthanasia."

Adequate staff support for the school's computer capabilities should have met this need routinely. It's essential that educators recognize that *information systems are there to serve people and that the systems must be designed around the needs and activities of people.* This is one of the basic tenets of information system management. But, unfortunately, it is one still to be learned in many schools and districts. Educators must learn to treat computers for what they are—*tools* that can expedite and literally multiply computational and information processing capabilities of people.

One old adage of the computer industry seems appropriate here: When he was chairman and president of IBM during the sixties, Thomas J. Watson, Jr., was fond of explaining that the computer was a tool that did nothing that people themselves couldn't do with lead pencils. The differences, Watson would explain, were in speed and capacity. Today's students need to learn this lesson, which appears to have been forgotten in many quarters. Their education needs to help them understand what computers do and why, down to a level of lead-pencil simplicity.

Take heart, though. It isn't that complicated. The equipment within a computer system consists of interconnected components and working parts put together with wire, solder, silicon substrates with imprints of electric circuits on their surfaces, and electronic components that have microminiaturized functions formerly performed by much larger vacuum tubes. Computers perform few basic functions—addition, subtraction, storage of electrical signals with positive or negative values, retrieval of stored data, comparison of data elements, and the ability to follow sequential sets of instructions called programs.

The librarian at the visited site felt this kind of basic knowledge is irrelevant, that all students need is the ability to follow instructions to avail themselves of services delivered through straightforward use of off-the-shelf software packages. As is pointed out elsewhere in this book, mastery of existing software packages, by itself, assures students of nothing much more than obsolescence on graduation or within a short time thereafter.

While students can clearly benefit from training on precision of inquiries, the staff responsible for computer utilization should also be aware of systems potential. In this particular situation, an appropriate action might have included querying the vendor of the search engine on its capabilities, or even checking with other vendors if the response did not accommodate the natural patterns of student inquiry. As an alternative, the staff person could have referred the student to an on-line thesaurus and suggested inquiries on some of the synonyms for the topical term initially tried.

There are many capabilities within the area referred to as cyberspace, enough so that the old-school practices of fingerpointing or blaming students should be discouraged. Within each educational system—school or district—with integrated computer services, someone should be capable of providing adequate technical and information networking support. Admittedly, these people can be hard to find and expensive to hire. However, the computer industry has spawned whole armies of suppliers capable of providing system oversight and/or site management services on a fee basis. If computers are to assume their logical role at the hub of each learning-oriented school environment, the problem of care and feeding for these wonder machines has to be dealt with and solved.

ASSURING STUDENT DEVELOPMENT

If a school is going to eliminate social or grade-and-age-based promotions, provisions must be made to assure standard levels of achievements for all students. In particular, special provisions should be made to give students who need more time to master given academic content an opportunity to perform to the best of their capacity. The school's environment also should establish a level of comfort and confidence among all students, at all capability levels.

The prevailing culture in each classroom should establish that it is rare and unexpected that every student will understand everything about every lecture or reading assignment. It is natural, for a variety of reasons, for a student to be confused about or to miss some elements of a lesson. The thing that should **not** happen is for students to let potential failure develop without making some further effort to get on top of the lesson. Students who ask questions in class or who request special help should be praised, even thanked for contributing to the mutual success of the teacher and the class. Students should be acquainted with the sources of help available and encouraged to ask for assistance, at any time, on any topic. Teachers can even use descriptions with success-building connotations to help students realize that it is positive to recognize problems and ask for help. That's the intent behind the designation PAR for a student learning-assistance program. PAR implies standard, expected levels of achievement.

A PAR program fits naturally into a school that uses block scheduling. As an example, the last double-length period of each day can be left open for optional or elective activities. Students identified as needing extra time can be booked into an activity slot that provides time to review or reinforce lessons that may need further work. The session may be held in a library or resource room if appropriate and staffed by people who can direct student activities, including setting up special tutoring sessions as required. At the close of each special learning (or remediation) session, students should be queried about what they did and achieved. The tone should be positive, encouraging students to understand they are on the right track and that the school and staff are committed to the success of each and every student.

The PAR approach, as its full name implies, is intended to assure that each student progresses up to grade level and academic subject expectations. Such programs should encompass perennial achievement situations as well as special, including legislated, requirements. An example of a typical problem surfaces in the transition between elementary or middle school and high school. Almost universally, some entering students will read at lower—sometimes too much lower—grade levels. The classic challenge is to upgrade the student to standards, preferably without requiring that grade levels of instruction be repeated.

One typical method, often used by colleges as well as high schools, is to assign lagging students to special classes that remediate to overcome deficiencies while they also attempt to advance students to standard achievement levels. But a single class, even if a double period is used, may not be enough to bring deficient students to levels that meet targets for further promotion. When this happens, students can be assigned to separate, extended-day groups for additional instruction. In such instances, it is imperative that staff members help affected students understand their problems and the value of upgrading their individual performances. Students should understand both their deficiencies and the value of achieving PAR.

Language communication skills are especially important for ultimate student success. Staff evaluators should recognize that a student may have been permitted to advance into high school with unacceptable levels of language deficiencies. Students should recognize and be ready to expend whatever efforts are necessary to avoid entering the workplace with language deficiencies that will decrease their chances for success as adult citizens.

The need for special, early emphasis on language skills enhancement becomes especially important for students who want to participate in school-to-work programs in high school. Language communication upgrading can easily and effectively be integrated into special courses or academy programs designed to prepare students for direct transition into the workplace.

SPECIAL PROBLEMS

Diversity has become something of a buzzword for describing America's emerging demographics, particularly for enrollments in public schools. Public school districts, particularly in states such as California, Texas, Florida, New York, and Illinois, have reported enrolling students with 30 or more native languages other than English. The trend certainly can be dynamic and healthy in the long run as new groups of citizens enrich the country with their cultures and energies.

In the meantime though, American schools are taking a bad rap over the programs for education of ESL (English as a Second Language) or EFL (English as a Foreign Language) students. In particular, the system has been challenged by the number and the extent of difficulties experienced with Hispanic students from Central and South America.

For more than 20 years, school districts across the country have been using a bilingual approach for Hispanic students. Students entering the first grade are taught initially in Spanish, including language literacy and most academic subjects. The theory is that English is to be introduced gradually, carrying students through a transition to full English fluency by the end of the third grade. Students who enter at an older age are taught bilingually for an interim period, theoretically leading to fluency after two or three years.

In practice, achievements have ranged from much slower than anticipated down to a virtual standstill. Very few students have made the transition in three years. Even when they are moved into mainstream English programs, they fall so far behind in English that few ever reach real proficiency. Dropout rates for Hispanic students have run 30 to 40 percent. Very few, even among those who graduate from high school, are qualified for skilled or white collar jobs.

In recent years, a strong backlash has developed against bilingual instruction. Among other objections, there have been a number of complaints alleging that segregating Hispanic students as is done under bilingual programs violates the 1954 Brown vs. Board of Education Supreme Court ruling that ended segregation on racial (and implied ethnic) grounds. In a 1997 survey, 84 percent of Hispanic parents in Southern California favored ending bilingual education in favor of immediate concentration on English. A number of cities and counties have opted to discontinue bilingual education.

While disagreements rage over what should be done to educate and prepare Hispanic students for productive citizenship, schools face a dilemma. The approach described earlier, with a special course for remedial or introductory English within a block scheduling format, shows promise for accommodating ESL students in secondary schools. Students who attend one class during the academic day and an added course given during the extended school day should be able to come up to English proficiency without having to repeat any grades.

SPECIAL EDUCATION

Block-scheduling and extended-day programs can do well in accommodating physically or learning-disabled students whose disabilities are at a level that qualify them for mainstreaming in public schools.

Within a learning environment that uses study-team assignments, the prevailing culture encourages each student to contribute to the limit of his or her ability. Learning disabled students can gain through their presence in small group sessions where team members collaborate to gather information or solve problems. As necessary, the LDA students can receive extra help in special study or tutorial sessions held toward the end of the school day.

It is, of course, to the advantage of both the students and

the district to include LDA students within regular course structures. The district's responsibility to provide "appropriate" educational experiences is more effectively met, where feasible, through mainstreaming. If students cannot be accommodated in standard school facilities and courses, the district could be responsible for covering tuition in appropriate private schools, potentially at far higher costs.

Over and above the physical and financial aspects of mainstreaming, the achievement of helping special students adjust to society at large through their school experience can be highly rewarding.

BELIEVABILITY AND CONFIDENCE BUILDING

America's young people are exposed to enough cynicism without having their school experiences pile on additional negatives. Academic failure can be the worst of all confidence deflators.

Schools can fail students in a wide variety of ways. The most obvious is through an unsatisfactory grade. But negative attitudes also are promoted when a gifted student who expected to be challenged finds classwork dull, simplistic, and/or boring. Each "turned off" student will acquire cohorts as negative reactions lead to destructive attitudes.

For effective learning to happen, ***each student must be involved in setting his or her own achievement goals within acceptable frameworks established for their schools*** and must understand the challenges and performance standards to be met. This understanding should be part of a larger context in which each student looks forward to graduation as a threshold to satisfying, productive adulthood. A significant number of students today, possibly a majority in some areas, are exposed to depressing levels of negative views about America and the career opportunities open to young people. Counselors and teachers should avoid delivering rosy images that are unreal and probably unattainable for the student. The idea is to help establish a vision that is both attractive and attainable by the individual student. Then, and only then, will students participate actively and willingly in establishing academic schedules and striving to deliver pride-building performances.

Experience has shown that introduction of program major course sequences and/or career-oriented academies within high schools can help build enthusiasm and enhance performance. The point is that it takes programs that students can understand and regard as beneficial and attainable to establish the kind of credibility that helps mold positive student attitudes.

SYSTEMATIC TROUBLE SHOOTING

Most educators agree readily that Dr. Murphy must have had schools in mind when he devised his famous law about things that go wrong. That's the bad news. The good news is that you don't have to sit back passively and let the calamities descend. Success in educating young people requires a continual monitoring of the present to anticipate and head off the things that can go wrong.

Traditional teaching and testing methods, were designed largely for the convenience of adults charged with developing grades, issuing report cards, and creating a rationale for promoting students in response to their ages and social/political factors, without full regard to performance or other conditions.

If educational processes are to become truly achievement oriented, teachers and other staff cannot wait until the end of a term, or even until midterms, to evaluate student progress. The learning approach and the instructional techniques this methodology fosters should promote real-time review and monitoring of student progress.

In part, this progress takes place because fewer class presentations involve teacher lectures and more information comes in the form of reports that share findings of student study teams. As part of this process, each student builds a portfolio of documents that trace his or her progress. Included are written reports recounting activities and research findings. Class handouts may require entries that reflect student knowledge acquisition, feelings, or preferences for further work. Special assignments for written or oral presentations should also be included as a basis for ongoing assessment. Under this philosophy, assessment happens on a timely basis that permits adjustment or revision of curricula to assure student comprehension and mastery. A later chapter deals with some specifics of real-time, performance-based assessment, including a technique for measuring the level of performance as a factor in grading.

SOURCES OF HELP

If the ultimate goal of education is successful entry into the community at large as employed, productive citizens living satisfying lives, the community can and should play a role in forming and delivering appropriate educational experiences. The more active the participation by community resource people in the ongoing education of the children who represent the community's future, the greater the achievements that can be anticipated.

A management of change planning process like the one described in earlier chapters puts a high premium on participation and active contributions from representatives of business organizations at which students will eventually be applying for jobs. The value of school-business partnerships can be enhanced with such activities as arranging visits by teachers to facilities of sponsoring companies. These in-service exchanges are most productive when teachers are exposed to the working experiences of typical employees. Ideally, teachers derive an understanding of such factors as how companies and workers involve themselves in lifelong learning requirements for survival in the face of dynamic changes experienced by society and business entities.

Students also benefit directly when scientists or executives from local companies lecture to classes or mentor individual youngsters. These interactions lend a feeling of reality to a program which, after all, should be designed to prepare students for survival in the real world of work.

To be truly successful, a school's academic program must reflect and be modeled upon the knowledge base and systems that drive the economy at large and the specific community in which the school operates. Teachers must become aware of such factors as obsolescence of the content presented in today's classes as the working world faces a general half-life for all existing work-related knowledge of three to five years.

BUILDING SCHOOL-TO-WORK BRIDGES

Possibly the happiest learning-oriented circumstance of all occurs when students at high school age know exactly what careers they want to pursue and are ready to make commitments. In the past, these goal-oriented youngsters had, too often, to mark time during their last year or two in high school because there was no way for them to pursue their special interests.

In increasing numbers of schools, students who know where they want to go can opt for enrollment in a special school-within-a-school, usually called an *academy.* An academy is typically a two- or three-year program taught by special faculty, generally in special or separate facilities. When the school uses block scheduling, students can be booked into as many as six or eight double-period courses in the specialty they pursue. In addition, regular academic classes such as English, science, or history will typically be adapted to include content of special, career-related interest. An academy program, where feasible, will include coursework at actual job sites. For example, as described in the previous chapter, health academy students will receive school credit for internships at hospitals. Some students may even line up part-time jobs in fields of their choice.

THE MAJOR ADJUSTMENT

Of all the adjustments necessary to complete the transition to a learning-based environment, the greatest demands of all are faced by the classroom teacher. When teaching is de-emphasized and learning is stressed, the role and responsibilities of a teacher must go through a transition that, in its own sphere of reality, is greater and more difficult than the challenges required of students. Under a commitment to learning, the student is catered to and the teacher, in becoming a facilitator or coach, is the caterer. Responsibilities for academic achievement shift markedly, with the heaviest burden of change falling on the teacher.

Things are bad enough under a traditional approach that involves integrated, multi-disciplinary instruction at elementary grades and specialized-discipline instruction at middle and high school levels. In the new, learning-oriented world, things can be reversed. As described earlier, elementary teachers can be asked to specialize while high school faculty can be asked to generalize and take on block scheduled, interdisciplinary, team assignments. As these transitions happen, teachers must acquire attitudes and habits that accommodate new levels of flexibility and adaptability. In this kind of situation, resistance can lead to major levels of frustration and unhappiness. The challenges of interdisciplinary instruction are covered further in a later chapter. For the purposes of this discussion, however, it is important to recognize where and what kinds of changed expectations faculty members are facing.

IMPACT OF TECHNOLOGY

A special challenge faced by teachers lies in the rate at which computers and other high-tech systems impact required knowledge and skills students must be prepared to acquire. While half-lives are generally portrayed in ranges of three to five years, the information technology field faces an obsolescence factor that's much shorter. In general, it is safe to assume that any computer hardware or software on the market today will be replaced by something faster and more sophisticated in 18 months or less. Some implications of this rate of change and the responsiveness that should be happening in modern schools are covered in the chapter that follows.

Chapter 10
Computers as Learning Tools

Computers are fascinating gadgets that appear to be mesmerizing educators. In turn, schools have come up with billions of dollars in apparent hope of acquiring a panacea cure for all of education's ills. In schools all across the country during the 1990s, computers by the hundreds of thousands have become ubiquitous.

As the feverish rate of new installations continues, there seems to be no question about the logic of or justification for the vast commitments that have been made. After all, computers dominate the American workplace and are continually increasing their prominence in our homes. So American students should enter the job market and society ready to deliver computer capabilities. So far, so good. But will computers deliver up to the wishful forecasts that have been made for them? Will they truly revolutionize education as we have known it?

SUCCESS IS NEVER AUTOMATIC

Computers are not the first technology to promise miracles in education. Revolutionary breakthroughs were promised throughout most of the twentieth century by a succession of wonder devices. The phonograph was on scene early, duly heralded as a major conceptual breakthrough in education. Other wonder devices followed in quick succession: 16 mm motion pictures, audio tape recorders, 35 mm slides, electric typewriters, audio cassettes, sound/strip film projectors, VCR, and CD-ROM. Each of these technologies, in its turn, arrived with a promise that education was in for serious change, that school would never be the same again.

One after another, these technological marvels faced unpredicted lethargy and fell victim to high levels of disinterest. Eventually, most of the equipment was relegated to venues such as broom closets and faded from the scene. Are computers immune from this kind of fate as proponents claim?

OFF TO A SLOW START

The level of enthusiasm for computers currently being shown in schools may truly be unprecedented, as claimed. However, things haven't always been this rosy. Think back just a few years. In the mid-to-late 1980s, tens (perhaps hundreds) of thousands of computers were installed in schools. For a wide range of reasons, including the favorite claim that schools and teachers just weren't ready to harness their potential, these early computers suffered the same kind of fate as 16 mm projectors and other predecessor technologies. Today, the 1980s vintage computers, many of which are still in schools, are disparaged as potential boat anchors or various forms of scrap because they lack the features, speed, and capacities of today's models.

That's probably too hard a rap for computers like the Apple IIe and its companions. It's true that newer, faster, flashier units are available today. But, if they still work, they should have some potential for getting students started on computers. Even more serious is the willingness to disparage and discard devices that aren't the newest or latest. That kind of thinking could lead to a mindset for demanding billions of dollars of replacement equipment every few years.

Part of the danger is that each computer is a system and each is potentially part of a larger information processing and delivery system. If educational decision makers are thinking in terms of requiring the most current gadgets, it could be a symptom indicating that too little attention is being given to the role of computers as tools of an information-dependent world.

COMPUTERS ARE SYSTEMS, STUDENTS SHOULD BECOME SYSTEMS THINKERS

As with any system, computers are part of a larger whole composed of interlinked parts that deliver results potentially greater than the sum of those parts. It's important that educators learn to focus on the functions of computers and software in the world of information workers. From a realistic outlook, all computers perform a basic set of functions, and all have some lingering use, regardless of the year of their manufacture. It's time to focus on the work that can be performed rather than on the larger numbers for measuring bits, bytes, memory or storage capacities, or processing cycles.

If the objective is truly to prepare students to learn to learn, it's time to focus on some basics. In the past, objectives were described in terms of computer literacy or fluency. This is the time to adjust perspectives. Teachers must become **information-system wise,** then turn their attention to transferring this outlook to students. This book starts with a reference to an innovative curriculum that scored a major success built upon recognition that the basic **transaction** is at the heart of every functional business system. ***Teachers and other present-day staff are going to have to focus their learning and their vision beyond the hardware on the desk in front of them and learn to understand the significance and impact of the computer's role in society generally and in the future of their students specifically.***

The way things are going, American schools may well be graduating a majority of future workers who will find themselves obsolescent within 12 to 18 months after they leave school. This is a likely prospect if schools continue practices of basing instruction and training on individual, current software packages without imparting any sense or understanding of the computer as a system on its own and also as part of a much larger system. Students must learn to see beyond the clerical details of rote operations and recognize the wide range of implications involved in perfecting the many interpersonal and business transactions for which computers play critical roles.

People who decide on what students need to know should recognize that the mechanistic, application-specific approach to instruction trains students in specialties that are likely to be superseded before they ever apply for their first full-time job. As a result of the short-sightedness of the curricula through which they are being processed by well-intentioned but ill-informed faculty and staff, many students are being set up for future frustration and major disappointment.

GETTING DOWN TO BUSINESS

One area of education where computers must acquire greater respect and use than they have had to date is business education. Consider that, since the advent of computers, enrollments in high school business programs have shrunk drastically. There are reasons, of course.

High school business departments used to hold students captive for up to four semesters of instruction in typing alone. Today, with the computer acting as tutor as well as the object to be operated, students can acquire adequate touch keyboarding skills in as little as 20 hours, sometimes less. In the modern world of desktop computers, many of the manipulative functions that students had to deal with on typewriters are handled automatically by the computers themselves. The decline in registration for keyboarding courses is thus understandable. With current methodologies, it is possible, for example, for students to master touch keyboarding as part of a writing sequence in an English course.

Another losing battle involved the defense of instruction in shorthand, which became irrelevant in an era when executives dictate into machines or keyboard their own correspondence. The rearguard defense of handwritten shorthand, along with another losing cause in the form of handwritten bookkeeping, absorbed energies that could have gone into modernizing practices through introduction of computers with software that replicated the trends that were rapidly revolutionizing business practices during those years.

The computers that did find their way into business departments tended to be misused or virtually unused. During the 1980s, one of the major preoccupations with computers in high schools was for the teaching of program writing in the BASIC language. For many years, it was an article of faith in the publishing industry that no introductory computer book could sell without an appendix on how to program in BASIC. The main value of BASIC, it turned out, was in academia. This line of instruction was a throwback to the days before general-purpose software packages became practical. At one time, companies had to program all of their applications from scratch. But most companies used languages other than BASIC. Thus, this teaching emphasis turned out to be chiefly a one-way ticket to obsolescence.

As personal computers became mainstay business machines of the modern office, business educators hopped a new bandwagon. They selected popular packages for office applications, particularly word processing, spreadsheets, and databases. To a great extent, this is still happening, making for a commitment to continue producing students whose skills will prove to be obsolete in 18 to 24 months, by which time a new version of each package can be expected.

Under such programs, students are learning about machines and specific procedures. With few exceptions, they don't acquire the basic knowledge and skills they will need if they are to learn to learn. To qualify for the twenty-first century workforce, students will have to acquire a scope of knowledge that encompasses the basic transaction patterns and processing systems that underlie all effective business information systems. In other words, future information workers will have to be able to think about processing systems and their capabilities; it will not do for them to be limited to individual machines and their working parts or specific software packages without being aware of the larger world of the organizations that employ them. They will need these capabilities to qualify for thousands of jobs that will classify them as information workers.

THE CHALLENGE OF 'DOING BUSINESS'

The idea that students are being prepared for computer-related jobs in business through exposure to so-called "office" software packages, accepted in many secondary schools, probably represents gullibility more than practicality. These packages combine programs for word processing, spreadsheets, and databases. As featured in a number of high school courses, they are represented as replicating conditions in real-world businesses. As noted earlier, a song title covers this situation as well: *It ain't necessarily so.*

The inclusion of these three applications in one package has more to do with competition among software vendors than with the natural order of things in business operations and management. Some background: In the late 1970s and early 1980s, a spreadsheet package became the first major success for a standard software product. Spreadsheets are standalone management tools for budgeting and operational reporting. Thousands of desktop computers were sold to businesses just because the package became available.

In those days, most word processors were designed as sales tools for use on specific makes or computers—they ran only on the equipment of individual manufacturers. They also were mostly "command driven," meaning that operators had to enter specific instructions from the keyboard to control the width and length of a document, size of type, tabulator settings, and other features. All keyboard entries were displayed in the same format, with variations entered only when text was printed. The

command structure represented just enough complexity to discourage executives, teachers, and other professionals from taking the time to master word processing skills. During this era,
word processing computers were limited predominantly to use
by secretaries, as typewriter replacements.

In those days, introduction of a new software package and
formation of a new company that provided product to make
computers more useful was a major event. One significant development of this type came when a new software house was
formed and grew rapidly around development and sale of a standard database package. A database is a specialized file structure within a computer that organizes and retains information
for operational use and/or management reporting. Examples
include employee paychecks and management of inventories.

Payrolls use employee databases with information items
that identify workers, Social Security numbers, tax deductions,
pay rates, and other essentials. The computer retrieves items
needed to compute pay, print checks and status reports, then
update the database with newly computed figures.

An inventory database contains records of stocks on hand
for products, parts, or supplies. Also included are costs, identification for suppliers, and records showing quantities used for
each item. With this information, the computer reports to managers when it's time to reorder items or if some units are not
selling as planned.

Applying technology that evolved partly through development of spreadsheet and database software, suppliers moved to
expand capabilities of word processors and make them more
"user friendly" by providing on-screen menus for selecting operating features.

By this time, a number of independent suppliers were offering improved word processing, spreadsheet, and database
software. Concurrently, one company, developer of the dominant operating system software that guides basic microcom-
puter operations, applied a strategy that called for incorporating word processing, spreadsheet, and database programs into
the same package as the operating system. The idea of a three-
way application package helped secure a position of leadership
for the operating system developer, which had entered the market for application software late and at a disadvantage.

FOLLOWING THE WRONG LEADERS

Now, what does all this mean to secondary educators and their students? It means that schools that install and purport to teach from full "office" packages are conforming their curricula to marketing strategies of software companies rather than to patterns of use in real businesses.

What approach would best serve students headed toward entry-level positions in computerized offices?

Different considerations apply to hardware and software purchases by today's business organizations. The current hardware acquisition pattern calls for serious policy reconsiderations by educators. As schools have moved, often tentatively and minimally, to install computers in classrooms and labs, it made sense to purchase standalone units. That is, each computer contained its own memory, hard disk, floppy disk, and full compliment of software, making it a complete system within itself. Earlier, businesses had moved in this direction too. Eventually, though, the myriad of standalone, independent systems led to a kind of anarchy in which it was difficult to keep track of what processing was happening and to oversee protection of data files.

In time, businesses have gone more to configurations in which user workstations are networked and supported from a central file server. This makes it possible for a technically qualified person to oversee the status of the full system and to monitor security and integrity of data files. Some schools are beginning to follow this same course. But many are lagging. For a school, networking makes economic as well as operational sense since network computers are available at far lower costs that standalone workstations. Further, the network approach keeps a system current for longer periods because updating of software and file management capabilities is done at one or a few central locations rather than at each workstation. Replacement of workstation equipment can be done less frequently and at far lower costs.

One dramatic example of major expansion of computer capabilities at minimal costs: In Winston-Salem, North Carolina, an enterprising middle-school technology coordinator discovered that the state prison had a program under which inmates refurbished used desktop computers from state offices. This discovery led to acquisition of 120 computers still quite viable for use on the school's network—*at no cost.* Similar deals are available all across the country, from large business organizations happy to donate equipment due for replacement to schools in exchange for income tax credits.

GETTING REAL

For realistic school-to-work approaches, schools would do well to adjust course content more realistically to the way real companies use computers for transaction processing and management decision making. For example, students who elect courses such as bookkeeping or accounting—or future college students who plan to major in business or accounting—may realize some benefits from learning about constructing spreadsheets and databases. However, a more directly applicable learning experience might come from exposure to a transaction-driven business recordkeeping program such as *QuickBooks*. This package supports typical business recordkeeping by processing transactions, creating its own supporting files, and generating needed documents and reports, all on a seamless, integrated basis.

An advantage of an instructional approach that uses transaction-based software is that students gain an understanding of how businesses operate and how computers meet business information needs. By comparison, instruction in spreadsheets or databases without a connection to realistic business transactions can be too abstract to impart real job-related skills.

Word processing, of course, is of universal value. All students should be proficient word processors by the time they leave high school. This skill will be valued in so many present and future jobs that it should be considered as essential as driving a car. Proof that this recognition is happening: In North Carolina, word processing proficiency recently became a high school graduation requirement. In most instances, it would probably be profitable to add a requirement for minimal proficiency in touch-keyboarding for all students, with job-qualifying proficiencies stipulated for business majors.

THINKING SYSTEMS

Understanding of basic procedures and information structures is far more important than rote training about which buttons to push for use of narrowly applicable software packages. Systems thinking is going to be an essential for real success during the twenty-first century. If students possess these requisite knowledge bases and skills, they will be able to master any updated or revised software application package within a few hours. So, it is important for educators themselves to understand and impart an understanding of what systems are, why they are important, and how they are designed or developed.

Basically, *a system is the sum of the actions, elements,*

equipment, and procedures that make up a perfected trans-action and/or an ongoing relationship. The result of an ef-fective system is a satisfied expectation for performance and/or project completion. A *systems thinker* concentrates on results rather than parts or interim steps within a transaction. Some examples of a systems thinker's outlook:

❏   A family shopping for a house doesn't buy a structure. It is shopping for a lifestyle, for happy surroundings, for an en-vironment that will promote happy experiences and memo-ries, and for a convenient home-to-work commute.

❏   People who choose to eat in a service-type restaurant aren't after nutrition only. They are looking for an overall enjoy-able experience. Similarly, occupants of a first-class hotel seek more than shelter. They want comfort, enjoyment.

In summary, systems thinking results from an attitude that includes a committment to get a job done and to meet stan-dards or expectations for efficiency, effectiveness, and satisfac-tion of identified customers. *Where computers are concerned, a systems thinker is committed to accomplishment rather than the individual functions that lead to acceptable re-sults.* The interim steps that lead up to results delivered by a system are necessary, of course. But those steps are contribu-tory. They are not the end results for which students should be educated or workers should be trained.

COMPUTER BASICS

Computers are going to play an important part in the lives of today's students—for the rest of their lives. Certainly comput-ers should be accorded a respect and a level of importance far higher than toys or trivialized pursuits. This is sophisticated equipment that should be accorded a level of respect that serves as a basis for building an understanding of the power and po-tential that lie beyond the keyboard and the mouse. At the very least, this kind of understanding should be basic for future in-formation workers. That designation, on average, will eventu-ally take in more than 70 percent of graduates in any given school system.

Why should students know about computer processing methods or capacities? Why should they be interested in memory size, disk capacity, cycle speeds, or the makeup of the software library available to them?

Very simple! The computer a student sits at in a school lab, library, or classroom will not be identical to the one encountered in an office, factory, or even a fast-food restaurant. The main link between lessons acquired in school (or even at home) and profitability in the workplace is the understanding of basic functions that will enable a worker to adapt quickly to the equipment, procedures, and application designs encountered on real jobs.

Consider an analogy. Before a young person is issued a license to drive an automobile, he or she must complete some basic instruction covering safe, sound operation of an expensive and potentially dangerous system of mechanical equipment. Of course a computer is different. It can't cause traffic accidents or run anybody over. But, in real work situations, uninformed, improperly trained computer users can generate some real, costly catastrophes. Carelessness or ineptness at a computer keyboard can destroy assets and cause damage that, literally, could put a company out of business or cause losses that could range into millions of dollars. In the real world, computers are serious business. People entrusted with their operation require knowledge and skills they should begin to acquire in high school but that, unfortunately, many are not getting.

So, what should students learn about computers and information systems? What are the basics?

Students should learn that, in modern society, information is a prime asset for any business, a necessity for any governmental entity. They face examples in their own school every day. Attendance reports must be accurate, reliable, and on time so the school can receive its operating funds from the state. Course completion information and grades must be kept accurately and safely because they support college admission applications. Students should understand the massive demands of information management when they are led to consider the job of registering and keeping track of millions of vehicles in individual states or a composite of some 50 million vehicles or more nationwide. They may be interested in the computer system that supports local law enforcement agencies, down to and including computer terminals in patrol cars, extending to more than 1 million felons in state and federal prisons. Certainly, all teenagers will be aware of computerized sales registers used to enter their orders in fast food restaurants.

As for examples of how computers function as a system, counterparts can be cited through living examples that relate to their own experiences. Each student is a self-contained learning system that replicates the basic computer functions of input, processing, output, and storage. Inputs are acquired through visual and auditory responses to surroundings—hearing lectures or explanations, seeing information on blackboards or in books, and writing entries in notebooks. Computers can replicate all these input functions.

As for processing, each student possesses a brain that is a far more sophisticated and efficient processor than anything that exists in even the most advanced computers. The brain processes information that gets people to their destinations, guards their safety, and also builds a knowledge bank that helps to assure their place and value as information workers. Comparing the human mind with even massive computer memories is a no-brainer. Memory is the immediate support resource for everything a computer or a person does.

Output for the student is achieved through speech and writing, also through actions and reactions, as occurs when a person drives a car or operates a keyboard.

The criticality of the storage function should be explained carefully and understood thoroughly. Students store information assets in notebooks or in computer systems and, of course, in their brains. For a computer, storage takes place in one or more recording devices that maintain accumulated information and support retrieval as required. The so-called computer revolution really began to happen in earnest when managers realized that stored files covering the operating status and financial value of a company were accumulated and maintained by computers more efficiently than through any previous means.

There, those are the simple basics that students should understand and be able to elaborate on and relate to their own operating experiences. A computer, any computer, is a processing system. Humanity relies on and is at the mercy of such processing systems. The scale and capacities of computers vary. But the same basic functions take place in systems that direct airplane traffic around the world, cook meals in the home, or monitor the skies for alerts against possible missile attacks. A student should never be told by a teacher or adult staff member that understanding what happens inside a computer's box is irrelevant and doesn't matter. This happens too frequently. It should stop.

COMPUTER-DELIVERED INSTRUCTION

One of the computer benefits promised for many years beginning in the early 1980s involved direct instruction on academic content. Results to date have been spotty at best, clearly not sufficient to justify the expenditures of billions of dollars to set computers in front of students. Certainly it is safe to say that equipment with the potential to become the greatest teaching aide in history is presently being underutilized. There are individual exceptions and bright spots. But the findings are largely that computers are underutilized for direct student instruction.

Sadly, one of the most immediate ways in which computers can help build the knowledge and skills of students has been belittled and/or shunned in many facets of the educational process. This application is on-line content reinforcement, often scoffed at as drill and practice and seen as boring, therefore of little interest to students. A lecture on the discipline requisite to learning should not be necessary here.

Reinforcing Learning

What should happen is a recognition that cognitive capabilities are enhanced through practice that refreshes and reinforces retention of acquired information. It certainly is no less boring for whole groups of students to have to sit in class and take turns, one at a time or in unison, reciting drills that could be completed in a small fraction of the time if they were performed at computer keyboards. The materials for enhancing learning processes are readily available through existing computer hardware and software. If their use is not incorporated into classroom activities, this important potential benefit from computers could quickly go the route of the movie projector or other past potentials.

A dramatic example of the potential for review-type instruction delivered by computers was observed a few years ago in a juvenile detention facility in California. The school portion of the facility had a room equipped with six computer terminals that administered course materials stored in an off-site file server. The young inhabitants of the facility signed up for turns at the computer terminals during every available moment of each day. When they were seated at the terminals, their attention to each entry they made and every response they received was closely focused and intense.

When our observer noted this situation and asked the teacher about it, the explanation was straightforward. These kids, residents of a disciplinary facility, had bad recollections of their school experiences. Most were from rough neighborhoods where it was socially unacceptable to demonstrate an interest in learning before their peers. But now, with the computers, they were experiencing, for the first time, attention to their needs and responses. The programs anticipated their answers and responded immediately to their entries. In short, they were getting a degree of attention that was new in their life experience and they were enjoying it and responding in kind.

The Right Way to Write

A frequently heard criticism about the Internet deals with the abysmal misuse of language in chat rooms or e-mail channels. Even people who don't object to purple prose are appalled by the sad state of the spelling, grammar, and general language usage they encounter. Many students, and teachers as well, tend to make a joke of this tragedy.

But there's also some potential good news. One of the heartening facts of the current drive to upgrade the quality of American education is the focus on future adult roles of today's students. These adult roles must be understood as requiring the ability to communicate clearly and accurately, personally and electronically. A strong, positive effect from the widespread use of computers in schools has been that their availability has led to increases in student writing practice, accompanied by increased skill levels in many instances.

The opportunity is virtually universal. After all, word processing is the most popular application installed on desktop computers. Couple this with the attraction derived from the newness of computer experience for many students. Assignments to prepare written compositions or reports represent a natural justification to acquire computer time and many students have taken advantage of this opportunity.

For whatever reason, lack of practice in writing, accompanied by quality levels generally judged as unsatisfactory, has been a perennial problem for American schools. Now, computers are providing a stimulus to write and teachers, given the neater appearance of student work as compared with handwritten documents, are able to deal more effectively with the workload of reading and critiquing more submissions.

Writing skill is one important area where proficiency is enhanced by practice. In general, the more words a person captures in written documents, the more productive he or she will become in completing future assignments and the better the quality of the work will be, giving the computer great potential to enhance student capabilities as communicators.

But improvement doesn't necessarily come automatically. It takes a steady stream of constructive criticism and suggestions for improvement to build real writing skills. This means that educators have to work particularly hard to help students understand that criticism can be positive, helpful, and a source of encouragement and growth. Advancement comes with practice and accompanying recognition of improvements and opportunities for further personal growth. There's no substitute for diligence. There's an old saying that writing proficiency begins by learning to keep the seat of the pants on the seat of a chair; success requires application.

The need for diligence is particularly important because computers also offer opportunities for sloppy thought and excuses for skipping or avoiding necessary work. A good example lies in the availability of programs that check the spelling of entered text. This can lead to a false sense of security that should be put into a realistic perspective. Students should understand what happens when they run a spellchecking program: The computer compares the presented text, word by word, with a dictionary brought into memory for high speed reference. Any word not found in the dictionary is highlighted and a suggested correction is displayed. The operator must then decide whether to accept the correction, enter another word to replace the entry, or ignore the suggestion because the word is correct even if it's not listed in the dictionary.

A problem: Use of a spellchecker does not guarantee that the writer has used the correct word. A typographical error that makes a word wrong within textual context may still pass dictionary comparison. Suppose, for example, the writer wants to enter the word **two** and strikes **tow** instead. The computer-referenced dictionary will pass this entry as an acceptable word. Without careful, intelligent reading, the overconfident student may turn in a paper loaded with incorrect, badly chosen words.

On balance, the fact that computers encourage more writing by students qualifies as a positive result of their availability.

Delivering Instruction

The ultimate potential benefit of computer-delivered learning—actual, interactive delivery of instruction—is still being realized only sparingly.

One underused source of help is available without cost. Most textbook publishers have computer-deliverable software supplements to augment content of their textbooks. These are generally available without cost to schools that adopt their books. Included are supplemental lessons that add to the content coverage in the book, sometimes through presentation of new information that has surfaced since the book was published. Also available are assessment materials such as research or report assignments or test banks. No claims for the quality of these materials are implied here. What can be said, though, is that they represent a vastly underused resource that is widely available, for the asking.

On the other end of the publishing spectrum, consideration is overdue for using on-line server files as a source of text materials. Almost unavoidably, many textbooks are out of date by the time they come off the press. The very process of book publishing also means that costs, which have risen sharply over the past two decades, will undoubtedly continue to go up as color production becomes standard and gimmicks abound. Wouldn't it make sense, in the light of current technologies, if text materials were housed in on-line files so they could be downloaded and reproduced locally in school or district offices? Teachers could specify acquisition and reproduction of individual chapters or book segments, as appropriate for lesson plans. Before long, it may even be possible to arrange to access chapters from books or on-line services from multiple publishers whose materials reflect different views or different content strengths on subject areas.

It could also be possible to assemble book-type materials to correspond with the knowledge base or learning patterns of individual students. For example, consider the situation of a six-year-old entering first grade. The typical first-grade student has a speaking vocabulary of perhaps 2,000 to 4,000 words. When this youngster is subjected to the conventional wisdom of a school system, he or she is presented with a reading vocabulary deemed suitable by adults. Why not let the child leaf through computer displays of a number of pictures and words to build an individual reader?

Also why not let the computer take part in programs to teach reading rather than recitation? Seated before a computer, the student could point to images or definitions that match presented or spoken words. At higher grades, students could enter definitions or descriptions of materials that have been read, extending exercises to comprehension rather than limiting them to recitation of words based on sounds alone.

Also imagine what the future might hold if computers presented special, up-to-date maps to students in a geography class.

The potential for imaginative education gets even more exciting as schools follow the logical move toward interdisciplinary classes. This is an ideal place for computers to step in instructionally, particularly since little has happened in preparation of textbook or other traditional materials for interdisciplinary courses.

In business courses, for example, documents could be displayed that represent realistic company operating problems. Using computers, students could deal with transactions matching those encountered in real world business situations, responding with writing assignments that encompass knowledge of accounting and management.

In a combined history-English program, students could be presented with copies of newspaper articles on elections, wars, or new laws. They could be instructed to write about them as though they were working for newspapers or magazines published during the same time frame as the events.

Electronic mail capabilities of computers could be used to create conference situations in which students from multiple schools cooperate on study projects.

GETTING THE MULTIMEDIA PICTURE

Many of today's kids, having lived entirely within a television age, think naturally in multimedia terms. It is natural also for imaginative faculty to provide opportunities that permit students to incorporate multimedia production into their learning activities.

In the real worlds of motion pictures and TV, computers have become mainstay tools for creating pictorial and animated entertainment or educational products. Many schools already have computers with sufficient capacity for multimedia production. These systems can often be adapted for multimedia outputs with relatively small investments in peripheral equipment.

Student enthusiasm in multimedia production is easily directed toward active learning. Teams of students can be allowed to submit videotapes or computer disks with multimedia shows as substitutes for term papers or oral reports on study projects.

FIT FOR PRINT

Today, most newspapers and magazines are edited and produced through computer graphics techniques. In school, students with special interests in design or journalism can develop market-related skills through use of computers outfitted with relatively inexpensive graphics and page-makeup software.

School newspapers and yearbooks provide obvious, economical applications for both computer equipment and student talents. It can be highly profitable to incorporate practice in use of graphic software in art or journalism classes for students who produce the school's publications.

Beyond these special situations, almost any student or study team may want to use graphics output capabilities for anything from routine class reports to graduation projects.

SOURCE OF KNOWLEDGE

The potential of computers for student research needs no elaboration but is worth stressing nonetheless. Entire libraries can be placed at the disposal of students, including hundreds of current and historic publications. Effectively directed and used, these facilities can add significant depth and motivation to student learning.

Students need little encouragement to wade into networks and to explore the realm of cyberspace anxiously and endlessly. Getting them to use the Internet or special library services is rarely the problem. More to the point is the need to impress on students that computers are not toys. They are expensive, sophisticated tools that hold important keys to their future. Some form of accountability should be established to impress students that their time at computer keyboards should be put to productive use and should contribute to their learning experience. There has been enough publicity about the negative effects of some Internet content to create an almost irresistible attraction for many students. Appropriate safeguards against misuse are available and should be put to constructive use.

NETWORKING

Computers can be highly effective in promoting networking by people as well as through equipment and telecommunications circuits. When computers throughout a school or district are linked via communications circuits, physical boundaries to learning experiences can be virtually eliminated.

Two or more classes can participate in joint learning exercises. Students can receive expert help from business leaders or scientists who are usually happy to share information with them.

There are also many pragmatic benefits. Students who are

absent due to illness can be invited to pick up study and home-work assignments via e-mail. Student writing assignments can be e-mailed to outside resource persons for review and revision suggestions. School news can be delivered to newspapers or broadcast stations.

On graduation, students will emerge into a wired world. Effective use of computers for interpersonal networking can help prepare them for one of the inevitabilities in their future.

INSTRUCTIONAL EXPECTATIONS

There are many specific places where computers fit and can contribute to student learning. In general terms, however, there are three main benefits we should be looking for:

1. Computers can help schools deliver better instruction on content already covered in the curriculum.
2. Computers can help prepare students to travel along the so-called information superhighway toward success, or at least accommodation, in the cyberfocused world where their futures lie.
3. Computers can play a special role in helping educators to introduce new streams of learning into our schools, content that hasn't been taught in the past, including integrated application of knowledge from multiple disciplines.

SELECTING THE RIGHT TOOL

Computers have brought an economic culture shock to schools. Institutions that have operated under severe limitations in the past—such as having to reuse the same textbooks for at least five to ten years—are finding themselves in a whole new world of technology-driven finances. Computer equipment can be both expensive and short-lived in terms of productive life cycles.

At the time of this writing and for the past few years, schools have had a lot of public interest and special support for acquisition and installation of computers. A good policy is to enjoy this level of help and make the most of it while it lasts. Sooner or later, somebody, or some powerful entities, are going to point to expended funds and question the returns realized by schools. If the answers aren't favorable in the public eye, look for restrictive or repressive measures, such as exploration of alternate, private sources for delivering education to students portrayed as underserved.

This is a good time for schools to be looking at the economies and practicalities of computer systems. Significantly, the business community has already traveled a fair distance down the road of expenditure downsizing. The most recent stimuli have come from both equipment configurations and bandwidth breakthroughs. Bandwidth is a measure of how much data can be transmitted on a communications carrier. Capacities for data transmission have multiplied as carriers have increased use of fiber optics cables and satellites, as well as digital formatting.

Increased bandwidth, in turn, has led to heavier reliance on network links. Until a few years ago, most desktop computers used in business were standalone systems, each with its own memory, disk storage, and rapid processing capabilities. In reaction to the mounting costs of workstations, vendors have opted to shift software storage and file maintenance functions to specialized computers that function as **network servers.** This has made it possible to place workers in front of less expensive desktop systems because they can download software and files from the server. User workstations can now have fewer peripherals, reducing costs through reliance on the network servers.

As these trends continue, schools will find themselves faced with the same pressures that business leaders are already dealing with. They will have to overcome the instinctive belief that, where computers are concerned, bigger and faster is automatically better. The day of pragmatism, which has already arrived for many businesses, is well along the route toward decision making about what methods and equipment schools really need. Equipment selection and network configuration in schools should increasingly be directed to understanding and appreciation of the role of computers within information processing systems.

LISTENING-TALKING COMPUTERS

Computers have finally found their voice. For at least 15 years, IBM has been investing heavily in a technology that progressed gradually toward a longstanding, science-fiction-like dream: a computer that can "listen" to human speech and generate text from input it "hears." The state of the art in computerized voice recognition was reviewed in a predecessor book, *Education Is NOT a Spectator Sport.* The finding then was that the technology was getting close. But the ability of humans to talk to machines in natural tones at natural rates was not yet deliverable.

At the time, it was necessary for the speaker to pause between words for one-tenth of a second. This level of constraint made it difficult for a person to maintain a train of thought. A proficient typist could input text as fast as a speaker, usually more accurately and reliably. At that time, levels of discrepancies between speech and text were too high.

All that's changed. With processor chips now operating hundreds of times faster than a few years ago, computers have acquired new ears and a voice. A person can speak to a computer at normal speed and in normal tone. Corresponding text is displayed a fraction of a second after input. In a recent demonstration, discrepancies between text and speech averaged one per line. But they were minor. (Spoken "some day" came out "Sunday.")

Before speech input can happen, a computer must be "trained" to recognize a user's voice. Following instructions, the human user speaks a series of specific, identifying phrases to register his or her voice patterns for the recognition program. This process can take as little as a few minutes for a brief introduction and up to four hours for the full treatment. Obviously, this sets the computer up to react to just one person. The decoding file is stored on a floppy disk and entered as needed. Other users must create and load disks of their own. Only one person can talk to the computer at a time, meaning that the process won't work in a situation like a school's computer lab, a business meeting, or a courtroom.

In education, this technology can have important benefits for special situations. For example, hearing-impaired students could read the text of a lecture as it was being delivered. There also may be cases in which students can benefit from a printed text of a faculty lecture or other audio input.

As much value might be realized by reversing the process: The same system can read aloud from captured text at a near-normal rate of speech, providing a valuable tool for visually handicapped students or a way to deliver information orally to study groups.

At any rate, the technology has arrived. This means it is a potential tool ready to challenge the creativity of educators and meet special needs of students.

BIG CAPABILITIES, SMALL COMPUTERS

The closer a computer can be moved to an actual site of student learning, the more valuable a tool it is apt to be. The ultimate convenience, on this basis, is the computer that moves wherever the student goes—the *laptop.*

Dozens of districts across the country have secured laptops

for student use through a program co-sponsored by Microsoft and Toshiba. With their portability, laptops conform conveniently to activities of the classroom, adding flexibility to instruction.

Many schools also have arranged for students to purchase, rent, or borrow laptops to be carried home as well as being used in school. This kind of program helps integrate computers into everyday life experiences, replicating lifestyles and experiences of increasing numbers of real world information workers.

CARE AND FEEDING OF COMPUTERS

As technology continues to change the direction of business computing, schools are going to have to rethink management of their computer facilities and capabilities. Under established practices in most schools, decisions about equipment selection and use were driven by the capabilities, configurations, and costs of standalone desktop systems and their ever-increasing capacities. That's changing. The driving force for computer operations is or will soon become the configuration, design philosophy, and operating reliability of the network that links student terminals to needed information and to connections with the outside world.

When the emphasis was on standalone workstations, management of information systems was relatively simple in comparison with today's challenges. In the recent past, many schools have been able to assign responsibility for supervision of computer-related activities to teachers, librarians, or other members of existing staff.

Look for this to change in the future. When a network philosophy is implemented, responsibility for management, control, and safety of information assets moves from the user's desktop to the heavy-duty servers. These units now function much like the central office of a telephone network. That is, all control and support functions are centralized. Technically, this elevates the job of network management far beyond the limits of the typical teacher or school staff member.

In the future, then, school administrators would be well advised to look to the model of community and four-year colleges. Long ago, virtually all post-secondary institutions placed management of central facilities of their computer networks under specialized, technically qualified people with responsibilities similar to those of information specialists in industry. Given the costs of new equipment and software and the frequency with which acquisition and installation decisions have to be made, finding a qualified technical person for this role promises to be a wise, money-saving move for most school districts. As an alternative, schools may opt to follow the example of many companies and hire outside vendors to provide "site management" services.

The bottom line: management of information resources is an essential. Some arrangement must be made to handle this function.

Chapter 11
Broadening Learning Horizons

When a school makes a commitment to a learning orientation, the old class schedule and structure—one discipline per course, 45 minutes per class—becomes outmoded. The learning-oriented school sets itself up to emulate practices and conditions in the working world, where narrow occupational specialties are dissolving in the face of the need for generalist-type people whose main asset is a capability and commitment to lifelong learning.

For students moving into the information society, lifelong learning begins by breaking down the one class, one academic discipline syndrome that has dominated throughout the history of American education.

ESSENTIAL KNOWLEDGE AND SKILLS AS DRIVING FORCES

On information age jobs, every transaction has multiple consequences. Even a transaction as mundane as selling a hamburger or cheeseburger leads to multiple consequences. Information on the sale is recorded in a computer system that automatically determines when and how many hamburger buns, beef patties, cheese slices, onions, and supplies of mustard and catsup are to reorder. The time of each sale is also recorded and will be used to let headquarters of the fast-food chain know how many employees are needed to handle expected volume, at what hours. The amount of the sale is incorporated in the financial records of the business.

In other words, everything that happens in business is related to something else that has to happen to keep things running. As schools gear up to ready students for the modern workplace, broader implications must be considered for learning transactions.

For example, students must recognize the value of knowledge they acquire about the English language. On adult jobs, language skills become keys in enabling them to follow instructions or to function as members of working teams and social groups. Students must appreciate further that the English language is the main vehicle for all current and future learning experiences. Regardless of academic discipline—math, science, history, or even an athletic sport—English is the basis for building required knowledge and capabilities.

In a school committed to preparing students for the workplace, academic courses should be designed and scheduled to promote capabilities for the interrelation of information content. Instruction should become interdisciplinary or multi-disciplinary. In setting up multi-topical classes, faculty and students need to recognize that expectations for student achievement are different from those in single-discipline courses.

In a single-discipline course, achievement expectations are relatively narrow, limited to the one subject covered. There is little preparation for the kind of learning required on information-age jobs. Today's workers have to respond to information stimuli involving products, customers, colleagues, equipment, and materials. Then they have to integrate meaning about all these factors. Academic courses can help prepare students for such workplace challenges by including multiple categories of information in regular, team-taught classes. Multi-disciplinary classes of this type emulate real life by requiring students to relate two or more content areas into a unified set of interpretations and reactions like those expected in today's workplace.

ANTICIPATE PROBLEMS

Be warned! Success is neither simple nor automatic when people are required to apply combinations of knowledge and skills to unexpected or unusual situations. As noted above, this is the kind of adaptability and flexibility expected in business. But that doesn't mean that business organizations find it easy to impart such skills. Quite to the contrary, it's a hard job that takes a lot of patience and extensive training.

To get the idea, think of a company that manufactures automobiles. For decades, employees were segregated into crafts, specialties, or departments that had little or no contact with the routines or challenges of other groups. Most workers had little interest in what happened in other parts of their companies. Many resisted changes that involved new responsibilities or greater challenges. However, over time, thinking changed. It became apparent that customers buy vehicles, not collections of parts. A buyer doesn't focus separately on fenders, bumpers, engines, transmissions, or interior design elements. The finished car is a system, an entity that becomes more than a combination of parts to the ultimate owner. Transactions are about cars that appeal to buyers.

When automakers formed integrated design teams that brought workers together from different departments, the result was a smoother, more efficient flow of manufacturing and assembly operations. Specialists had to acquire a general view of the vehicle and their role in its production. When this happened, quality improved, manufacturing operations became more efficient, and costs came down.

Today, many secondary schools are going through a parallel process. Faculties are made up of specialists trained to be comfortable within their own specific disciplines. A typical teacher is not trained to be concerned about whether students relate lessons on scientific discovery to the impact of this knowledge on contemporary society or ongoing human history. A history teacher may touch on the role of the Industrial Revolution in bringing workers into cities where living conditions were horrible. But the lesson becomes far more vivid if a student reads a novel by Charles Dickens about life in nineteenth century London. History, art, science, and technology co-exist and are inter-dependent in real life. Why shouldn't they co-exist in a learning environment?

The topics aren't the problem. As usual, where problems arise, the trouble is generally with the people involved. When teachers of interdisciplinary courses play on the same team, the experience can be beautiful. But when teachers assigned to teams don't develop the coordination necessary to integrate instruction effectively, results can be devastating. For students caught in classes experiencing faculty dissonance, the double-length period turns out to be less than an opportunity. It can be more like an extended sentence.

The source of the problem is simple to identify: Integrating academic content represents a major change. And change inevitably encounters real difficulties as well as less logical resistance. Schools are now encountering this same kind of predictable resistance in setting up multi-disciplinary learning experiences that replicate workplace-type thinking. As teachers unfailingly point out when school-based teams confer to redesign courses, academic subjects are different. According to tradition, each subject area has its own, distinct body of knowledge, professional societies, achievement tests, and even special licensing requirements for teachers. Nonetheless, there's no denying the ultimate consideration: Businesses hire whole people, intellect and all, not segmented elements to deal separately with language, history, math, science, technology, and so on.

RECOGNIZING THE NEED FOR LEADERSHIP

Possibly the single most critical obstacle to effective structuring of interdisciplinary courses in high schools has centered on how to mix or match two (or more) separate sets of content into a digestible serving. One workable answer, which apparently is not applied as regularly as it should be, is based on a sound principle of small-business startups: Every venture needs a leader. Equal partnerships rarely succeed; somebody has to have the authority or power to break any decision-making ties. This is true for management of any enterprise, from legislatures to giant corporations to a conference on what to teach in a multidisciplinary course.

Now, how do you identify leadership or power sources when two teachers get together to confer on course content? The answer begins with a look at the students. The teachers should be able to agree on what they want students to achieve from any given course. With that established, the next step is to figure out the relative influence of each subject on the desired results. Leadership should go to the teacher of the subject with the most critical part in the mix. This principle is critical. It's not about personality or force of will. It's not even about who would rather be in charge. Student achievement is the only guide needed. Criticality of outcome should be the determining factor.

Say, for example, subjects to be covered are English and history. Teachers should ask: Is it more important that the student gain communications skills or a knowledge of world or American history? Both cannot be equated equally. Either the student will build knowledge of history supplemented by language communication exercises or the driving force will be the student's mastery of English with history as a source subject. The decision can go either way. The key point is that the status and needs of the students should be primary. It might even be possible to vary the mix, with some students concentrating more on written communication and others stressing historic content.

Given the identified emphasis, the targeted achievements of students should lead to such decisions as which textbooks to use, what kinds of assignments will be used for assessment, how student study teams will be configured, and so on.

ACADEMIC ADVANTAGES

Knowledge application is well and good. But is it worth the hassle involved in breaking down existing academic traditions to build new, multi-disciplinary structures?

Absolutely! There are other, vital circumstances that favor content combinations. Far from the least of these is that the multi-disciplinary approach makes it possible to cram additional subject content into already crowded curricula. Students today are expected to deal with a greater number of academic subjects than they did even one generation ago. And they are also expected to absorb new and more extensive knowledge about each subject. Yet, in most places, schools operate on the same 180-day annual schedule as they have for more than a century. One way to increase curriculum breadth without increasing costs to a point of public resistance is to combine learning experiences, enabling students to overlap content and to use one learning experience to reinforce another.

COMMUNICATION, VERBAL AND NONVERBAL, AS A BASIS FOR LEARNING

Education is—or at least should be—a profound human experience. As such, education is communication-dependent, relying for success on the senses that accumulate information and covert it to knowledge. In this context, the term **communication** implies its broadest possible meaning. Academically, there is a temptation to assume that language is involved in all exchanges of knowledge, ideas, or experiences. In reality, communication among students and faculty in any given school extend far beyond language-based, or media-carried exchanges.

A school is a community within which communication takes place in many forms. People form relationships and rely on one another, often without even being aware of the special kinds of interpersonal communication that takes place, much of it nonverbal. Teachers support one another as friends and/or colleagues, through personal crises or tragedies. Students gravitate naturally into peer groupings. And, where students and teachers are concerned, shared feelings can acquire special depths of support and understanding. These all represent unspoken, unwritten interactions that help form a kind of hospitable climate of shared impulses and experiences that create a natural habitat for transmission of feelings and knowledge. Learning is shared through these special networks of human vibrations. All this is separate from and in addition to the communication promoted in any school: the transmission of ideas, images, and information through use of language and graphic images.

These characteristics of a communication-hospitable environment are identified separately from formal academic subjects for a specific reason: In referring to communication within an educational context, it is too easy to assume the reference is to language as an academic pursuit. Realistically, language instruction should be separate from the feelings that grow among people who inhabit the same space.

If you find this caliber of closeness and the associated intimacy of nonverbal communication improbable, consider the circumstances. From age five or six onward, children spend most of their working hours in school, generally with the same group of youngsters and adults. This goes on year after year, with youngsters spending more time with classmates and teachers than with their own family members. The attachments that result can have profound effects on feelings, thoughts, and reactions to other members of affinity groups. If the school environment is positive and constructive, schoolmates and teachers become part of an extended family. A learning approach should capitalize on this natural interaction for the benefit of the entire group.

LANGUAGE COMMUNICATION

Academically, greater levels of formality have to be introduced to the communication processes that promote learning. Structured language of the type acquired under English curricula becomes the basis for exchanging or acquiring the ideas and information to promote learning.

Instruction in English plays a unique role in the overall, interdisciplinary knowledge-acquisition process of the school years. English is both a core academic subject and a medium for acquisition of knowledge in other curriculum areas. At a core level, the study of English involves the acquisition of factual knowledge such as spelling, punctuation, rules of grammar, and customs governing usage. Beyond that, though, there is a dimension of relating basic factual knowledge to describe experiences or explain ideas, and also to apply knowledge to human activities.

These facets of knowledge can be thought of as *factual* and *procedural.* Factual knowledge comes to the fore when a student makes multiple-choice responses on a test or when a person participates in an activity such as a game of *Trivial Pursuit.* Educationally, the learning of factual content can be vital, as occurs when a child is coached to recite a home address or phone number.

Procedural knowledge governs performance, using sets of information to govern actions, including choices among possible actions. Educationally, procedural knowledge can become a component of skill development. Application of procedural knowledge lies in the demonstration of capabilities. Procedural knowledge elements are combined, or compounded as learning levels become more sophisticated. Thus, for example, English holds the key to learning in such content areas as math, science, social studies, technology, and career preparation. The reason is plain: Successful performance in these academic areas requires a student to relate elements of procedural knowledge and to communicate an understanding of the more complex content. However, the role of language as an integral part of these courses is typically unrecognized or under-recognized in syllabus content for most schools.

Thus, for example, students get no academic credit—and too often no valid guidance—for written work they do in, say, a history or science course. In math, the lack of connection made between language and subjects such as arithmetic or algebra is even worse. Possibly the most dramatic example of this myopia occurs at the fourth or fifth grade level. Regularly, parents are advised that fourth or fifth grade students who may previously have been doing excellent work in arithmetic are suddenly experiencing difficulty, possibly failing. Parents may even receive recommendations about arranging for math tutoring.

On close inspection, it is not at all unusual to discover that the child still understands arithmetic just fine. The difficulty, it is likely to develop, is that word problems have been introduced into the math curriculum in fourth or fifth grade. Sadly for many students, this is the first indication that they have not learned to read.

This example shows one of many sad consequences from the fractionation of English language instruction in early grades.

Too often still, reading is treated as a separate discipline from the other, closely related segments of language proficiency. Then, the emphasis on sounding words too often leads to a situation in which reading is not taught at all. Instead, students practice recitation without due regard to the meaning of the words they enunciate with care—but without concern for content. In other words, **American schools tend to teach recitation which is misrepresented as reading instruction.** As evidence, consider how common it has become to encounter a student who has been an A reader who cannot figure out what the newly encountered word problems mean or what is to be done with them.

American education has tended in the past to disassociate language from other areas of academic learning. This hasn't worked! Every teacher should be alert in appraising student skills in expression and comprehension through use of the English language. All teachers should recognize the impossibility of teaching other academic subjects when students lack the fundamental language skills to understand even the most basic lesson content.

It's time these skill-based relationships are understood and recognized. Some dependence on language skills is implicit in any course of study. It makes simple, sound sense to take advantage of writing and recitation portions of courses in other subjects to enhance language skills. The potential benefits are important enough to transcend any inconvenience to the adults who staff any given education system. Experience has shown that it pays huge dividends to apply stringent standards to written exercises in all academic subjects. Making this principle work, in turn, results from an understanding of the separate, distinct phases of English instruction as: (1) an academic content area on its own and (2) as an essential ingredient in all learning experiences for every student.

This is not a plea to distort the weighting of academic content. Rather, the purpose is to recognize interrelationships among areas of knowledge acquisition. In turn, this understanding is a basis for determining where and with what degree of mixture curriculum content can be blended profitably through multidisciplinary instruction. The discussions that follow address these opportunities.

ENGLISH FOR ITS OWN SAKE

On its own, English rates as a vital core subject within any viable curriculum. Elements of the English language are just as basic to a student's body of essential knowledge and skills as arithmetic functions or atomic structures. Proficiency with language requires mastery of a basic vocabulary, plus certain rules about spelling, grammar, and usage that make the language uniform and understandable among an educated, workplace-ready audience.

Although the lessons learned about language structure and usage are universally applicable across all instructional areas, this segment of English instruction is unique enough to stand alone academically. Other aspects of English are also unique to a language-centered class. Examples include a sampling of great literature, poetry forms and great poems, drama, and the role of literature and theater in society. In some instances, this area of English content can be mixed with or should be taught in parallel with history classes.

Basic instruction in language is a discipline onto itself. Beyond that, day-to-day, practical use of language should be monitored to reinforce proper usage and positive habits. Thus, though it could be counterproductive to teach grammar and usage in a science or history class, it would be entirely constructive and positive for an English teacher to review writing done for any of these classes.

Often overlooked in the emphasis upon instruction in basic language structure and usage, as well as in reading, is that *language is communication.* Whether it is written and read or spoken and heard, the purpose remains communication. A basic part of the communication process is **comprehension** or **understanding.** The reader or listener must understand the **meaning** of the spoken or written message, **not** just the words. By the same token, the speaker or writer must communicate his or her message so the intended meaning will be understood. All too often, this interrelationship of language and communication is forgotten or neglected in emphasis upon structural elements of language. **Communication is a vital, integral part of all curriculum content areas** and English is a vital communication tool for today's students and tomorrow's citizens.

Because language is so essential to learning, English instruction offers a logical basis for discussing the feasibility and desirability of multi-disciplinary instruction. If instruction and disciplined practice in writing were limited to classes of English-only content, the written submissions would be limited to literary-type, academic styles and approaches. Such writing has its place in an overall array of academic skills. But academic writing (and reading) practice doesn't prepare the student for the kinds of communication exchanges demanded in the modern workplace. For such preparation, multi-disciplinary practice in writing about other content areas can be a major factor in a rounded, modern educational experience.

In a curriculum-planning activity for faculty members, English content can be either a mainstay skill that stands alone or a support for student learning in other disciplines. No matter what subject matter is involved, however, English can play a role in contributing to student achievement.

ENGLISH AS A LEARNING CATALYST

No matter what lesson is to be learned, and no matter what the subject or content, the main delivery vehicle will be language. Therefore, English has an implied role in every session in each classroom, regardless of subject matter.

In history, for example, key words may lie in slogans that stir people to action. Students can be asked to consider the slogan, "No taxation without representation." What were the issues that helped trigger the Revolutionary War? Were the Colonists simply upset that they didn't have representatives seated in parliamentary sessions in London? Or were the taxes too high and the representation issue simply an excuse?

By focusing on words, students can be led to diagnosis of events and partisan positions that give rise to historic phrases. Take the infamous tax on tea that led to the famous tea party in Boston Harbor and the conflicts that followed. The British saw the tax as benign, possibly as a benefit to the average New England resident. At the time, tea sales were being made to a small group of wholesalers who added a profit as they distributed tea to consumers. The British-imposed tax added the equivalent of the merchants' markups, then arranged for the tea to be sold directly to retail outlets serving residents. The protests that ultimately contributed to ill will and war were instigated by the wholesalers who lost their monopoly.

In math, some students are helped when mathematics is regarded as a language or communication method. Putting symbols and numbers into words early in the student's experiences can help later when entire problems are described in words. Some students understand the processes better when mathematical functions are described verbally. This understanding is then carried forward to ease the transition when arithmetic problems are presented in words rather than in numbers alone.

Even as the level of math instruction becomes more complex, language-oriented instruction can help build understanding of the principles being applied and the results sought. A language orientation helps students to understand that the purpose and value of math lie in its application to problem-solving and practices related to everyday life. Success in the study and application of math, therefore, requires the ability to understand instructions, requests, or explanations through the use of language, application of knowledge to devise a solution, then use of language again to explain solutions. Thus, success in learning math can be connected directly to the extent to which language communication is used as a vehicle for learning and application of the principles involved.

In science, notations of experimental observations and discoveries hold a potential key to understanding for many students. In science-related courses particularly, an important tool for assessment of student understanding can lie in the clarity with which a student explains scientific principles and their consequences to both peers and lay persons. It may help students to point out that success in scientific endeavor lies in the ability to understand descriptions of needs and to convey ideas for solutions or the benefits of new advancements. Thus, a study sequence in science might benefit from review and interpretation of newspaper or magazine articles intended for lay audiences. Students may also be challenged to prepare written and oral presentations about results of their experiments. In such exercises, students should be helped to recognize that the assignment reflects conditions that scientists encounter in the real world.

In all these areas, overall educational achievements can benefit from recognition of the interdependence of topical knowledge and language communication. By including language-based evaluation of written exercises in these other courses, educators can contribute to higher skill levels and successes for future scientists, mathematicians, or engineers.

There's also another potential advantage to enhancing English instruction within other subject areas: By awarding credit for language activities completed in courses such as history or science, educators streamline the curriculum. It may become possible to devote fewer hours of class time to the writing and correcting of compositions, making it possible either to add content to the curriculum or to add reinforcement for students who are experiencing difficulties.

MATH AS PART OF THE SUCCESS EQUATION

A common complaint among students who fail to reach standard achievement levels in math centers on boredom in class. All too often, math instruction bogs down in abstractions that lead to student reactions that range from boredom to gross lack of comprehension.

Such reactions are regrettable because they are, potentially, so easily overcome. It's a matter of order of pedagogical presentation. Two approaches are used regularly and defended, sometimes fiercely, by partisans within the educational community. The approaches involve presenting information from general knowledge to specifics or, conversely, from specific to general.

Traditionally, most math instruction has run from general to specific. For example, a given lesson in algebra or geometry may begin with a theorem or hypothesis that students memorize. Only later will students learn the application of the principle to real-world kinds of problem solutions. That's how the general-to-specific presentation approach works. Some minority of the general population can learn effectively through this approach.

Most people, however, learn more naturally if they start with the projected result and are led through the steps needed to make it happen. This approach is as straightforward as involving students in baking a cake. Once they can envision the end result, they are able to relate naturally to a series of steps that assemble ingredients, mix them in a specific sequence, then apply heat.

Sensitivity to student learning patterns is perhaps one of the greatest, and certainly among the most important, challenges facing educators today. Remember always that each student learns individually. Also important is the tendency of learning instincts to fall into some predictable patterns. Where math is concerned, it can pay great dividends to try presentations that proceed from both the general to specific and specific to general.

At the simplest levels, learning can be patterned in terms of tables for addition, subtraction, multiplication, and division. Some students do grasp numeric values in the abstract. But others may do better if they have manipulatives and can count or view the relationships of quantities of items. Adding practicality, as is done in descriptions involving money and purchases, may help still other students. Even at higher levels, some students will respond better if they analyze known results as a basis for understanding principles than if they begin with abstractions.

Given an understanding of varying learning styles, it follows that it can be highly beneficial to combine coursework in math with other academic disciplines that call for application of mathematical skills. Examples include science, business, and technology. Each of these disciplines depends on application of mathematical principles and skills. Why not, then, combine content to help clarify student understanding?

In a school dedicated to promoting learning, it can be an advantage to combine multiple disciplines in a single course. For one thing, this approach provides an opportunity for two or more teachers to pool their knowledge and skills in both academic disciplines and understanding of student needs and learning patterns. Each such team effort is potentially greater than the sum of the separate parts. A particular challenge lies in developing presentations about how math functions as part of everyday human life. All students will be aware of natural functions such as gravity, friction, electricity, power, speed, and flight. These characteristics are basic to such academic disciplines as science and technology. The related disciplines can enhance mathematical learning by providing the general results that can be diagnosed and understood with the aid of mathematical specifics.

Mixing content from multiple disciplines should be regarded as a two-way process. Math can be a starting point for course design. But the process can just as easily start in related areas such as science, technology, or business, as reviewed below.

SCIENCE AS A FOUNDATION OF KNOWLEDGE

Today's students live in what can be considered a golden age of scientific discovery. **Discovery** is a key to the concept of why scientists do their thing. Throughout history, curiosity has led to exploration, exploration to discovery, and discovery to knowledge. Within a multi-disciplinary outlook, it can be beneficial to help students see the relationship of science to other aspects of their lives. For example, curiosity about the stars has led, in the lifetimes of today's students, to a telescope in space and to earth-launched explorations of the sun and planets of our solar system. Before that, curiosity about the shape of the earth and the extent of its oceans led Europeans to venture to a distant land they eventually called America.

Curiosity is a good place to establish the interdependence of science and other disciplines. Scientists use microscopes that are built to precise mathematical specifications. For at least some students, introducing the mathematics of a microscope's optics will add both understanding and curiosity to the study of micro-organisms. Similarly, each mission into space represents a triumph for mathematical precision. Then, when photographs from space are processed on earth, they are composed from a series of scale-related mathematical values.

In each of these brief references, the approach is essentially the same. Students can start with generalities they relate to readily and extrapolate to a clear understanding of specific underlying principles.

TECHNOLOGY, A DRIVING FORCE IN MODERN LIFE

Students must learn to understand, appreciate, and live with technologies because they are part of a society that is technology-dependent. These lessons should be put into a perspective that illuminates the truly dynamic developments that have made America what it is today. In imparting technology-related knowledge and skills, educators should avoid the temptation of over-simplification, permitting students to think it's all about computers. Rather, computers are an effect rather than a cause of the accelerating rate of change students and their parents have endured.

For a true perspective, it might be profitable to interrelate lessons of technology with a large measure of history. The technology that surrounds us today traces deep roots back into the nineteenth century. Today's advances are successors of such elements as the invention of a way to generate electricity by Edison, the discovery and harnessing of radio waves by Marconi, and to the simplification of methods to capture photographic images by Eastman. Beyond that, consider the railroad, automobile, and airplane and the impacts they have had on society.

What's the value of understanding the history of modern technology? By understanding the progression of discovery and the building-block nature of scientific and technological development, students equip themselves for future leadership. That's because this perspective can help them to look forward to anticipate and prepare for a future in which change will, if anything, accelerate further.

Take computers and the fascination they engender. The devices on student desktops today represent only a foreshadowing of capabilities to come. That's universally accepted. But it's also true that the developments of the future will be built upon a foundation of today's realities. And that's the value of establishing a realistic, developmental perspective for instruction involving technology.

Computers offer a good example of the gradual development that underlies virtually all human progress. Most computer and history textbooks mark the beginning of the computer era during World War II. In 1944, a lab at Harvard University was equipped with a supercalculator called Mark I that weighed some 15 tons and could perform three calculations per second. The machine was used to compute artillery targeting tables for the Navy. The Mark series of calculators was superseded within a few years by electronic computers that were far faster. But the legacy of Mark I still persists. The Harvard lab devised techniques for programming the functions of computers. Refinements of these techniques have, in turn, given life to the multi-billion-dollar software industry without which today's wonderful computers could not exist.

That's where most background descriptions of computers usually end. But, as so often happens, reality can be far more interesting and can also help impart a perspective of potential value for tomorrow's leaders. The reality is that the Mark I system installed at Harvard in 1944 was actually designed in its entirety in 1843 by an English scientist named Charles Babbage. The Mark I implemented Babbage's design in every particular except for use of electric power instead of a steam engine. In 1844, a young Englishwoman named Ada Byron (Countess of Lovelace) devised a complete system for programming Babbage's machine. The basics for modern computing thus lay dormant for almost a century until they were resurrected by a Harvard graduate student, Howard Aiken.

The point: Intellectual progress in human society is inherently cumulative. Appreciating this nature of technological development can help students prepare for a future in which electronic technology becomes ever more entwined with human existence, and even human anatomy. Electronic systems of the future can be expected, for example, to react to human touch (reading fingerprints), human sight (recognizing eye formations), and human speech (computers already exist that recognize human speech and generate text).

Breakthroughs already under way may well introduce capabilities for computers to simulate human thought. Far fetched? Consider the 1997 chess match in which a computer trounced the world's outstanding chess champion. Sophisticated observers of this event recognized that the computer was "learning" and adjusting its strategies in reaction to moves by the human champion. Implications of such capabilities for promoting learning by tomorrow's students can stagger the imagination.

The point at this juncture in time: Technology does not exist in a vacuum. Technological development is closely enmeshed with most aspects of human life. Computers and other technological devices are tools that extend human knowledge and the ability to apply that knowledge. In the study of science, for example, Babbage's motivation to provide for additional computation power in the 1840s still drives today's scientists and engineers. Through a century and a half, technology has added muscle by replacing digital gears with vacuum tubes, vacuum tubes with transistors, transistors with printed circuits, and printed circuits have become microchips.

Over time and in the face of technological progress, however, the imaginations and perceived needs of people are the driving force. By understanding the history of these developments, students can appreciate the basic role of and challenges faced by people. The technology of today and the future is driven by the force of human motivations. Scientists, on one hand, need more computational power. Engineers find an answer with a smaller, faster device. Then the engineers drive the process when they continually seek faster, more efficient devices. In between, programmers are challenged to harness the new capacities and figure out ways to produce more sophisticated results, faster.

Parallel developments occurred as people discovered the potential of and applied computers to enhance human communication. Computers became switches for telephone exchanges. They became transmission devices for communication networks. And they became mainstays of communication through broadcast and publication media.

In a real sense, then, technology, history, and society are intertwined and mutually involved. Educational curricula should reflect this reality.

SOCIAL STUDIES, A SOURCE OF MUTUAL IDENTITY

The case for interrelating instruction in history or other areas of social studies with the writing and oral reporting aspects of language arts has been cited above. It is also worth noting, and incorporating in academic studies, that science, mathematics, and technology all have evolved in response to human desires, needs, crises, or tragedies.

Medical breakthroughs have evolved from every major war since the middle of the nineteenth century, when society's leaders started valuing human life. Medical scientists have reacted to battlefield tragedies to shape opportunities for improved health care through innovative treatment of injuries and illnesses. The continuing race for improved weapons stimulated development of motor vehicles, aircraft, and missiles. Students might even benefit from discussion of the atomic bomb, including its influence in discouraging widespread use of weapons of mass destruction. Outbreaks of diseases have led to intensified medical research that have, in the overall, led to increased human longevity.

There's also some potential for linking history and literature. Society's understanding of social atrocities, particularly those associated with living conditions in burgeoning cities like London, New York, and Chicago, has been built largely through major works of fiction. Today's reader, for example, can gain a better understanding of life in nineteenth century London from a Dickens novel than from any history book. The same is true of Industrial Revolution abuses in cities like New York and Chicago through works of fiction by authors like Sinclair Lewis or Frank Norris.

Carried far enough, mastery of technology becomes a factor in conflicts between commercial entities and even competing societies. Within a historical context, people who figured out how to use spears gained combat advantage over those who fought with clubs and primitive tomahawks. Then somebody invented the bow and arrow and dominated the balance of power. The process continued through the ages as weapons became more sophisticated—until computers were introduced into the power equation.

A new trend is already apparent that could make control of information systems technology a major, dominant weapon in future conflicts. Future wars, for example, may well be waged by scientifically trained soldiers in bunkers, combatants who never see one another or even engage in actual battles. Rather, technology can establish a new balance of fear that restrains hostility commitments. At the very least, such prospects can represent interesting topics for challenging, thoughtful studies by students raised in a technologically dominated era.

In preparing students for post-graduate life in American society, social studies classes can function as something of an intellectual melting pot.

ARTS FOR APPRECIATION AND FULFILLMENT

Throughout history, art has been a vital form of communication that has contributed to human development and survival. Even today, courses that cover American cultural heritage should impart knowledge that equips students as future citizens. Art courses should not be frills; content about the arts should be integrated within the total body of knowledge and depth of understanding that tempers each student's attitudes and outlook. Artistic expression can also be valuable as nonverbal, graphic representations for understanding and internalizing lessons from academic courses.

Certainly, it is relevant for students to understand how drawings on the walls of ancient caves communicated life-support information to budding human communities. In effect, these drawings were maps guiding fellow inhabitants to sources of food while also warning them away from dangers.

In their turn, music and drama were used throughout history for religious and secular expression and story telling. Poetic meter that made long tales easy to remember became important vehicles for reporting information through entertaining performances by traveling minstrels. In a technological, money-dominated time, courses in arts, integrated with other studies, represent an important thread by which future citizens can cling to their ethnic and national heritages and build empathy for others. Again, the point here is that it is not necessary to treat arts and culture as sidebars in the knowledge base acquired by students. Rather, this content should be part of a blend that supports each individual as he or she strives to become a whole person.

BUSINESS, CAREERS, FUTURE CHOICES

Career-oriented programs have become a front-and-center focus of modern education. Note the difference between the presently preferred term *career* and the old-line designation of *vocational education.* In too many cases, *voc ed* courses were a shunt that removed students who were not candidates for transition to college from higher-ranked academic tracks. Male voc ed students were assigned to what were typically called shop courses where they used hand tools and performed work that didn't even resemble then-current practices in industry.

Female students were assigned to **home ec** programs where they learned the rudiments of cooking, sewing, and other home-making activities, skills that have turned out to be too limited in an economy of single-parent or dual-income families. Female students also were directed into courses in typing and short-hand long after those classes should have been phased out.

Net result: American high school graduates were insufficiently equipped to function in the real world of their day. So-called vocational education courses frequently didn't cut it as practical occupation preparation. Graduates of these programs, for all intent, entered the workplace as unskilled laborers. Concurrently, college-bound students acquired virtually no help with practical lifeskills.

Change has been happening. Perhaps schools have re-sponded too slowly. But the case situation referenced at the very beginning of this book serves to establish that some edu-cators have recognized and acted upon this need. Through the years, secondary curricula have become increasingly respon-sive. Under the impact of technological applications for busi-ness functions, coupled with the downsizing and restructuring of business organizations, career education programs now play in an entirely different arena. These are times for special rigor and relevance in secondary career education. Young people en-tering the workplace after secondary school or two-plus-two tran-sitions to community colleges need to be prepared to step right into productive jobs. Their capabilities on high school gradua-tion, both academically and occupationally, must meet even more rigorous standards than those in college-prep programs. A col-lege-bound student, after all, is still something of a work in progress. A graduate of an occupational prep program should be a finished product ready for marketing.

ENHANCING THE SCHOOL-TO-WORK TRANSACTION

An important conceptual breakthrough in secondary career education has come through school-within-a-school programs that provide actual work experience and career qualification as part of high school curricula. Offerings such as academies or program majors in high school have proven the value of main-taining high standards and eliminating social promotions. Ex-perience has established beyond any doubt that, when chal-lenged, students headed directly to the workplace from high school can turn in world-class performances as long as they can see a return on their efforts.

This is a time for educators to be aware of the similarities in requirements between academic and career-oriented programs. Consider language skills. The day of the semi-literate, unskilled worker who can achieve a solid middle-class income is long gone. There are no longer significant numbers of jobs for the unskilled and unread. High levels of reading, listening, writing, and oral presentation skills are basic to success in any segment of the workplace. Also basic is a comfortable level of computer-competence. Where computer utilization is concerned, career majors need at least the same, often higher, level of skill than the academic student who will use computers primarily to write college papers. Add all these elements together and they come to a single, central requirement—pride of achievement.

To deliver this caliber of results, the faculty members who develop the new, advanced curricula—hopefully with help from area business representatives—need to respect all students for the contributions they will be expected to make. The modern American school must truly become a classless society.

DOING MULTI-DISCIPLINARY INSTRUCTION

Under any circumstances, the curriculum devised for any student today is going to be crowded. American students are expected to cover more subject matter and to gain a breadth of knowledge that provides a basis for the lifelong learning that has to happen in their future. To accomplish all of the defined tasks that constitute a high school education, some doubling up of subject matter in multi-disciplinary course offerings is going to be virtually necessary. For most teachers who have functioned alone in the past, team instruction can be something of a culture shock.

There are no hard and fast rules about how to team teach effectively. But there are some steps that can be followed profitably in getting started.

1. Study your students. Their needs are primary. Be analytical. And don't hesitate to talk to them about their own objectives and targeted achievements. Their involvement can contribute greatly to your mutual success if they "buy into" the program.
2. Determine the mix and relative importance of each content element toward achieving the goals you have defined. On any team or other cooperative human effort, somebody has

to be the leader, to take primary responsibility. You can make this kind of agreement on the basis of experience or personality of the teachers involved or on the predominance of one subject area. Consider the alternatives. Build an understanding. Commit to a plan of work.

3.   Stay flexible. Keep in mind that it's up to you to assure student learning. Build realistic assessment activities into your learning program, then be guided by results of these assessments. Based on your reading of student needs, establish a workable mix of individual and study-team activities.

4.   Learning is an ongoing process that will be different for each student and for each group within every class. Make it a rule to teach students, not curricula. Don't be afraid to vary your plan or to follow detours based on student interests or motivations. Work continuously to promote a rapport among students and between students and teachers that will create a healthy environment to promote learning.

Time available for education will always be limited. The educator's challenge lies in making the most from this critical resource. Cooperation among educators can go a long way toward delivering greater, higher quality results within the available framework.

Chapter 12
The Assessment–Learning Connection

A mericans seem to have an obsession with keeping score. In sports contests, for example, we develop fixations with measurements in inches, with increasingly complex rules, and with the ultimate end result, **winning.**

The fixation carries over into performances in our schools, where our traditional scorekeeping methods are known as tests. Put any group of kids into a new classroom, let the teacher explain why they're there, then open the floor to questions and at least one of them will unfailingly ask about what tests will be given, when, and how they will count on grades.

It isn't the kids' fault. It's one of the imperfections that's bound to creep into any system with 25-plus-million customers. As a result, **American students have become the most tested and least evaluated in the world.**

STANDARDIZATION VS. INDIVIDUALITY

In the late-1950s, a boy of seven was, along with scores of other kids, handed a list of questions and an answer sheet to be marked for machine grading. When the teacher-proctor said "go," all the other kids proceeded prodigiously to read the questions and mark answers correspondingly.

But this one kid was fascinated with the answer sheet and the processing it would undergo. From the simplified explanation the group had received, he recognized that a machine would scan all the answer positions on the sheet and arrive at a score by sensing the correct-answer positions that were marked. In a course of action that seemed logical to him based on the information he had received, he went through and marked every answer position on the sheet, reasoning that he would thus have a correct answer to every question.

In the 1950s, the kid was earmarked as a troublemaker, a reputation that stayed with him for at least the next 10 or 12 years. If the same thing happened today, we might hope that someone would recognize that the kid was thinking—that he had some natural talent for analysis and trouble shooting. In a number of the schools visited in gathering data for this book, he would today be identified as having some creative potential worth nurturing.

ROOT PROBLEMS

The 1950s, for better or worse, were not like the 1990s. The country had just recently been through a war during which some 10 million potential fathers and more than a million prospective mothers experienced batteries of tests classifying them for military service. In each instance, their responses were marks on columnar answer sheets. Just a few years before World War II, IBM had come up with a machine to process these sheets of paper and produce punched cards with grading information. Military personnel were sorted like so many punched cards, matched to available slots in a global war machine, and sent on their way. Nobody said the system was equitable or efficient. But it did support building the largest war machine that inflicted the greatest destruction upon people and environment in history.

In some ways, the ability to test people and assess their capabilities and potential has not progressed a whole lot since World War II and its aftermath. The machines that grade tests now have greater throughput. But the idea and methodologies are still pretty much the same, except they have been extended to schools in every cranny of the United States, with tens of millions of kids marking hundreds of millions of answer sheets.

We now call the methodology **standardized testing,** and we count on it to serve three major purposes in American education:

1. **Student Selection and Sorting.** At an early age, every American student is set on a course that will guide the educational direction and options open during the rest of his or her life—all as a result of a series of pencil marks drawn under pressure and in strange surroundings. These marks, of course, represent answers to standardized tests

purporting to measure learning and achievement potential as well as existing knowledge. Throw in images of massive, impersonal computers processing answer sheets and determining destinies of millions of children and you develop a picture of a futuristic, impersonal, science-fiction kind of world where life is like a lottery in which impersonal, chance decisions spin endless webs in which people are entrapped. Most people like to think there's more to it than that. In a number of cases there is. But those cases have tended to be exceptions rather than rules in the history of American education. Within education, test scores function much like a rail switching yard. Railroad freight cars, occasionally but with embarrassing regularity, can and do wind up on the wrong track. When this happens, a car is carried along a misdirected journey that can run thousands of miles before the mistake is uncovered. Then the car has to be re-routed additional thousands of miles before it gets back on course.

Is this analogy extreme? Answer for yourself. American schools now accommodate more than 25 million students. The millions who transfer to new schools during each year arrive as strangers. Since it is impossible for administrators and counselors to get to know and evaluate each student individually, it is inevitable that classroom placements be based on some objective measurement tool. So, they form judgments from the test scores the kids bring with them as a kind of intellectual baggage. Far too often for some observers, these cursorily evaluated students are placed in academic programs that guide substantial portions of their learning opportunities. Adjustments are made in many instances by observant teachers and/or counselors, particularly when high-performing or low-performing students differentiate themselves from their peers.

Although it is said to happen less frequently than it used to, it is still possible for an early misdirection to lead to a long-term, inappropriate effect, as in the case of the unfortunate youngster identified at the beginning of this chapter. Once a student is launched and under way, there are more tests, administered at regular intervals along the academic superhighway. The main testing objective is to measure student achievements. Other tests determine the grades assigned to students, setting parameters for each individual's future by determining colleges or careers for which admissions will be open. In short, standardized psychological and achievement tests have become mass-production tools for control of human destiny in an age that is nominally striving for a rebirth of individuality.

2. **Auditing School Quality and Performance.** There is also a group dimension to the application of test data. If all or most of the students in a given school test below an anticipated norm, the system tends to conclude there must be something wrong with the school as an organization and with the teachers and administrators who run it. There are ample supplies of tar and feathers to cover one and all.

The apparent assumption: Multiple-choice tests are fair and equitable because they are impartial and impersonal. Some students and schools do well on these tests. Therefore, those who do less well are judged to be less deserving.

3. **Evaluating and Improving Instruction and Curricula.** Generalized statewide and national tests, unavoidably, tend to be disconnected from the instructional content and methods to which students are exposed. In a world undergoing continuous change, standardized tests are monuments to the status quo. The culture of standardized testing defies responsiveness to educational challenges or changing needs.

Look at the typical cycle: Tests are prepared under isolated conditions that combine traits of a time warp and an intellectual vacuum. The character of any national test, along with the content of its questions, are established with little or no input based upon instructional programs or expectations of student knowledge and capabilities. At this writing, 47 states now create tests of their own based upon specific curriculum standards. Selected working groups of teachers typically provide input in the form of a pool of questions available for inclusion. However, the competitive dynamics of committee activities and the general lack of proficiency in the technology of testing among teachers still leads to a separation between tests and the realities of student performance expectations. In any case, the reality of uniform, objective tests is the same at the individual classroom level: it's all highly secret. Teachers and students have no inkling about specific questions to be asked. Packages of sealed test instruments are kept under lock and key until the appointed performance hour.

Completed response sheets are then carted off to a remote grading facility, maintaining an information vacuum broken only weeks or months later when gross scores are received. From these reported results, individuals have no way of knowing which questions they answered correctly or missed; all they get is an impersonal number. For classes or schools as a whole, the grade reports deal in averages, providing little or no guidance on where curriculum modification or remedial instruction could benefit students.

The point: Existing, standardized testing methods are of no help in adjusting or revising instructional programs to correspond with educational objectives. Clearly, some other, more responsive approach to measuring and evaluating student achievements on a timely enough basis to guide revision of teaching/learning processes would be handy. That method, which can and should coexist with standardized testing, is ***performance-based assessment.***

CONSIDERING ALTERNATIVES

The current situation, then, is that objective, multiple-choice testing represents a *status quo* while instructionally integrated, performance-based assessment is seen by traditionalists as a distraction from what's really important, a threat. Closer to expanding educational frontiers, creative assessment that promotes intellectual exploration is seen by proponents as a new wave, a harbinger of progress.

The probable reality, as noted above, is that a program of educational change needs a balance between standardized testing and integrated assessment. But co-existence inevitably leads to frictions that, rather than enhancing results, can obstruct both methodologies. Standardized testers may feel that qualitative assessment, in promoting creativity and exploration of new learning venues, distracts students from full mastery of basics on which they are tested. Learning-system advocates who tend to support integrated assessment feel that standardized tests inhibit intellectual exploration by students.

Does this add up to an opening salvo of a fight to discredit and disregard objective, multiple-choice tests administered on a state or national basis?

Absolutely not!

Standardized tests are part of our culture, part of the way we do things in American education. For at least as long as we can foresee, standardized tests will remain a major basis for decisions on college admissions or for selection of students for educational programs or special schools. Also, the function of auditing school quality and performance won't go away—at least any time soon. The public remains guided in their assessment of school quality largely by cumulative scores on standardized tests published in newspapers, too often along with articles voicing displeasure about achievement levels of local schools.

Thus, for better or worse, standardized tests are still viable tools for sorting students and auditing schools. The third avowed purpose, however—adjustment of instructional programs and curricula—is not about to happen if testing methods remain as they are. This rationale for testing has actually not been valid for some decades.

Herein lies the tragedy. Possibly the greatest single benefit that could accrue from imposing the most-tested status on American kids would be to use the examinations to assess the shortcomings of instructional content and adjust curricula to enhance achievement. As described above, this potential benefit is unattainable under standardized testing.

DEALING WITH TYPES OF KNOWLEDGE

A phenomenon of multiple-choice testing is the student with a high test score who has trouble with practical application of his or her knowledge. In part, the student may be showing the effects of a personal tendency or educational emphasis on *declarative knowledge,* which is highly specific and fact based. Beyond that, however, there's always the element of chance in multiple-choice answers. A response made in uncertainty or through shear guesswork looks like any other on an answer sheet.

Of course, there's also the student who studies facts without delving into their meaning. We have all seen youngsters who know all the facts but don't understand the connections between those facts. The best performance-based assessments ask youngsters to explain and justify their work, not to select and/or conform raw facts. If American schools are to upgrade themselves into rigorous, relevant, learning-oriented institutions, a method of assessment is needed to evaluate more than recitations of facts. They should be led into acquisition of *procedural knowledge,* or the ability to recall and/or devise sequences of information and actions to deal with application of knowledge to reach decisions or solve problems. This kind of procedural knowledge doesn't show up on standardized, multiple-choice tests. So, a method is needed to measure student understanding of course content, a method capable of delivering results in real time so teachers can adjust courses of study to enhance student performance.

Assessment methods also should be sufficiently flexible to accommodate the continuous exploration of the frontiers of knowledge by today's students. Because of concern over impending tests, there is not always time for in-depth exploration of new knowledge areas that are not covered on the tests. Further, a direct correspondence does not always exist between curriculum and test content. Therefore, the curriculum does not always prepare students for standardized tests the way some observers may assume. A good rule of thumb: Do a good job of building student understanding and content will take care of itself.

This problem has come up in faculty conferences where teachers struggled to enrich curriculum content to match real-world standards. The prospect: If we spend time on new content areas that parents and community leaders say we need, how will the community react if these efforts result in lower scores on standardized tests? Do we expand knowledge horizons or do we restrict instructional content to conform to established syllabus outlines that may be outdated?

There are no totally definitive answers. Expectations and appropriate actions will vary state by state and, sometimes, district by district or even school by school. What does seem apparent is that national curriculum standards won't work. A national standard-setting mechanism would, of necessity, be so cumbersome and slow that course definitions would be outdated before they were published. Such standards would discourage, possibly even suppress, creativity or intellectual searching by teachers and students. Clearly, some balance is needed between objective testing and assessment techniques that challenge students to expand their horizons.

PERFORMANCE-BASED ASSESSMENT, DEFINITION AND ROLE

Critical differences between administration of standardized tests and ***performance-based assessment*** center around the timing and purpose for their use. Timing is significant because assessment becomes an integral part of the learning program for an individual course or for overall curriculum content. An assessment exercise can actually be part of a learning sequence for students because a key purpose is to promote, as well as to measure, acquisition of knowledge and skills.

Another important characteristic is that assessment instruments, as contrasted with objective tests, challenge students with problem solving activities that require application of logic, judgment, and identification and evaluation of alternatives. In other words, an effective assessment measures the way a student thinks about and applies acquired knowledge and skills— over and above the ability to recall factual content. Putting it another way, the purpose of assessment is to improve, not just to audit, performance. Also important: An assessment activity can lead to alternative or variable conclusions; students aren't channeled to come up with one specific answer to each question. In this respect, performance-based assessment adds to the student's learning experience while measuring achievement. In the long run, it is also healthier to avoid having students go through an entire educational sequence believing that each question should have only one answer.

For example, the following is an explanation to a teacher covering an assessment of a middle school English language course. Two standards are addressed:

> A typical performance assessment in middle school English language arts is given below. It addresses two standards: (1) Students evaluate their personal responses to literature, and (2) Students write persuasively to a real audience. The scoring guide is given to students at the same time as the assessment.

The accompanying student assignment calls for specific performance actions, as follows:

> Re-examine your reading notebook (the record of your personal responses to individual and assigned reading you have completed this year). Select three books that should be included in the classroom library. Write a friendly letter persuading your teacher to order these books for next year. In your letter, provide (1) the titles and authors of the three books you recommend, (2) the reasons why you think these books should be included, (3) the kind of students who are likely to enjoy the books you selected, and (4) specific mention of passages from the books that seem important.

This example pretty well speaks for itself in differentiating between standardized multiple-choice tests and performance-based assessment. Standardized tests classify students, groups, and schools on a gross basis. A student's individual score, for example, says nothing about which questions were answered correctly or incorrectly. Thus, there is no measure of the student's content comprehension or of specific strengths or weaknesses. This means, in turn, that there is no opportunity to use test results to adjust instructional methods for either current or future students or to identify students who require remediation.

By contrast, the assessment above calls for an expression of the student's conceptual grasp of the full content of a language-arts course, as well as analysis and synthesis of acquired knowledge. The assignment also requires the student to perform research to identify potential titles for addition to the classroom library, then to evaluate candidate titles and to apply judgment to come up with specific recommendations. Clearly, an assessment like this can become an organic part of the student's total learning experience. Assessment occurs in a real-time context. Evaluations are quickly available to adjust instruction for individual students or cohort groups, fulfilling an important role for performance-based assessment: enhancing the quality of instruction.

Perhaps the most significant difference between standardized testing and performance-based assessment lies in what actually happens in the two processes. Multiple-choice tests attempt to measure what a student knows. Performance-based assessment gives the student a chance to demonstrate what he or she has learned and how.

SETTING STANDARDS TO ASSURE RIGOR AND RELEVANCE

A special advantage of qualitative assessment is that, under the method described here, the relative levels of rigor and relevance can be pinpointed for application through reference to the ICLE Relational Model, described earlier. This point is critical. It is too easy, in the name of qualitative assessment, to call for work that amounts to little more than a routine essay or composition. Such assignments can encourage *subjective* evaluation by individual teachers. In turn, subjectivity can lead to inconsistent instructional guidance and unreliable, unrealistic grading. In worst cases, grade inflation, a major rap against American schools, can easily persist.

To demonstrate the value of the Relational Model as a guideline for rating the rigor and relevance of the assessment task for the middle school English student, the evaluator would deal first with the Bloom's Taxonomy scale on the Knowledge Axis. Since multiple evaluations are required, the assignment qualifies for a 6 rating on the Bloom's scale. On the Application Axis, note that the task involves a real-world predictable situation, or a 4 rating, as shown in Figure 12-1.

Recognizing the challenge represented by the need to develop and evaluate student progress on performance-based assessment tasks, ICLE catalyzed formation of the Model School Assessment Network (MSAN), a national consortium that shares information and implementation guidance. The network is supported by the ICLE staff, which coordinates consortium activities. Educators within member districts are encouraged to use any suitable instruments from a pool of several hundred pre-evaluated assessment documents. Faculty members or resource specialists are also encouraged to devise their own assessment instruments and submit them to the ICLE support group. Each submitted assessment instrument is reviewed according to established, objective guidelines. Appropriate instruments are then published and distributed to members.

SCORING STUDENT PERFORMANCE

To help minimize subjectivity in grading—and also to make evaluations highly relevant to students—each MSAN assessment in-

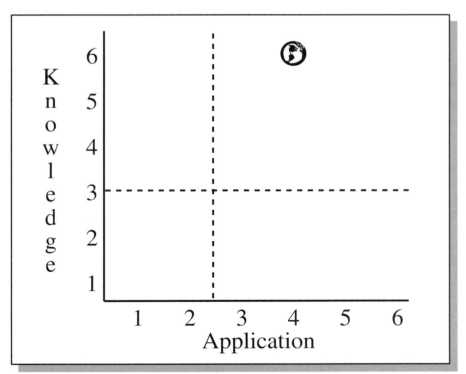

FIGURE 12-1. USE OF THE ICLE RELATIONAL MODEL FACILITATES PINPOINTING OF THE LEVELS OF RIGOR AND RELEVANCE FOR AN ASSESSMENT.

strument incorporates its own assessment criteria. A unique feature of the ICLE approach to performance-based assessment is a standard recommendation that grading criteria be shown to students *before* work begins. The idea: Learning achievement is potentially enhanced if students understand expectations for their performance.

To illustrate, the following are the scoring guidelines for the middle school English assessment cited above.

Scoring Guide

4 (superior performance). You have maintained a complete and thoughtful reading notebook throughout the year. You are able to select and evaluate three books to recommend. You can cite several specific and convincing reasons for including the books. The writing is on the whole well organized, clear, fluent, persuasive, and mechanically accurate.

3 (good performance). You have maintained a complete reading notebook. You are able to select and evaluate three books. The evidence is not always entirely convincing, specific, and/or ample. The writing may not be tightly organized in spots and/or may contain minor errors that detract only slightly from meaning or quality.

2 (performance needs reworking). You have maintained a notebook that is not complete. You selected fewer than three books. Arguments and specific references are missing or somewhat weak, unconvincing, and/or perfunctory. The writing lacks a sense of organization and/or has serious mechanical flaws that impede meaning.

1 (incomplete performance). You have maintained a notebook that is noticeably incomplete and apparently hastily written. One or no books are selected. Reasons for selection lack specificity, are inaccurate, and/or are unconvincing. The writing is seriously disorganized and mechanically flawed.

Notice that in this task students are aware of what is expected. They understand what curriculum standards are addressed. The letters may become part of the students' writing portfolios and available for parents to examine. There are no secrets.

The reading notebook is assessed frequently during the course of the year. It is not a one-shot evaluation at the end of the year.

BASIS FOR PERFORMANCE-BASED ASSESSMENT PROGRAMS

Note the reference in the middle-school English example above to a "reading notebook" that each student is expected to maintain. The assessment process is, in a sense, a logical outgrowth of a student-accumulated recap of learning experiences. The process is an ongoing, integral, historic, cumulative part of an effective learning experience.

Notebooks, or accumulations of content-and-experience summaries into a **portfolio,** should be a primary activity of a learning-oriented student experience. This is a proven, traditionally underused learning reinforcement and study technique. The principle is simple: As part of routine reading, study-team projects, or research assignments, the student writes summaries of newly acquired information, knowledge assumptions, and/or conclusions. These notes are accumulated throughout the student's academic career, at least from the time the individual's written communication skills warrant (typically by middle school). Periodically and as an integral part of each course, every student's portfolio is reviewed. This can be done either through a reading by a responsible teacher or counselor or through an oral presentation before an entire class or smaller peer group.

The portfolio should function as a kind of database that helps the student reference and interrelate content of his or her acquired body of knowledge. By reviewing these summaries, the student reinforces memories of all the covered content. This kind of review can be an excellent preparation for a content test or written assessment exercise (which also should be incorporated in the portfolio).

Over and above other considerations, the portfolio is a constant reminder to the student of how far he or she has come and how much has been accomplished. As such, the portfolio is a tool for self-assessment, part of a continuous improvement process. A student's total educational experience is formed into a continuity that bridges content areas, grades, and memory lapses that commonly occur from one school year to the next. In effect, the portfolio becomes a bridge across the student's total span of educationally acquired knowledge. In these times of emphasis on self-esteem, a well maintained portfolio can provide a foundation for self-confidence that is legitimately earned.

On graduation, the portfolio, which can consist of multiple looseleaf notebooks by then (or possibly a set of floppy disks), becomes an instrument of transition. Final projects incorporated into the portfolio can reflect studies of career opportunities, a plan to pursue college education, a commitment to life-long learning, and a resume and job-application letter. In other words, the portfolio concludes with a student's commitment to the next reality in his or her life.

ANOTHER EXAMPLE: A CLEAN-UP PROJECT

For a different, more rigorous view of an assessment activity, consider the following unit, entitled "Garbage! Garbage! Garbage!" This assessment is intended for high school science students. Student performance in completing this assessment scores as a 6 on the Bloom's scale and as a 5 on the application axis, placing it at high levels in both theory and application.

The performance task stipulated for the Garbage! assessment task is as follows:

Students will investigate solid waste management and its impact on their community/region and make recommendations for the future.

Working in small groups, students will select an area of solid waste management, e.g. sanitary landfills, recycling practices, mass burn plants, reuse of products, reduction of waste. Each group will research positive and negative aspects of the topic and its impact on the region. A written report and class presentation will be required. Each group must also develop a model of its recommendations for the future in the form of drawings, a physical model, or a detailed implementation plan, for example.

Background knowledge and skills to be demonstrated in this assignment are listed as follows:

Research scientific information using a variety of resources

Identify a community concern that has a scientific basis and propose and defend plausible solution

Recognize society's impact on the local ecosystem

Scoring of performance on this assessment is based on five separate evaluation factors, as follows:

Scientific research is complete and exposes information that is new to the student.

The problem identified demonstrates a comprehensive understanding of the science concepts and societal impacts.

The proposal for the future is plausible and creative.

The written report is complete, mechanically correct, well organized, and conveys the important information appropriately.

The model is an effective representation of the proposal for the future and is well executed.

THE ASSESSMENT-LEARNING CONNECTION

Though assessment is often treated as a separate element of an educational development program, it is important to stress that assessment should not be isolated. Specifications for assessment methods should be integrated with those for instructional design. Under this approach, the assessment instrument becomes a tool in an approach known as **problem-based learning.**

This methodology, discussed further in a later chapter, was derived from a highly successful approach to the first two years of medical school instruction for fledgling doctors. Applied to middle and high schools, instruction in selected subjects—math and science initially—is centered entirely on problem-solving activities. Problems are designed so that students must perform research and acquire curriculum-required knowledge in the course of their solution.

Within the present discussion, relevance centers on the role and value of assessments as activities that promote learning as well as validating knowledge acquisition. Thus, qualitative, performance-based assessment serves to:

1. Guide instruction.
2. Evaluate student progress.
3. Validate learning progress.
4. Involve students in their own progress—all within a framework that promotes learning and enhances teacher professionalism.

SUPERASSESSMENT: THE SENIOR PROJECT

As an extension of qualitative, performance-based assessment programs, many high schools are introducing a final, extra-rigorous requirement—a senior project as a prerequisite for high school graduation. This involves a year-long set of activities for high school seniors that culminates in meeting three requirements:

1. Each senior conducts extensive research and prepares a

formal paper on a topic of special personal and intellectual interest. During development, the paper is reviewed, critiqued, and revised under guidance of a faculty adviser or committee.

2. Each student undertakes a project involving content or information that correlates with the subject of the paper. Extensive research and/or preparation time is generally prerequisite for the project. The project can culminate in an end product, such as a physical model, a VCR tape, or a handicraft item. Or, the project could culminate in a performance or oral presentation.

3. The project is presented and reviewed rigorously before approval.

An organization based in Medford, Oregon—Far West Edge, Inc.— is both a leading exponent and source of information and training about senior projects. According to documents from this organization, hundreds of public and private high schools across the country now use a senior project as a graduation threshold.

The currently recommended form of the senior project was originated for public education by the Medford (Oregon) School District in 1986. However, the authors are aware of senior project requirements in private schools dating back to the 1960s. Those requirements were at least as rigorous, possibly more so, than current requirements. In one instance, students were required to prepare a thesis of at least 35 typewritten pages, this in the days before computerized word processors were prevalent.

Regardless of origins, the senior project is seen as having a number of important values for students. One is that students are encouraged to pursue learning in an area of sufficient personal interest so that it often impacts their career choices. Another is that a project adds relevance and stimulation to a student's senior year, which is often spent going through final motions after most academic prerequisites have been satisfied. Students also benefit when outside resource people are enlisted both to guide research and to review papers and projects. A final noteworthy value is that students leave high school on a high point of personal achievement, self-esteem, and pride.

DEVELOPING QUALITY ASSESSMENTS

To achieve acceptance and to establish a comfort level with students, assessment instruments need to be structured so that students clearly understand what is expected of them and how their performance will be rated. To illustrate a form and format that has proven workable, Figure 12-2 presents a typical example of an assessment instrument distributed by the Model Schools Assessment Network. Note that the format establishes specific places to present students with a title for the task and an indication of the subject area covered. Assessments can be interdisciplinary, but identification of the primary content area helps focus the student's attention.

An entry under a **Standard** heading relates the assessment task to the corresponding element in a local, state, or national instructional framework. Other entries describing the **Performance Task** are posed in language as close as possible to the kind of instructions a worker would receive from a real employer.

The assignment form also identifies the knowledge and skills the student is expected to be able to apply. A graph showing the Relational Model and the position of the combined knowledge and application levels also is included. Finally, a **Scoring Guide** advises the student on exactly how his or her work will be evaluated.

AN ASSESSMENT-DEVELOPMENT PROCESS

Performance-based assessment is a relatively late arrival on the educational-evaluation scene even though this approach is well proven in other areas such as athletics, art, music, and business management. Evaluation techniques that challenge students to apply knowledge, rather than simply repeating facts, have been regarded by some in education as being more informal and less exacting than multiple-choice testing. In fact, however, performance-based assessment can be at least as rigorous and, because of the emphasis on application of knowledge, more relevant than standardized testing.

In terms of comparison, performance-based testing has suffered because standardized testing has a long history of standards and methods for development, administration, and grading of test instruments. Recognizing this challenge and related requirements the Model Schools Assessment Network has enunciated a process aimed at assuring the relevance and rigor of assessment instruments. This process calls for a sequence of five steps, described below.

1. **Decide What Students Should Know and Be Able to Do.**

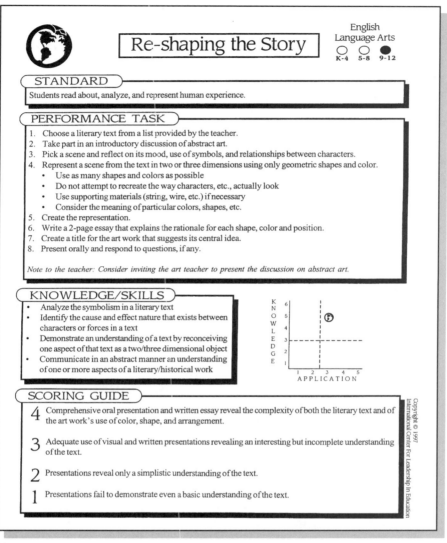

FIGURE 12-2. ASSESSMENT INSTRUMENTS SHOULD BE SELF-CONTAINED AND EXPLICIT IN THEIR INSTRUCTIONS TO TEACHERS AND STUDENTS.

Begin with a clear statement or series of statements that describe what students should know and be able to do by the time they complete the task. These statements reflect the objectives, benchmarks, or standards of the state or local curriculum that apply to student performance. The agreed-upon statements are included in the Knowledge/Skills section of the assessment instrument. This content differs from the instructional goal or standard, which is included in the Standard section. If local, state, or national standards are cited, identify their source.

It is often tempting to begin with some method, project, or activity that has worked in the past. If so, it is extremely important to pause, analyze the activity, and modify it if necessary. The important standard here is to comply with your own knowledge/skills statements, which must be clearly delineated and honored throughout the design process.

2. **Develop Your Task.** Create a set of instructions that, when followed by the student, will require application of the skills and knowledge identified in Step 1. The explanation of the performance task requirements should be written in clear, concise language. But the task itself needs to be rich and complex, requiring students to engage in planning, problem solving, and reflection. The task also must interest the students and reflect a real-world situation to which they can relate. Again, check compliance with your own instructional objectives, benchmarks, and/or standards.

3. **Design Your Scoring Guide.** Think through exactly what you will accept as evidence that students have mastered the skills and knowledge associated with the task. What will "top performance" look like? "Acceptable performance"? Include all aspects of student performance you consider important, then construct a scoring guide or guides that reflect the criteria to be evaluated. Choose levels of achievement that are easy to understand.

Some teachers work with their students to develop the criteria. Others first develop their scoring plans, then share them with students before work is begun on the task. Where scoring is concerned, it's important to keep an open mind and to be willing to adjust criteria on the basis of experience in administering the assessment task. These evaluations and adjustments should help to correlate assessment results with traditional grading systems.

4. **Ascertain the Level of Difficulty.** Include, as has been done in Figure 12-2, a format for the Relational Model. Mark the position on the graph that represents levels of difficulty and applicability of the skills and knowledge demonstrated in the task.

5. **Critique the Task.** Submit the document you have devel-

oped to objective reviewers. These people should be qualified to judge the appropriateness of the task for student performance and the fairness of your evaluation and grading standards. As appropriate, involve community resource people with real-world business experience in this evaluation.

After a representative group of students has performed the task, review results to determine whether students have understood their job, found the experience challenging, and performed up to expectations.

If a school or district is to succeed in creating a learning-oriented environment, qualitative assessment should be an integral part of how student progress is evaluated. The world at large will undoubtedly continue to insist that students be tested for factual recall. But, if students are to learn from their evaluation experiences, some form of qualitative, performance-based assessment should be an organic, integral part of the school's instructional design.

Chapter 13
Building Around a Solid Core

$\mathcal{E}$ very enduring structure needs a solid, reliable foundation if it is to survive continuing use and ongoing upgrading through maintenance. The structure of knowledge and skills that supports a student through a useful, productive life requires an especially strong foundation. This foundation must see the individual through the wear and tear of an extensive sequence of personal adjustment in society, work, and lifelong learning transitions.

An enduring educational foundation, according to current science, begins before birth and continues through a full lifespan. Since schools seldom have contact with or influence on children during the early stages of their development, all educators face unknown conditions, possibly barriers, in meeting educational expectations.

Thus, the knowledge structure schools are charged with building begins from uneven, unequal bases. As in construction, all parts of an emerging structure must be evaluated and accommodated. In a building, there are bearing partitions that carry the weight of the rest. In education, there are elements of core knowledge that are central to the composite that comprises an educated person.

CORE OF KNOWLEDGE

The core courses, those central to the totality of learning achievement, include English, math, science, technology, and the elements of culture and historic background that comprise a sense of identity. Those subjects, in addition to their focal role in all academic learning, are interdependent. Inherent relationships among these content areas require some ordering, or sequencing of presentation, particularly during early school years. For example, during the first three years of elementary education, a student must establish a foundation of language communication and rudiments of number systems. These are the tools for additional, more intense learning that follows. Failure to establish a foundation for further learning within the first two or three elementary grades handicaps a student and greatly increases the probability of an achievement shortfall or ultimate failure—an unacceptable outcome.

Unfortunately, the educational transactions designated for delivery of these early knowledge installments have not always been completed satisfactorily. Things have become increasingly difficult as educators who live within an information society are pressed to implement policies and practices enunciated in Horace Mann's day. At a time when learning is a critical ingredient of schooling, we still struggle under a system that makes attendance paramount. Average Daily Attendance (ADA) is the prevailing measure, the critical area of reporting—sequencing from classroom to building to state, with full recognition that these numbers become the primary source of funding. All this happens with no measure of what is being learned or consequences for the level of learning success. The main method for measuring learning is through *ex post facto* tests. It has been said, only partly in jest, that if attendance was taken on testing days, everyone would be present.

As a further constraint to learning, educators have been pressed into a race against time. Schedules have often become more important than student achievement. In the urgency to press students through the educational pipeline on schedule, many have been shortchanged. The quality and extent of their knowledge have led to widespread functional illiteracy and mathematical inadequacy. These shortfalls have led, in the longer term, to the presence of inadequately prepared graduates who have impaired America's competitive capabilities and burdened society with expenses for unemployment and welfare.

For a situation in which students and teachers are new to one another, as happens in first grade, a planned sequence of interactions can help to set students at ease, and also give teachers an opportunity to develop a feel for the students' capabilities and needs.

There are no hard-and-fast rules for getting started with a new group of students. Each teacher should operate within his or her personal comfort zone. But it is always safe, once children and their teacher are introduced, to get into a learning-oriented activity.

AN ANALYTICAL APPROACH TO CREATING LEARNING-ORIENTED METHODOLOGIES

There's a vast gap between saying a new methodology is needed and making it happen. Let's admit that and recognize what we're dealing with. Education as delivered in the United States and virtually everyplace else consists of a series of parts variously called disciplines, courses, or subjects. Through most of the twentieth century, educational and psychological scholars and researchers have defined and refined prevalent ideas about the accumulation and application of knowledge for each discipline-defined academic domain.

Now, with the twenty-first century approaching and with most people secure in assorted academic niches, education is being redefined in interdisciplinary terms that threaten most of these comfort zones. Within the emerging information society, convincing evidence indicates that what we really need are generalists who can interpret multiple facets of knowledge and amalgamate whole new sets of skills. The twenty-first century graduate will have to relate, analyze, and apply knowledge on a wide range of increasingly complex subjects. And this must happen within a whole new continuity of human existence now being called a worldwide economy.

How can we make this happen?

The simple answer: We need a new methodology to apply to the organization, integration, and application of knowledge. An inkling, really just a beginning look, of the shape of this new methodology emerged from a research project launched in early 1998 by a group of senior ICLE staff members. The initial stimulus was an outgrowth of studies concerning perceived needs for modified curricula to support emerging patterns for interdisciplinary learning.

Every educator today is aware of the disparate feelings building up around methods for measuring student progress and assigning grades. The entrenched approach uses objective, quantitative, standardized test instruments for which responses are recorded on multiple-choice answer sheets that are graded automatically. Without trying to settle the unresolvable, let's just note that the other major approach is for qualitative, performance-based assessment, which we are also calling ***Analyti-***

cal Assessment. This approach requires students to gather new information, apply existing knowledge, and think their way through to an answer that is appropriate to them. A major difference, then, is that standardized tests measure what students know and performance-based assessment demonstrates how they think.

If we want to measure students' progress by their ability to apply knowledge rather than to repeat raw facts, and if we want them to be able to interrelate knowledge of multiple disciplines, we're going to have to modify curriculum structures. The rigid, discipline-specific categories are going to have to be restructured to reflect the realities of current and future achievement expectations. We're also going to have to get away from the seemingly irresistible temptation to keep adding more and more topics to our curricula, apparently valuing quantity over quality. These practices have given American curricula a reputation for being "a mile wide and an inch deep." American teachers and students are expected to cover as many as *six times* as many topics on core subjects as students in countries like Japan and Germany.

That's what the ICLE research project set out to do. The initial instinct was to attack breadth by asking qualified panels of educators and business or community leaders to suggest items that could be winnowed from topical lists of curriculum disciplines. For each core area, 100 or more topics were listed.

SORTING OUT COMPLEXITIES

One reaction to the initial survey struck a spark that led to evolution of the new methodology for curriculum design and develop which, at this writing is being applied in an extensive ICLE survey on design and content of educational curricula and associated learning-assessment systems. One of our senior consultants, a person whose experience in information systems goes back to the early 1950s when punched cards reigned, recalled extensive work on systems design, problem solving, and decision making in which he had been involved through the 1960s and 1970s. These were the times when industrial, military, space-related, and societal systems seemed to grow more complex by the minute—times that led to enunciation of the still-famous Murphy's Law.

Some time around 1962 to 1964, systems designers were forced to refocus on the nature and challenges of their field. Until then, most references to management skills like problem solving and decision making were in the singular. The professionals in the field had established, comfort-providing methodologies for analyzing problems, evolving solutions, and/or reaching decisions—all strictly on a one-at-a-time basis. That is, the processes were designed to deal with such requirements as industrial trouble shooting or straightforward supply decisions. But they fell down in the face of the new dimensions of complexities that were arising. Faced with problems such as the design and development of an intercontinental ballistic missile or of meeting President Kennedy's challenge to put a man on the moon, existing problem solving and decision making methods came up short. The problems being attacked suddenly contained too many unknown elements to permit handling under singular methodologies.

Chewable Bites

The techniques that evolved called for breaking down the massive, complex unknowns into a series of digestible parts that could be understood and dealt with by qualified scientists or technicians. A major space exploration problem might involve the services of more than 100 teams of specialists dealing with separate increments of the overall mission. After close study of a number of projects and the emerging management methods, the ICLE consultant identified a similar need in education for a separate methodology for taking hold of a vast undertaking and breaking it down into chewable bites. This individual, who was also involved in evolution of the transaction-based approach to business education described in the first chapter, called this new process *Functional Analysis.*

The idea of Functional Analysis, which has been adapted to the ICLE curriculum review project, is to break the overall, massive undertaking into a series of separately attackable parts that can be dealt with individually, then absorbed into an overall approach. Each of the elements of the program can then be studied and dealt with by following an algorithm directed toward specific, individual problems or subsystems.

Within the education field, the goal will be to identify content areas based on key knowledge-application tasks and targeted competencies. This is a proven systems development methodology in which the end result is defined first. Then, the necessary components for a solution are identified and the steps needed to connect the sources with the results are worked out.

The ICLE study will concentrate initially on the core areas

of language arts, math, and science. Care will be taken to avoid going overboard on a vocational or school-to-work concentration that can overlook building an appreciation of the arts, culture, and traditions so essential in instilling a sense of pride and identity in young people. As elements of the core curriculum are identified, for example, a separate Functional Analysis will be conducted to define ways in which core-area learning can be integrated with and enhanced by studies of the arts.

This development will be evolutionary, the beginning of a long journey. To reach our targeted destination successfully, the working team will require flexibility, and also an extra dose of ingenuity. The tasks ahead will require that we take stock of multiple approaches and alternatives identified through extensive surveys, then evaluated through extensive brainstorming sessions. These steps will follow a process known as a *Delphi.* The name, Delphi, is derived from the Delphic Oracle, an idol set up on Olympus, in ancient Greece. People presented their problems to the Oracle, engaged in joint concentration, and came up with solutions, whether by miracle or human ingenuity.

Once problems or required decisions are isolated, an algorithm will be developed to deal with each, setting a course for analysis and resolution. This same approach, it is worth stressing, also has great promise as a tool for building a learning-oriented environment in which students build algorithms to lead them to conclusion of study assignments. This approach also will lead to forming habits that will stand all graduates in good stead when they enter the job market as information workers, and in their personal lives as well.

LANGUAGE AS THE FOCUS FOR LEARNING

It's time to be realistic about educational basics. The reality is that education must mount a full-court press to assure that achievement levels for *all* students are up to standards in language communication and arithmetic by third grade. These are the bearing supports for a sound educational edifice. Students should not be promoted until they have satisfactorily acquired these basics.

Note particularly the emphasis on language, our basic communication tool, and not on reading. The fact that reading has been singled out—designated as a separate academic discipline—may, in itself, represent part of the problem contributing to low levels of literacy. As a discipline of its own, reading has become a battleground of competing methodologies, each of which has demonstrated its own shortfalls.

Phonics, too typically, is treated as though it **IS** reading rather than a tool for the prospective reader. The reality: ***Phonics is to reading as spelling is to writing,*** a part, not an end result. Phonics can encourage emphasis on sounds rather than meaning. If reciting phonetically is treated like competent reading, real literacy may never happen. The real world puts a premium on comprehension of messages rather than the sounds of words. Words without meaning don't cut it. ***Recitation isn't reading. Neither is the proficient reciter of words a proficient reader. Recitation is not, in itself, an element of learning.***

Whole language, based on word and phrase recognition, can miss its target by teaching a syllabus rather than children. This is a classic example of lockstep instruction for students whose learning patterns are known to be individual. For many students, recognition, memorization, and recitation or repetition of extensive groups or sets of full words or phrases is more than they can absorb and retain at the expected rate. Students who experience this difficulty are in danger of being left behind, effectively abandoned by an inflexible system.

Either methodology can work for students with compatible learning patterns. But, if a school or district is committed to assuring that all students perform to established standards, a program based on lesser percentages of achievement shouldn't be acceptable.

What should be sought is a methodology that employs techniques that require students to engage multiple sensory learning skills. The learning-oriented approach should, through application of multiple senses, assure comprehension by every student at some point in a knowledge-acquisition sequence.

Getting Started

To illustrate, think of some activities that might be suitable for a first-grade class. Right from the beginning, it is a good idea to establish activity groups. Depending on the size of the class, these can include anywhere from four to six students. The teams can be dispersed to study sites around the room. Groups can be assigned to listen to tapes, watch videos, look through books, or possibly work with manipulatives. The students rotate among these activities. At any given moment, one team of four to six students can work directly with a teacher, aide, or volunteer who is seated in front of a computer.

A caveat: These discussions deal with possibilities. They are not intended as prescriptions.

CHANGING THE TEACHER'S JOB

Potential obstacles also result from the changes in role and responsibilities that teachers must accept to use this approach. For too many years, the teacher has been expected to function as part of a delivery system, presenting information prescribed by others in the form of a syllabus structured for implementation through books, lectures, or worksheets that generated shudders of resentment and boredom on all sides. (A funny thing about worksheets and reinforcement exercises generally: Put the same or similar exercises on an interactive computer and the kids find them fascinating.)

The learning-based, student-centered approach described here redefines the teaching job. Prescribed, inflexible methods are gone. So is the role of students as spectators. A learning-oriented classroom is an active place. The teacher's job may be more challenging. But the potential rewards are far greater.

A pessimist tends to regard these factors negatively: as problems. An optimist sees opportunities to stimulate the imaginations and problem-solving skills of children, to permit them to learn on their own terms, applying their own curiosity and sensory skills.

Even for optimists, though, it won't be easy. Public education employs some 3 million teachers and specialists. Obviously, all of them are not about to change their methods and, even more serious, their beliefs. That's okay. It's basically healthy for teachers to hold firmly to principles. What can be changed are expectations and standards for educational achievement. Any approach that results in enhanced student achievement should be accepted enthusiastically by any real professional.

Teacher participation in this kind of transition should be voluntary. Plans should be stated clearly and enrollments in in-service programs should be opened. Volunteers should be supported. However, coercion should be avoided. Unwilling participation is almost certainly the fastest way to assure failure.

An Instructional-Assessment Connection

The teacher-assessor or other resource person loads and works with a standard word processing program, such as MS Word or WordPerfect. Use a plain, Gothic type, such as Univers. Set up so that entries are displayed large enough so the whole group can see all the letters clearly. If the students are looking directly at the computer screen, a font size of 24- to 36-point will usually do the trick. Even more ideally, the computer would be attached to an overhead projector or large TV screen to display keyboard entries even more visibly and make it possible also to enlarge the viewing/participating group. With a TV set or projection capability, the teacher could be facing the students who are arrayed in front of the screen for viewing, enhancing the manageability of the learning situation.

Assuming that this is a first, introductory lesson, a good way to start is to key in the vowel letters in capital and lower case, with spaces in between on the display. This establishes an opportunity to introduce pronunciations for the key letters that appear in every word and also dominate the sounds of spoken English.

As the first entries are displayed, look closely at the members of the student study group. You want, quickly, to see if any kids are squinting, straining to see the letters, or trying to inch closer to the screen. Make mental (or written if appropriate) notes of any such symptoms. Check these kids again in other activities. If the pattern repeats, report these students through established channels as potential candidates for eye exams or corrective glasses.

Using an instructional approach to check student eyesight may be an unusual suggestion. But it is in keeping with the philosophy that schools should teach students, not curricula. The more aware a teacher is of student traits, particularly special problems or requirements, the better the prospects for learning achievement.

In observing the students as they review the first display, say the names of the letters and all the sounds they can represent. As you do, point to the letters or use the mouse to drag the cursor over each in turn, highlighting the text to focus student attention, as shown in Figure 13-1.

Get the students to recite the sounds. They can recite in groups. But it is advisable to have each student repeat what he or she hears individually. As this is done, note any situations in which students fail to hear or mis-hear spoken sounds. As with vision problems, these students should be monitored as possible candidates for special screening or assistance with hearing or speech difficulties.

The technique of displaying information for students through use of a computer should be considered as a generally available

FIGURE 13-1. USING A COMPUTER TO PRESENT AND DISPLAY READING LESSONS GIVES THE TEACHER IMPROVED CONTROL AND A BETTER CHANCE TO OBSERVE STUDENT RESPONSES.

presentation method usable for any topic and for students in any grade level. It isn't necessary for the teacher to turn away from students as is required with display boards or flip charts. And, as compared with the increasingly popular method of handwriting on plastic sheets placed on the viewing surface of an overhead projector, the computer provides an opportunity to format lesson materials so they can be printed out and given to students for content reinforcement.

Returning now to the initial reading lesson, once letter names and sounds of vowels have been spoken and repeated, instruct the students to print the displayed letters. Check this work, observing both the handling of pencils and the configurations of printed characters. The tactile exercise of printing gives the student an opportunity to reinforce the lesson. More important, by doing this review early in the student's school experience, the teacher has a chance to identify whether students need guidance on how they grip pencils. Further and more critical, by looking at the printed characters, the teacher can do a quick initial screening for possible dyslexic problems. Too often, dyslexia or other learning disabilities go unnoticed for years. The earlier such problems can be recognized, the sooner corrective measures can be applied.

Multi-faceted Learning

Consider the combined learning-assessment dimensions of this general approach.

1. Students are exposed to letters (later words, phrases, and sentences) in a focused, shared experience that includes opportunities for mutual assistance and/or reinforcement.
2. Learning encompasses multiple senses.
3. Students pronounce names and sounds of letters (later words, phrases, and sentences).
4. Students print the letters, words, phrases, or sentences covered, building tactile reinforcement into the exercise.
5. The teacher performs an initial screening for possible vision or hearing problems and also checks for possible dyslexic-type impairment.

As an added benefit, the teacher can note the students' reading/writing/language comprehension and skill levels for future classroom management guidance. Invariably, it will become apparent that one or more students in each group are reading beyond the expected level while others are clearly average or behind. These evaluations should figure in decisions about the makeup of future study groups. Based on performance evaluations, the teacher may decide, as only one example, to team more experienced students as leaders of groups in which the remaining students have lesser skills. This arrangement could lead to assignment of students to operate the keyboard and set up work for their teammates and also to provide some peer tutoring.

Another option might find students with comparable abilities as teammates. Teams of lower-level students might need more guidance. But the teacher might prefer to let them learn and grow together, challenging one another at their own level while avoiding competition that might become overwhelming.

Building the Reading Vocabulary

The free-wheeling, computer-proximity sessions provide an opportunity to build learning patterns unique to the students' own language-instruction needs. This approach makes it possible to build learning sessions around vocabulary students already know and understand. Each entering student will have an oral vocabulary that runs into thousands of words. Isn't it natural to build initial reading capabilities around what already exists?

As one example, assume the vowels have been displayed and reviewed as a starting point that is appropriate regardless of whether or not the students already know the alphabet. The students can then take turns offering words for display on the screen and inclusion in the accumulating record of their lesson. As each new word is displayed, the teacher notes the presence of a vowel and establishes the identity for the other letters. Learning is incremental, traceable, and verifiable.

Phonetic recognition can be built actively and easily during on-line sessions like these. To guide students in breaking down words into syllables and sounds, the teacher-facilitator can simply insert spaces between syllables. Then, by using the mouse to drag the cursor (or with corresponding keyboard entries), the instructor can highlight the stressed syllable in each word. This approach places phonetic recognition and sounds within a student- and learning-driven context. Thus, phonetic structures are related directly to reading activities based on student-presented vocabulary rather than diverting attention from the main language learning task.

As the lesson progresses, the displayed entries should be accumulated in as orderly a pattern as is practical. The idea is to enhance student recognition of covered content and the appearance and ongoing use of material that will appear later on a printed page. A file name should be recorded and entries should be saved to disk periodically for further uses discussed below.

Figure 13-2 shows a screen with accumulated vocabulary items separated into syllables, with one syllable highlighted for pronunciation emphasis.

Student Ownership

At an early, appropriate instructional point, students can be asked to spell their names for inclusion in the display (helped as necessary). The names can be shown prominently in the display, perhaps at the top or bottom of a page or inset among ruled lines. Clearly, the value of inserting names is to establish proprietary interest in the reading content. As time permits, possibly in succeeding sessions, students can propose new vocabulary words. At the teacher's discretion, some guidance might be applied to group words topically—nouns for family members,

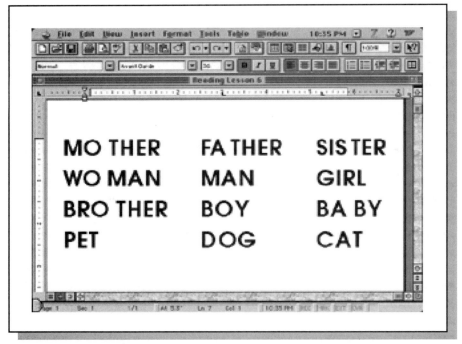

FIGURE 13-2. VOCABULARY IN READERS CAN BE SELECTED ON A STUDENT-DRIVEN BASIS.

classroom objects, favorite activities, home, games, outdoors, indoors, safety, foods, and any others that come to mind. If this is done, topical headings can be placed in the cumulative display.

As this language practice continues on an ongoing basis and at continuing, higher levels, students can be prompted to add vocabulary encountered in other studies. Terms from arithmetic can include the basic functions—*add, subtract, divide, multiply*—and others, such as *total, sum, difference,* and so on. Today's students may well add terms like *computer, television, video, disk, memory, storage,* or *printer.*

Somewhere along the line as pages of reading entries accumulate, the teacher should take steps to organize the captured text into a cumulative document—a personal reader for each student, if you will. One step should be to check the page format that's in place, adjusting margins as necessary. For readability, the margins should be fairly wide, such as 1.0 inch top and bottom and 1.25 inches on each side.

It's also a good idea to set up a header or footer to imprint a title and a number on each page. The title should establish a special, proprietary identification for the student team involved in its development. For example, the study group can select a team name—Reading Rebels, Righteous Readers, Wise Words, etc.—for inclusion in the title line for each page. Names of the team members can also be included in the header or footer.

To dress up a personalized reader, the teacher/facilitator may want to arrange to have a clip art picture file available on-line. Pictures can then be selected to correspond with the selected words. If line art is used for illustrations, young students may want to color the pictures, building pride of proprietorship for each reader.

Periodically, in installments, each team's reader can be printed and stapled or bound in another way. Blank or ruled pages can be interspersed and students can be assigned to hand-print the words they have learned, building tactile reinforcement into the learning system.

In the course of a typical school year, students can build a reading vocabulary that exceeds expectations of an average beginning reader. A thousand or more words can be mastered and students who proceed on this path should be able to both read aloud and cite meanings for a wide range of sentences, including problems or instructions on application of arithmetic.

ANTICIPATE AND PREPARE FOR OBSTACLES

When innovations of this type are suggested, the first responses among experienced teachers or other staff are inevitably objections or reasons why the ideas won't work.

If the school has used a specific reader for some time, there may be objections over the possibility that some prescribed words may not be covered if the students get to establish their own vocabulary. Preconceptions about methodology and/or challenges about differentiating between recitation and reading may arise.

Teachers who've lived entire careers wielding chalk or felt-tip markers might not see how it might be easier or more efficient to do their notemaking with both hands on a keyboard. Obviously, there will be hesitations and uncertainties at the prospects of such a transition. There's no denying that a major change is involved. Computers, after all, are new and strange for most classroom teachers, especially in early elementary grades—particularly for use in live, interactive presentations.

Beyond that, most teachers do what they do at least partly because they enjoy personal, direct contact with kids. Understandably, there may be a feeling that inserting computer technology into the relationship might break the mood or contact they enjoy and consider important.

When problems are anticipated, it invariably becomes easier to deal with them. Such anticipation is essential any time a new system is being introduced. Bear in mind that, **ultimately, every system belongs to its users.** Therefore, it is necessary to give teachers new to any methodology a chance to internalize its features and to "buy into" the new approach.

THE STRAW MAN OF COST

Yet another source of resistance is a long-standing staple as an educational excuse or obstacle. When a computer-coordinated approach is described, a typical, reflexive response is that classrooms don't have the equipment for computer projection and that the stuff would cost far too much.

Promoters of educational change have heard all this before. Consider: It has become generally accepted that placing at least one computer in each classroom is a present-day necessity. In worst case, this is enough to get the job done. However, TV sets and overhead projectors are also common classroom accessories. Linking a computer to either of these devices should present a trivial cost (a connecting electrical cord) in light of practices under which most schools overspend on computer equipment. Don't confuse this approach with more sophisticated and expensive systems that link computers to high-priced video projectors. Most schools already have software that can drive a connection to a TV set or overhead projector.

The great majority of computers placed in schools since 1995 or 1996 are high-powered, high-tech systems with massive memory, rapid processors, extensive disk storage, a modem, and enough resident software to run a good-sized business. On top of that, most of these self-sufficient systems are linked into either or both, a local-area network (LAN) or wide-area network (WAN). Access to the Internet, Wide World Web, and subscription databases are commonplace.

By the hundreds of thousands, the units installed in schools are top-of-the-line workstations. As is commonplace in the computer industry, many of these workstations present concerns over technological obsolescence almost from the day they are installed. This leaves teachers and administrators with the prospects of upgrading or replacing them in a relatively short time, often as little as two or three years.

A common belief among many educators holds that schools

need to provide this caliber of equipment for students so they will be ready when they are positioned in front of the very latest gear in job situations. This is an understandable theory. But, as has happened so often, educators are again running behind the prevailing practices in the real world. A major trend in the business world has seen replacement of expensive, standalone workstations with less costly but adequate network computers. Software and file-maintenance support are provided by high-performance file servers linked to workstations throughout a network.

With inexpensive network computers, costs of user workstations can be reduced by at least 50 percent. System management is improved because the central file server can be monitored and supervised by a professional. Security and availability of information are upgraded. If schools followed this efficient, economic alternative (as many have begun to do), costs for buying display equipment for student presentations would become trivial. More important, student preparation for information-industry jobs would be enhanced.

As in so many situations, progress requires rethinking that opens the way to student-responsive learning programs. Defense of the *status quo* for its own sake should have no place in modern education.

A LEARNING ORIENTATION FOR MATH

A typical problem scenario has a fourth-grade child who has been doing fine up to that point bringing home a note that he or she is having trouble in arithmetic. The parents quiz the child, who reports he or she just doesn't understand the subject any more. A teacher conference reveals the youngster does just fine with worksheet exercises. But when the same kid tackles simple problems presented as narratives—the infamous word problems—he or she is totally lost.

Too often, reported math problems emerge as reading problems. This kind of occurrence, on its own, provides proof of the interdisciplinary nature of all learning. Divorcing math instruction from concerns over English literacy has hurt dually, with reduced performances in both math and reading.

How can courses be structured to enhance both math and language communication skills? Easily! Start by recognizing that mathematics is a language. Then teach math accordingly, as a discipline that depends on clear use and understanding of verbal descriptions and instructions. Recognize that learning activities must focus on the communications functions of language. As things stand, effectiveness of math instruction suffers from the practice of teaching recitation rather than reading in early elementary grades. Clearly, the so-called "math problem" that typically surfaces in fourth grade indicates a need to stress meaning of words rather than accepting pronunciation only. Reading and writing are natural companions to mathematical content in the early elementary learning of arithmetic. Further, math itself is a language that can benefit from being treated accordingly.

Mixing Words and Numbers

For example, suppose beginning instruction in reading and writing treated numbers as part of a student's basic vocabulary. Possibly the figures 0 through 9 and their meanings could be introduced as extensions of the alphabet. Then, multidigit numbers and their values, illustrated with appropriate diagrams and/or manipulatives, could be added as increments of a growing verbal treatment.

Carrying this forward, when instruction begins in mathematical functions, students should describe the operations verbally. For example, students could read the addition operation $4 + 4 = 8$ as "Four plus four is equal to eight," or "The sum of four and four is eight." The idea is to establish that math operations can be stated in sentences and that they have meaning that is part of each student's essential vocabulary. With this approach, students can move seamlessly into verbally stated problems. After extensive practice in stating math operations as English sentences, students will adapt readily to deriving mathematical expressions for verbal statements, building the kind of understanding needed to solve math problems presented in words. Interrelating language with math can also help the student gradually to enhance information processing and problem-solving skills.

Computerized Instruction

Objections to a traditional tribulation of mathematics instruction, the worksheet of numeric exercises, can be overcome (or at least diminished greatly) by shifting these assignments to computers. Part of the difference stems from the power of the computer to mesmerize children. Routine drill-and-practice exercises that become dull and boring on worksheets fascinate kids when they are administered by computers.

Interest-holding power can be increased exponentially if the computerized exercises are embellished with animated illustrations and accompanying sounds. Something as simple as having a smiling face or applauding hands, accompanied by congratulatory sounds, appear after a correct answer greatly enhances interest levels and responsiveness. Positive results also come from immediate feedback on performance for individual exercises, which can result in far greater levels of satisfaction and self-esteem than when papers have to be turned in and graded by teachers who resent such chores.

Traditional, drill-and-practice exercises can admittedly be boring. But some sort of memorizing is requisite to establishing proficiency in basic arithmetic. Any approach that removes this burden from teachers should be welcome. Simple reviews of this type can be carried out on inexpensive equipment, even outdated units no longer used for prime instruction operations.

As students encounter serious word problems, a new learning opportunity becomes available. Solutions of these problems require input analysis, determination of the outcome required, and specification of processing steps. The new opportunity lies in training students to develop algorithms that guide them to solutions of these problems.

Building an Algorithm

An **algorithm** is simply a set of instructions stated in order of performance. An often-cited example of an algorithm is a recipe. These days, one of the most common uses of algorithms is for creating outlines, or working plans, for development of computer programs or processing procedures. In education, algorithms are valuable as outlines for instructional or assessment tasks—and also for application of acquired knowledge to real-world purposes.

Algorithms can be developed by following a few simple steps which even elementary grade children can learn readily:

1. Identify outcome or desired result (the answer).
2. Identify your givens or inputs.
3. Determine the processing steps that will lead from input to output.
4. List problem-solution steps in sequence.
5. Solve the problem.

Developing and using algorithms are essential skills for serious computer users. Applying algorithms to word problems in math serves both to improve performance immediately and also to contribute to future success in a computer-dependent society. It's relatively simple to encourage students to think in algorithmic patterns, building habits that can improve their learning and knowledge-application skills. Just have them write out algorithms to go with problem-solving assessment or study assignments. To help get them started, students can begin simple descriptive sequences.

❏ Describe how you tie a shoelace.
❏ Describe two different routes you can take from your home to school.
❏ Describe the steps in setting a table for dinner.

In the learning process, language comprehension and expression are key to all progress. In this sense, therefore, all knowledge acquisition is interdisciplinary. Responsibility for enhancing language skills should be shared by all concerned teachers.

SCIENTIFIC SUPPORT FOR LEARNING ABOUT SCIENCE

Study of science represents a confluence of knowledge-acquisition experience for the student. In science, the student encounters new dimensions of language—expanded vocabulary, precise meanings, and a broad scope of content that can be fascinating, confusing, or both. Much of the information to be mastered is through illustrations—photographs, drawings, graphs, and charts—all qualified as nonverbal communication. However, communication between people about graphically represented information still requires verbalization.

In another dimension, the study of science is naturally interdisciplinary: Scientific investigation depends on mathematical measurements and analyses. Mathematics is a basic tool of the scientist. A student needs to understand math to learn science. Frequently, the calculations, tables, curves, or charts encountered in science textbooks are accepted as factual content— unexplained and unchallenged. It takes a little extra effort to review and reinforce knowledge of the math a student encounters during a science course.

There's also another interdisciplinary dimension to the study of science: Information has to be communicated in words. The student needs to develop the specific skills for reading and writing scientific information. This communication capability should be viewed as a workplace-essential survival skill.

In reading scientific content, it should be absolutely essential for students to prove they understand the text. One way to assure understanding is through peer group discussions (structured through a simple algorithm) in which students work out their mutual understanding of text content. An additional approach (not an alternate, but an extra reinforcement technique) is for students to write summaries of science lessons and add them to their portfolios.

COMPUTERS AND CURRICULA

The idea that computer technology has become an academic discipline in its own right needs no elaboration within this discussion. Business-type, job-related instruction in computer operations—such as word processing, spreadsheets, and databases—has become almost universal in high schools that are installing increasing numbers of workstations. The computer has also become the primary tool for instruction in touch keyboarding.

Consider these as givens. Now consider the role and function of the computer within the present context of interdisciplinary or multidisciplinary learning opportunities. Use of computers for direct instruction of academic subjects is a largely unrealized potential for most schools. For clarification, this is not a reference to instruction in the use of computers. Rather, the computer has great, largely untapped potential for the delivery of information and the validation of student learning. This potential remains largely unrealized.

Asked about the value of computers as learning tools, many teachers react with what passes for enthusiastic support. Pressed for explanations, most cite "research" activities through Internet and library access. While these are valid supplementary benefits, there are still precious few examples of computer use for direct support of academic instruction.

Instructionally, software developers are still just scratching the surface of the computer as an educational delivery system. Initially, major portions of instructional computer time were devoted to straightforward drill-and-practice exercises. Although this application is still valid and constructive, computers are potentially capable of a lot more. Many schools use word processing software for student writing assignments. This application encourages communication proficiency and holds major potential for enhancement of literacy levels. But there's still a missing link. To really pay for themselves, computers are going to have to support acquisition of academic knowledge.

Increasingly, interactive instructional software is being developed to support delivery of academic content in areas such as English, math, and science. A number of large computer and software companies are spending millions of dollars on product development, much of it in collaborative or joint efforts with educators. These efforts are sincere, committed. And, at this writing, efforts appear to be approaching a breakthrough, with developers seeking the combination that will unleash a huge, still-unrealized potential market. But results are still far short of achievable levels.

Putting it another way, there are still gaps to be bridged between practitioners of pedagogy and technology. Teachers are torn between pressures of curricula and standardized tests and their desire to enrich the learning experiences of their students. Many teachers recognize that computers are tools that can help them do their jobs more effectively. For them, the gap lies between their understanding of the content to be imparted and the complex processes associated with organization of information, presentation to students, and actual learning.

Computer and software specialists are eager to help. But they face a gap of a different nature. Their focus is on the special dimensions of information delivery attainable with computers—animation, interaction with users, responsiveness, and the ability to store, organize, and retrieve relevant information from mountains of knowledge stored around the world.

The brightest current prospect lies in the hope that the essential compatibility will evolve gradually. Teachers will, over time, acquire enough computer sophistication to recognize where and how technology can serve them. Concurrently, technologists will learn more about dealing with the weakest link in computer processing systems—people. They are gradually settling for less elegance in presentation and focusing more on connecting the computer to teachers and students and dealing, at the same time, with the challenges of integrating instruction on multiple academic disciplines.

Promising Start

Given the circumstances described above, computers and curricula have come together along lines of minimal resistance.

Two computer applications that have become commonplace, most commonly in high schools but also in middle schools, are

Internet access and proficiency in use of word processing software. Both these applications promote interdisciplinary learning. Internet research assignments lead to information acquisition across the full spectrum of academic subjects. Although information access can be slow and sources hard to find and possibly inaccurate, the net effect is still positive; students do more research, covering vastly more sources than could ever have been encompassed in a high school or community library.

PUTTING TECHNOLOGY INTO REALISTIC PERSPECTIVE

Too many people, students and educators among them, treat the terms *computer* and *technology* as synonyms. This practice falls somewhere between major misconception and simple misunderstanding. Computers do implement technology, particularly electronic technology. But there is more, much more, to modern technology than the personal desk-top computer that receives the undue credit.

Students experience an important interaction with technology during however many hours a week they spend watching television. Now add in the hours they spend on the telephone without recognizing that they are using a massive computer system to connect them to the recipient of their verbal wisdom. A modern automobile generally thought of as a mechanical source of transportation now incorporates dozens of microchips that control everything from the suspension to steering to fuel consumption to a climate-control system. Ride an elevator in a modern building and electronic technology helps get you to your destination.

In the course of a rounded education, today's students should acquire an understanding and appreciation of the larger scope of technology in their lives and in their working futures.

THE ART OF LEARNING

Despite strong emphasis on so-called "core subjects" by such prestigious pronouncements as the *Prisoner of Time* report, a number of schools have discovered a new emphasis and value for the arts. As curriculum elements, the arts add tactile and intellectual support to the learning process. In effect, arts-based instructional programs add a coordinated, multi-disciplinary systems dimension to student learning experiences.

Arts-related activities provide an opportunity for the student to personalize and internalize the content of academic core courses. For example, students in a fourth-grade class develop brightly colored maps tracing the expansive pattern of El Nino currents. In a seventh grade science class, student teams each "adopt" a galaxy that they represent graphically in scale models or paintings as well as in written reports shared with the entire class. In another situation, fourth graders build time lines showing the history of human communication from crude cave drawings to modern telecommunications and computers. A fifth grade class uses computers to prepare a series of reports and posters on local history and pioneers who contributed to development of their county and town.

In other activities, human experiences are interpreted in dance, drama, and music. In each instance, the representation, or acting out, of acquired lessons makes learning more memorable; school experiences become more interesting. In North Carolina, as described in a later chapter, a public-private partnership has launched a series of 27 schools that use the arts as common focal activities for instruction in all academic subjects.

Aside from reinforcing other areas of study, emphasis on arts helps build a sense of pride in culture and heritage for students who act out or picture the lineage of their people and/or area.

DOCUMENTING PROGRESS

Learning is part of a system for *organizing, retaining,* and *applying* knowledge. Within this system, learning is a process that involves stimulation of interest, discovery, and assimilation of new information into an existing and always growing body of knowledge. The long-term value of acquired knowledge, then, lies in the measures used to assure retention and application.

A proven method for promoting retention of learned content involves reinforcement through recording new lessons through written or graphic representation. One successful vehicle for achieving this reinforcement is an individual, personal *portfolio* maintained continuously by each student. As described in the previous chapter, a portfolio documents each unit of study a student completes, with separate portfolios typically assembled for elementary, middle, and high school—hopefully with greater levels of sophistication at each level. Reinforcement takes place with the recording of new knowledge content resulting from current learning.

Application of knowledge, the basis for this discussion, comes from the intellectual cross-pollination of portfolio content. Study projects, either assigned or student-devised, call for application of knowledge across disciplines in problem-solving situations. In effect, then, the portfolio becomes a database for retention and retrieval of student-accumulated knowledge.

THRESHOLD TO REALITY

In the world of work, and also in college, a premium is placed on self-motivation and self-direction in the completion of complex, multi-faceted tasks. On the job, employers value a "self-starter" or "take charge" person who initiates new potentials, solves problems, follows through, and delivers results independently as part of a well coordinated team.

Many high schools are now emulating this kind of real-world experience by requiring a senior project as a prerequisite for graduation. Each project is approached as an independent commitment. Subject selection is virtually unlimited, though each project must be accepted and approved by a faculty adviser. Typical requirements stipulate at least 15 hours of research, preparation and delivery of a speech (which can be supported by a multimedia presentation) and a written paper of at least eight pages. Within the context of this discussion, the senior project should become the student's ultimate encounter with multi-disciplinary acquisition and application of knowledge.

Each project should be designed to replicate the kinds of expectations students will meet as college students or information workers. Thus, the senior project reinforces one of the important challenges in every student's future: Every student must learn to learn, and keep learning throughout his or her lifetime.

Part 4

In the
Right Direction

Chapter 14
Educational
Choices

I t's the American way. Consumers expect options for their investments. This applies across the board, to cars, houses, toothpaste, or breakfast cereal. Today, education has become no exception. Education is clearly one of the most critical investments for the average family. At the post-secondary level, a qualified student can choose to apply to any of thousands of available schools. So, the logic goes, why shouldn't there be choices among elementary and secondary-schools?

Readers of this book will be aware that this can be an emotion-charged question, one that begets other vital questions:

❏ Do Americans owe a moral allegiance and responsibility to support and work for the continuous operation and/or quality of public schools?
❏ Should parents have the right to apply the tax money allocated for the education of their children to enrollment in schools of their choice?
❏ Should Americans follow the British concept which holds that tuition money follows the child to any school chosen by parents?

Questions such as these will undoubtedly excite—and upset—the American public and its educators for years to come. This discussion cannot and does not suggest definitive answers or resolutions. Rather, it seems worthwhile to recognize that educational choice is an issue that merits attention and to take a realistic, pragmatic look at things the way they are.

PUBLIC SCHOOLS

Too often, public schools don't even figure in discussions of educational choice. The reality, however, is that public schools now offer the most diverse range of selections of educational alternatives.

This may be due partly to a development that may be the most significant change of all—the sometimes slow but clearly perceptible shift in attitudes toward the relationships between schools and parents. Today, widespread, open dialogues exist between parents on one side and teachers and administrators on the other. Advice and guidance from community and business leaders is being sought actively. And, even more remarkable considering some past antagonisms, educators are listening and changes are happening.

In many school districts today, all interested parties share a single focus that is defining the expectations for student achievement: America is engaged in international competition encompassing wide ranges of products and markets. To succeed, we need a workforce with world class capabilities for productivity, innovation, and quality output. The primary supply source for the future prosperity that represents a universal American goal is our public school system.

Under these pressures, today's parents, as customers with school-site-selection authority and responsibility are often surprised by the options open for placement of children in special programs within local public schools. In general, the closer the student moves toward graduation and entry into the workforce, the greater the number and type of options there will be. However, alternatives now exist over the full spectrum of educational grade levels, including growing numbers of preschool and open-enrollment programs within public schools. Significantly, available options seem to be increasing in every part of the country.

Discussions of options and innovations in education also continue in the two chapters that follow. The topical separations implement a decision of the authors to conduct a major case study aimed at demonstrating the kinds of innovation and quality attainable if top-level government and business executives make the kinds of commitments that promote a climate for improvement.

OPEN ENROLLMENT POLICIES

If American parents prefer competitive choice in education, they can find a wide range of opportunities in the public schools within many districts. The old world of local or neighborhood-restricted choice is either over or on its way out in many areas where parents are free to enroll students in public schools of their choice.

Magnet Schools

Selection factors may include some sites designated as magnet schools that are intended to attract enrollments from outside the immediate district because of academic or other program excellence. An outstanding example of this concept is the operation in Wake County, North Carolina (in and around Raleigh), where 34 of 105 schools offer magnet programs differentiated for a range of factors, including emphasis on arts, technology, programs for gifted students, year-round operation, or extended-day services. Descriptions of these schools and their operating concepts are presented in discussions that treat North Carolina as a viable example of improvements that can be realized when government, industry, and private citizens commit to creation of an education-friendly environment.

Flexible and Alternative Schedules and Structures

So many new approaches and methods are being introduced that they can be seen as an effort of educators to redefine the processes and structures of education. Recognizing the criticality of what happens to kids in early elementary years, a number of schools are focusing on teacher-student relationships.

Hernando County, Florida, for example, has a plan under which students and teachers stay together for three years at a time. In a K-2 sequence under this plan, three teachers work continuously with the same children. Each of the three teachers has one group through all three grade-levels as his or her special charges. However, each teacher on the team has a specialty—reading, language arts, or math. The rooms in which the teachers work are equipped and arranged to support the designated subject specialty. The reading and language arts rooms have six computers each, math three. Each room has six **stations,** each set up to support a learning activity. Students rotate to these special classes, spending one hour a day on each subject.

Among other advantages, teachers who get to know a group of kids in kindergarten then stay with them through second grade don't experience the lost time in getting acquainted at the beginning of each new school year. Where teachers function as a smoothly integrated team, the students are evaluated and assisted from different viewpoints. There is a higher probability that students will establish a sound personal rapport with at least one teacher in a three-member team. Students have clearly benefited from this arrangement, which will gradually be expanded to additional classes and schools. As experienced educators would anticipate, the greatest challenge with this plan lies in finding teachers who can and are willing to collaborate on behalf of the kids even though the work may be more challenging.

Other plans under which students spend multiple years with the same teachers also are being introduced. Some of these assign students of varying age levels to the same group. For example, there may be K-2 students in one class, 3-5 in another. This arrangement makes it easier to assign work individually and let students proceed at their own pace. It also arouses some complaints from parents who feel their kids may be held back if they are grouped with younger children. Considerations like these serve to demonstrate the need for full parent-community-school cooperation.

Optional **year-round** programs also represent a growing area of public school choice. An example of this type of program is referenced later in this chapter and described in depth subsequently. In some instances, districts permit parents to select any school they prefer, for any reason, as long as their children qualify for enrollment. Options include special education programs for children with disabilities, special emphasis on arts as focal points of education, schedules that provide extended-day programs, and commitments to academic excellence for gifted children.

As noted above, choices open to students at public schools seem to expand as grade levels advance, with the greatest number of choices occurring as students move closer to workforce entry. So, because of the criticality in preparing students for the workplace, this review covers high schools next. The selection below presents only some of the more prominent options currently available.

SCHOOL-TO-CAREER PATHWAYS

Recognition that future employers are the primary customers of education systems has come fairly recently. As one consequence, schools all across the country have collaborated with representatives of business and governmental entities to establish rigorous, relevant career-oriented or job-training programs. These activities are aimed at preparing students for either direct entry into the workplace or development of background and appreciation to establish a mindset for college or graduate study leading toward professions. Conceptually, an important outgrowth of these efforts is recognition of a phenomenon identified earlier: Students proceeding directly into the workforce from high school need preparation that is at least as rigorous, often more so, than college-bound students. That remains an inescapable consequence of the information age, a factor schools are going to have to live with from now on.

Discussions below cover some of the major approaches through which high schools are providing direct career preparation.

Career-Dedicated High Schools

Large districts particularly have, for years, provided career-preparation or professional-indoctrination programs through specialized high schools. New York City pioneered this movement with specialized schools that provide standard academic training and also add in-depth work in career areas. Similar programs have been under way for some time in Chicago, Los Angeles, Detroit, and other metropolitan areas. Specialties for such schools have included performing arts and music, graphic arts, math/science, biological sciences and medicine, economics and finance, engineering and technology, automotive, construction trades, and even academic specialties such as literary and social studies programs.

The very presence of such schools encourages young people to give serious thought to careers earlier than they might if such options weren't available. The curriculum emphasis of such schools also encourages articulation of transitional arrangements between high schools and two- or four-year colleges.

A major advantage of such specialization lies in the opportunities created to bring people with extensive real-world experience into teaching positions. Typically, career-directed schools will offer six to eight electives in their specialty areas and are permitted to hire instructors for these units on the basis of job or professional experience. This makes it possible for students to emerge from high schools extensively briefed on what will be expected from them in real-world job situations. The presence of specialists on the faculty also helps build an appreciation for a school's occupational orientation among the teachers who handle traditional academic subjects, and also by prospective employers, of course.

Invariably, applications for admission to such schools exceeds the number of openings available. The rigorous competition, in itself, helps promote the quality of instruction and job preparation.

In fairness, it should be noted that direct school-to-work programs also have their doubters and outright critics. The most-voiced complaint sees children committed to vocations at too early an age. Concerns include fear that students may be enrolled in direct school-to-work classes to fill slots to please administrators and teachers in a kind of rush to judgment or job-maintenance action.

Even heralded successes for school-to-work programs do not justify involving any student in a lifelong commitment, particularly if there is unwillingness or reasonable doubt. Any assignment of students into career-oriented programs should be preceded by counseling and definitive conferences with students and parents. In the proper, validated cases, students who are not motivated or fully qualified for college entrance (more than half of all freshmen entering four-year colleges do not graduate) preparation for a profitable working specialty can be both intellectually beneficial and financially profitable.

Career Academies—Schools Within Schools

In less-densely populated areas or in specialties for which demands for training are lower, specialized *academies* are being created within existing, traditional high schools. In effect, an academy is a school within a school.

An earlier chapter provides information on a typical example within a public high school—the Health Careers Academy of Oakmont High School, Roseville, California. Similar programs are provided by many schools that offer ROTC training to prepare students for military careers on graduation. Muir High School in Pasadena, California, operates an aerospace academy in which staff members from the nearby Jet Propulsion Laboratories mentor students. There is also an Air Force ROTC program on campus. In high-tourism areas, a number of academies provide training in the hospitality or food service fields.

Beyond that, many of the career areas cited above have been used as a basis for creating special school-to-work courses or two-plus-two transitions with community colleges that fall short of academy-level concentration in high school.

All of the advantages cited for specialized high schools apply to academies, which serve primarily to make the same kind of preparation for career specialties available in districts that can't support special schools or for fields with limited personnel requirements.

Skill-Based Vocational Programs Within Regular Schedules

These activities take place either as course offerings within traditional academic high schools or at multi-specialty schools set up specifically for occupational training. Earlier descriptions of programs in food preparation and auto mechanics at the Roseville (California) Joint Union High School District illustrate this kind of offering. Many high schools are set up specifically for vocational training. Typically, these schools include shops or special facilities for such occupations as carpentry, heating and air conditioning, electrical, food preparation, convalescent health care, publication, TV production, photography, or electronic assembly and testing. A school of this type in Mooresville (North Carolina) is described in a subsequent chapter.

Often, these programs operate in conjunction with job experience through release time or cooperative programs that award educational credits for work performance. In a number of instances, local trade unions sponsor and participate in these activities. Some programs of this type, often called ROP, or Regional Occupational Programs, are set up specifically for training in occupations or, for special students, survival-type skills. Emphasis in these facilities is on practicality. In some areas, these programs provide something of a safety net for students who have experienced difficulty in traditional academic settings. Often, these students prosper under the combination of discipline and opportunities provided through alternate, vocationally oriented programs.

Independent or Continuation Schools

A *continuation school* tends to be similar to the ROP programs described above, except it is administered through established school districts rather than as a separate county or state activity.

Independent-study high schools fill a special niche, providing supportive or last-resort educational opportunities for students who, for a variety of reasons, can't attend school on a regular daily basis. A highly successful program of this type is conducted at Independence High School, which is part of the Roseville (California) Joint Union High School District.

Students may enroll if work or special conditions make it impossible for them to attend regular high school classes routinely. For example, a number of young people who live in the district work as models or entertainers, requiring that they travel irregularly and often extensively. In other instances, economic conditions may require students to work up to 20 hours weekly. Still other students may have emotional or physical problems, including periods of recovery from serious illnesses, that mitigate against regular daily attendance. The school offers a full range of courses replicating the curriculum of other high schools in the district.

Independence High operates with a one-on-one relationship between each student and an assigned teacher/program coordinator. Each student has a scheduled weekly appointment with his or her teacher. The coordinating teacher arranges for all of the work assignments and receives homework and mandatory activity reports that students must turn in. The combined work-study schedule must be equal to or greater than the time requirements for attendance at a regular high school.

Students must pass tests covering all academic courses and also must take and turn in satisfactory scores on curriculum-based content tests. Graduation qualification or GED tests also must be passed to qualify for a diploma.

ADVANCED PLACEMENT AND BACCALAUREATE PROGRAMS

A heartening number of schools recognize and provide special programs to support gifted youngsters. The principle is straightforward: Students with high levels of intelligence and motivation hold future leadership potentials in business, government, or society generally. It is to the advantage of the district and the country as a whole to nurture their development.

In Wake and Mecklenburg Counties, North Carolina, and in other districts across the country, there are magnet schools designated specifically as gifted/talented. They offer enrichment programs that challenge students to proceed through the curricula at their own, often accelerated pace and to pursue knowledge in areas that are of special interest to them.

Accelerated or gifted-level courses are provided to qualified students by middle and high schools. The students are encouraged to complete most of their graduation requirements early in their high-school careers, then go on to take college-level work. In all parts of the country, selected high schools support either the International Baccalaureate or Advanced Placement programs. Under these plans, a student can complete most of his or her first year course requirements before entering a cooperating college.

Making a program of this type work calls for close cooperation between committed teachers and parents. Teachers and counselors have the contacts that can lead to recognition of special potential in individual students. Conferences with parents review both the potential of the student and the opportunities of special course offerings. Final decisions remain with parents. But it takes cooperation to monitor student progress and to provide the encouragement that is an essential ingredient for success.

CHARTER SCHOOLS

While they still represent a small fraction of publicly funded educational sites, **charter schools** have a number of characteristics and sources of support that mark them for potentially significant future growth. A recent report calls the charter movement the fastest growing segment of education and places some 475 charter schools in 26 states. Sources of support have come from such prestigious locations as the White House and the leadership of the National Education Association (NEA).

In part, this support seems to derive from the lesser-of-evils traits that charter schools present to educators and influential public leaders. The charter structure incorporates features of public support and accountability that doubters interpret positively to mean these institutions are subject to at least some of the same control factors as regular public schools. On the other hand, there is enough independence to permit curriculum creativity and operational flexibility that can lead to high levels of instructional quality and student achievement.

In reality, a charter school represents a type of entrepreneurship within the educational establishment, the equivalent of a small start-up business putting itself up against an entrenched behemoth. A permit to begin a new school—officially a charter—is issued to a group of educators, parents, or local citizens, independent agencies, or community partnerships who form a nonprofit corporation and apply to a state agency or local school board for a charter that will permit the organization to form and operate a school. The typical charter school is small, flexible, and adaptive to the children it serves. In the case of education, smaller size represents special economies that facilitate more achievement at lower expense.

In many instances, the head of a charter school has a title such as coordinator, president, or CEO rather than principal. This individual, who may be actively involved in parent relations and/or actual instruction, will be assisted by a minimal office staff, often one person. Administrative costs are thus lower than for the typical public school. In one school visited for this project, the students collect their own trash and clean their own classrooms, eliminating the need for janitorial help. In this same school, the students bring their lunches, eliminating the need for a cafeteria. These economies, in turn, provide funds for computers, educational aids, and extra compensation for dedicated faculty members. Another charter school, in Northern California, makes extensive use of "distance education." Students plug into the school from home on laptop computers, receiving and completing their work assignments remotely, then visit the school periodically for conferences with faculty coordinators or fellow students.

Charter schools operate under enabling federal legislation that empowers states to create their own programs. Although provisions vary among states, the principles that apply to formation of charter schools are fairly universal. In some instances, the charter school operates under the supervision and control of its local board of education. In another, growing option, the charter school becomes a governing body on its own that is responsible directly to a state department of public instruction as though it was an independent school district.

The formation process has created a good deal of friction in different parts of the country. Problems have centered on policies and agreements for the hiring of teachers. Teachers' unions generally have sought to maintain priorities for tenure and seniority in hiring, while managers of the newly formed schools have tried for freedom to hire instructors who subscribe to the philosophies around which the school was formed.

Student admission policies must follow state guidelines. Typical policies invite open applications from a defined community, which can include a town, city, or limited geographic area. If applications exceed available openings, a lottery is held.

The curricula for most charter schools are rigorous and

usually creative and innovative. Since enrollment is voluntary, success lies in attracting parents and children committed to high achievement and challenging the students who do register. The nature of the goals that lead to formation of the typical charter school attracts active—unusually active—parent involvement, often including special financial contributions and also through direct classroom participation to assist in instruction. Local businesses have also shown a willingness to "adopt" charter schools by providing curriculum guidance, part-time instructors, materials, supplies, equipment, and even supplemental funding.

Even in states where charter schools are considered highly successful, enrollments are still insignificant in comparison with the massive structure called American education. At most, enrollments in any given state are less than 1 percent of total registrations. However, at this writing, the modern charter movement is only a little more than five years old and is felt to be gaining momentum. It seems fair to say, at present, that a charter school represents a potentially attractive choice for parents with gifted and/or motivated children who are also willing to involve themselves in their kids' educations.

SPECIAL EDUCATION

Under specific federal legislation, every American child (through age 18) is entitled to an education "appropriate" to his or her physical, mental, or emotional capabilities. The term **special education** is generally applied to programs that accommodate the disabled. Special programs, even special schools in some instances, have been created for physically handicapped (wheelchair access to schools is now a universal requirement), and students with visual, auditory, emotional, neurological, or learning disabilities.

Under the law, parents counsel with educators at their local school district to determine the appropriate way to meet each student's individual needs. As a rule, parents, along with their medical advisers and/or therapists, have a major voice in determining what constitutes appropriate facilities and programs. In many instances, districts arrange for tests and evaluations by state, county, or privately contracted clinics or laboratories.

In general, two separate tracks are followed to achieve appropriate education for the special student. One is called **mainstreaming.** Students participate in regular classrooms with "normal" students. In most instances, specially trained aides are assigned to assist with the care and instruction of the special students.

A second option lies in schools or institutions dedicated to learning disabled programs. In general, these facilities, which have at least a substantial part of their tuitions paid by local school districts, specialize in programs for the severely disabled. Decisions about the kind of institution a child should attend center around evaluations of *educability,* or the degree to which a child can adapt to a mainstream classroom or whether a special facility will prove more appropriate. For persons who are severely disabled, care and instruction needs often go well beyond the scope of a typical public school.

An outstanding example of a dedicated facility serving the severely disabled is the Wildwood School and Programs in Schenectady, New York. This full-service organization involves itself in the lives of its students and adult members from toddler age through to lifelong support. The school serves children from preschool ages through their teens. Built specifically as a special education facility, it features self-sufficient classrooms with their own kitchens, bathrooms, and private conference rooms for special tutoring.

Teenagers are served by the Wildwood Youth program, which trains its charges in basic societal survival skills, including riding public transportation, shopping, using a post office, opening bank accounts, and other everyday lifeskills. School-age children and teens are eligible to attend summer programs at Wildwood's own campsite. Members of a young adults group learn job skills and work habits, and also participate in organized recreation programs. Adults live in community-based residences and hold jobs for which they are trained and coached by the adult staff. Started in 1966 by a group of concerned parents, Wildwood now accommodates some 450 students in its school and many more in programs that serve adults through a lifelong commitment.

The learning-disabled population has recently been estimated at 8 percent of newborns. And the incidence of these disabilities may well increase as medical institutions improve their expertise with neonatal care and as more mothers engage in abusive use of drugs and other harmful substances during pregnancy. Under these circumstances, special education promises to be a growth area of concern for the country's school systems.

PRIVATE SCHOOLS AND THE VOUCHER ISSUE

The term **private school** can invoke a variety of images, depending on who's doing the invoking. For some parents, chiefly those considered well-off or members of professions, the private school has an exclusive, quality image. In some parts of the country, particularly the Northeast, it is common for parents to begin planning educational careers for two-year-olds. They plot paths that run through the "best" nursery schools, preschools, elementary schools, secondary schools, and target "top" universities, all while the kids are still in diapers.

From the educational viewpoint, these "exclusive" schools have undoubtedly earned their reputations. Some, such as **Montessori** Schools and **Waldorf** Schools, enjoy high reputations for creative, child-centered approaches to education and outstanding achievements. Others, including a number of East Coast prep schools, enjoy outstanding national academic reputations. In general, these reputations are earned and deserved. We know of one private school, for example, which recently graduated 80-plus students who turned in *average* SAT scores of 1425. Clearly, this institution has a reputation for high achievement and for the ability of its graduates to gain admission to the best universities in the world.

Schools of this type do offer scholarships for children from families that can't afford tuitions that can run to $10,000 or more annually. Any students who win such scholarships are certain to be classified as mentally gifted. Since the really "top" schools typically have fewer admissions spots than applications and also since most have long waiting lists, owners or administrators of these institutions generally have no direct stake and little interest in so-called **educational vouchers.** If parents with vouchers did apply, the acceptance criteria would have less to do with money and more with mental acuity of the child.

Other private schools cater to student bodies with more average social and academic goals. Their tuitions may be lower and academic achievement pressures may be fewer. A common denominator is that parents feel these schools are safer, protected from the violence that engulfs public schools in some urban areas. In most schools in this category, curricula and activities are secular. Even if they are sponsored by a religious group, prayer and attendance at religious services may be optional. In this range, some schools would like the option of accepting vouchers from parents who are willing to make up the difference between a state-funded stipend and actual tuition.

The other main category consists of *parochial schools,* some of which have been identified specifically as *Christian academies.* Virtually all of these schools have a direct connection with a religious sect. Many are housed in churches, synagogues, mosques, or other religious facilities, a factor that may reduce their operating costs and tuitions. Although there are no universal rules, most of the controversies associated with educational vouchers have centered around the willingness of many schools of this type to accept these stipends in lieu of tuition. Some are even willing to accept students who are not affiliated with the sponsoring religion and to exempt them from religious instruction that is otherwise mandatory.

Perceived benefits for schools in this last category include high degrees of academic rigor and discipline that support reputations for achievement levels higher than those of inner city public schools. Opposition to vouchers for such schools has centered on so-called "quality" issues. Many faculty members in these schools do not have full teaching credentials. Compensation levels also tend to be lower than in public schools. Some critics contend that the discipline level in parochial schools mitigates against creativity or imagination in instructional programs. Critics have to acknowledge that students from these schools generally do better on standardized tests than public school students in the same neighborhoods. But they maintain that students are subjected to rote instruction and memorization, making for a low quality of job performance when these kids hit the workplace.

Proponents of educational vouchers hold that the decisions about selection of schools for children belong to parents. They cite the British model under which tuition follows students rather than institutions. They maintain that, given parental authority for educational guidance, families should be able to apply funds from public taxes to any institution they choose.

To date, there has been no overall resolution or enunciated public policy on the issue of educational vouchers. Government-supported voucher programs are in effect in a few areas, with Milwaukee, Wisconsin, the largest. In addition, a number of business organizations and foundations issue vouchers privately. These plans operate as equivalents of scholarships. A recent report by the Heartland Institute indicates that 30 private sources with some $40 million in vouchers now provide partial tuition for some 13,500 students. Tuition values underwritten by private sponsors often are far short of covering full private school tuitions, some valued at only $800 to $1,000. Yet, private organizations that sponsor educational vouchers are said to have a waiting list of almost 40,000.

Evaluation of results for this segment is both premature and inappropriate at this time. Rather, this topic is significant because it clearly will not go away, and also because wider public attention is going to be required at some future time.

HOMESCHOOLING

Estimates indicate that somewhere between 500,000 and 1.25 million students are now going to school at home. The majority of this small-but-growing student segment have parents who object strenuously to unsafe conditions and/or the secularization and perceived loss of morality in public schools. Religious fundamentalists predominate in this group. However, a significant minority of homeschooling parents seek educational rigor and quality that they feel their children cannot get in public schools.

Controversies have stirred around the question of whether homeschooling is legal. Opponents have held that laws require actual school attendance for specified numbers of days and hours per day. Representatives of the growing homeschooling movement deal with mandatory education requirements pragmatically by advising parents to file affidavits with their local school districts setting themselves up as private schools. In most areas, parents can create a private school with one or a few students where parents serve as administrators and/or teachers.

Extensive networks of homeschooling support groups and active associations have been set up in most states and nationally. Major networks of suppliers have grown to provide homeschoolers with services that range from diploma-granting correspondence schools, to publishers of materials designed especially for this market, to local tutoring services, to multifamily pools that hire instructors or arrange for group enrichment activities. In many areas, public school districts offer independent study options that serve homeschoolers. This arrangement typically fits a pattern like that described earlier in this chapter for Independence High School in Roseville, California.

As operators of independent schools, parents also have access to sites where national and state achievement or graduation qualification tests are administered.

Negative comments about homeschooling tend to focus on the lack of credentialed teachers and student loss of social interaction with peers. Homeschooling advocates recognize these problems, particularly the need for social outlets, and generally create offsetting or substitute activities. The homeschooling movement has spawned a number of individual activists and groups that are vigorously encouraging and recruiting parents dissatisfied with public education. Though small, the movement shows signs of continuing growth.

CONTRACT OPERATION OF PUBLIC SCHOOLS

To varying degrees, public school districts all across the country have been subjected to expressions and demonstrations of dissatisfaction. In response to continuing, intensifying demands, a number of districts have authorized pilot implementations of alternate forms of school management and operation. Among the alternatives in the public limelight have been activities of companies offering to take over full responsibility for management and operation of existing public schools.

Under concepts introduced comparatively recently, school boards assume the right to consider alternative sources for educational management aimed at improving student achievement. Part of the basis for such decisions comes from the willingness of private contractors to accept accountability for student performance. In effect, the private firms guarantee results, an assurance not available from existing public schools, particularly where teachers are represented by unions. In effect, open bids are invited for proposals to take over and operate a given facility under contract. In some instances, public schools bid against private firms.

A flurry of such activity in recent years has resulted in strong performance on Wall Street of securities of educational management organizations, or EMOs. A survey of this field was published in January, 1996, by *U.S. News and World Report.* Four private companies were then operating 20 public schools with enrollments totaling 14,900. The contracts were valued at $92 million. Nonprofit entities ranging from universities to the National Urban League have also entered this field.

The most successful private organization managing public schools is the Edison Project, which has been awarded contracts in Massachusetts, Texas, Kansas, California, and Michigan. The firm is aggressively pursuing new contracts. An initially announced goal to expand to 100 schools has been modified. In 1997, the Edison Project held contracts for operation of 25 schools with enrollments of more than 13,000.

The Edison program espouses rigorous curricula, extensive use of technology, team pedagogy, and extended instructional schedules that add days to the annual school calendar and time to the school day. Students requiring special help attend tutorial sessions before and after the regular school day. Edison has operated largely in districts where existing schools were underperforming, including inner city Boston. The contractor assumes responsibility for upgrading the physical plant of the school and also insists on the right to screen and hire teachers, as well as to pay them on the basis of performance.

Edison schools offer open enrollment, which is usually oversubscribed with places awarded on a lottery basis. Each student receives a laptop computer to take home for open access through a national Edison network to special study resources or for direct exchanges with teachers. The course of study includes full bilingualism and completion of high school graduation requirements by tenth grade, with the last two years spent on advance-placement work. All but one of the Edison-managed schools achieved improved standardized test scores during their first and second years of operation.

Another area of private educational contracting, which is experiencing faster acceptance and growth than management of entire schools, is remedial tutoring. A number of schools and districts have awarded remediation contracts to organizations like Sylvan Learning Systems. Typically, the contractor sets up facilities in a public school and provides remedial instruction for underperforming students. Generally, the special fees made available by federal and state agencies for remediation cover the costs of these services. Decisions to assign private companies to this work are often based on the guarantees of results offered by the contractors.

The prognosis: Progress will be slower than advocates projected. But this movement will not go away. Private contracting will continue to expand.

SCHOOLS AT WORK

From the mid-1980s onward, private companies have become increasingly active in promoting and supporting quality in education. Active projects have included tutoring, mentoring, sponsoring teacher institutes, and, most actively, opening and operating child care facilities and schools on company premises.

As the labor market has tightened and competition has mounted to hire and hold specialized professional and technical people, benefits from child care and educational facilities in the workplace have increased apace. The clear benefits of quality child care and education right in the workplace where workers can share time and learning experiences with their children represent a major perk, an inducement for key people to stay on their jobs. One oft-quoted observation: "Parents who want to be close to their children and to take a direct hand in their education also make excellent employees."

For their part, increasing numbers of employers see sponsorship of child-care facilities and schools as sound investments. When such costs are folded into the general expenses of employee benefits and relations, most reporting companies have indicated returns of two-to-one or better realized through reduced turnover, lower rates of absenteeism, and improved productivity that comes with peace of mind. Scores of business-sited schools now accommodate tens of thousands of preschool and elementary-age children.

Logistically, workplace-sited educational facilities can be structured along one of three lines:

1. They can be set up as **satellite schools** that operate as branches of local public schools.
2. The sponsoring company can create a nonprofit foundation to open a charter school in company facilities.
3. The sponsoring company can open a private school or preschool care center in its own facilities.

The satellite school route has been most popular to date, largely because overcrowded public schools have welcomed the opportunity to expand enrollments without having to win support for bond issues or construct new facilities. Under this arrangement, a sponsoring company provides, at its own expense, the facilities, including ongoing maintenance, to run a school, often for children of the sponsor's employees.

The in-house facility is then set up as a *satellite* of the local public school, which appoints a member of its faculty as supervising teacher. The cooperating public school supplies books and oversees instruction. However, the sponsor retains a strong voice in determining the methodologies and levels of innovation applied.

Because this arrangement creates a win-win situation, with the local school benefiting from student attendance revenues and the sponsor providing incentives to employees, this approach promises to grow rapidly. County and state educational agencies in some areas have actively begun to seek sponsors for satellite schools. Companies that have been involved in this movement include Honeywell, Hewlett-Packard, American Bankers Insurance, and the Miami International Airport (Dade County, Florida).

The plan for company-sponsored charter schools is similar, except that the legal structure is different in that there is no direct operating connection to a local public school. Instead, a non-profit entity is created to apply for and be responsible for the charter application and ongoing operation. The Exploris School, described in one of the chapters that follows, fits this description.

The third alternative is for a sponsoring company to establish and foot all or part of the bills for operation of a private school. Such schools can be open to enrollment from the community at large on a tuition basis. However, scholarships are typically provided for children of qualifying employees. The Cary Academy, also described in an ensuing chapter, falls into this general classification.

INNOVATION VS. TRADITIONAL STANDARDS: IMMOVABLE OBJECT VS. IRRESISTIBLE FORCE

It's the look of the nineties. Long-repressed, innovative educators are being encouraged, or at least tolerated, in programs that change the look of local schools and offer options to excellence-seeking parents. On introduction, innovative programs start tentatively, then spread out as they gain acceptance. Prominent among the pioneering efforts encountered in the survey undertaken in preparation for this book (most of which have also been presented before Models Schools Conferences sponsored by ICLE) are block scheduling, year-round schooling, integration of technology into instructional programs, problem-based learning, assessment integrated with instruction, and schools that feature the arts as a basis for student learning experiences.

As has been true for businesses—for example, in the development of new computer information systems or the introduction and testing of new products—new educational methods are typically begun on a piloting or parallel basis. For example, Mooresville (North Carolina) Schools introduced the year-round program, described in depth in a subsequent chapter, as a limited pilot in a single school. The plan, briefly, sets up four nine-week intervals interspersed with *intersessions* of two or three weeks. The principle behind this design was that a nine-week session is short enough to eliminate the student burnout encountered routinely between eight and 10 weeks into a 16-week semester. Also, the shorter intersessions or summer vacations cut down on memory losses generally encountered over long summer breaks. In this instance, parent demand led to introduction of the plan in other schools.

Similar strategies were applied to the four-plus-four block scheduling methods described earlier for the Roseville, California, high schools. The method started in a single school, then spread as results led to increased acceptance.

For educators and community leaders open to changes in our schools, these innovations and others like them represent good news. They present evidence that some positive steps are being taken to enhance American education. For each new success, however, there are educators who feel they are being stymied, shackled if you will, by the specter of things as they have always been and are not about to change.

In contrast, consider the schools that build their instruction and curricula around problem-based learning, performance-based assessment, the arts, or community exploration and experiences. Educators in these innovative surroundings measure their success by such evidence of student performance as the ability to solve problems through original research, creativity, or application of knowledge. With justifiable pride, many of these educators point out that there is more to monitoring and measuring student progress than marking answer spaces on standardized, multiple-choice tests, or even performance standards enunciated and governed by traditionalists.

This is where the innovative, seemingly irresistible force of creative challenge meets the immovable object of objective testing and content-based standard courses of study. Should students be evaluated on their ability to reason and innovate or should multiple-choice test scores prevail?

A typical dilemma: Schools where teachers and many parents, and certainly students, feel learning achievements are at new highs are prone toward lower scores on standardized tests. Proponents of the new programs see such developments as penances or punishments for daring to be different. Opponents are of different minds. Some say, "Innovate to your heart's content. Just make sure your test scores go up." Others say objective testing is the only, or at least the most valid, method of measuring educational achievement. Among this group are many who offer direct comparisons between scores on international tests in science, math, or other content areas, scores that invariably show a cross-section of American kids scoring poorly.

How badly do we want innovation, creativity, or problem solving capabilities? If we value these traits and are willing to recognize their potential in the international marketplace, is it time to change the way we keep score on our children's progress? Should we consider a dual system that measures **both** objective content mastery and innovative and problem-solving talent?

Does, after all, the greater problem lie in the testing methodology rather than in the new approaches to pedagogy?

We are probably not yet ready to resolve this final question. But, we submit, it may be worth some serious thought.

Chapter 15
Doing Educational Change—Part 1

Americans see themselves as winners. We believe in ourselves, even in our ability to evolve formerly underperfoming schools into a credible, world-class education system. Abundant evidence indicates that significant changes, enhancements really, are already happening—and will continue to happen barring the ever-present prospect of mismanagement or overmanagement that has cost us dearly in the past.

Convincing evidence indicates that positive educational change is an *ad hoc* process. That is, effective change initiates with the subjects and/or objects that require change; it is not and cannot be mandated by fiat. America is not a prospect for creation of a nationally mandated and directed superprogram that determines what kids will study and when as they follow a gigantic lockstep algorithm. Among other inhibitors to such a plan is our Constitution, which leaves educational responsibility at the state level. For effective change to occur in American schools, improved student performance needs to start in the classroom and radiate outward.

However, this doesn't mean that the executive and legislative branches of government have no impact or influence on the quality of education that American students acquire. What it does mean is that education flourishes when a favorable ambiance for positive growth exists and when local innovators generate an environment in which communities and schools are free to make change happen. The notable public and alternative school successes recounted in the rest of this book evolved within the favorable climate and intellectual nurturing promoted in a single state, offered here as model of what can happen under positive leadership and extensive local commitments.

SUCCESS IS NEVER AN ACCIDENT

Progress starts with commitment. In North Carolina, commitment permeates everything in education. Observers attribute the state's commitment to schools to a regional bent toward economic growth, coupled with a recognition that business and industrial progress doesn't happen in a vacuum. The reality is that growth requires specific kinds of foundations, including sympathetic governments, natural resources, transportation, and, farthest from least, an educated, trained workforce. As shortages have surfaced for skilled, high-tech workers and managerial professionals, North Carolina companies, with strong support from governmental and private sources, have become increasingly generous in their willingness to underwrite programs aimed at educational excellence.

The current round of commitments and actions leading to the results in North Carolina schools chronicled below started in 1992 at the behest of Gov. James B. Hunt, Jr. The governor sponsored legislation that led to creation, as part of his staff, of a Commission on Educational Standards and Accountability. The work of this group led to updating and increasing the rigor of the state's Standard Course of Study. In parallel with the commission's work, and also in response to an encouraging ambiance generated by the fervor for upgrading an educational system that was not seen to be all that it could or must become, districts throughout the state took actions that led to innovation and improved performance. Some—only a sampling—of the programs that have resulted from this stimulation, are covered in the segments that follow. Public-sector programs are covered in this chapter. Then, joint public-private and private initiatives are covered in the following chapter.

RURAL SCHOOLS TAKE ON A COMPETITIVE WORLD

The Polk County (North Carolina) School district has become something of a poster organization for demonstrating how much constructive educational enhancement can occur when an entire community unites to serve its children. The activities associated with a commitment to and implementation of the ICLE Management of Change process are described in Chapter 5. As so often happens, the time and circumstances helped propel this district toward the excellence it now enjoys.

The triggering event came with the merger (voted in 1989) of the schools of the old county district with those of Tryon City, the county's largest community (but not the county seat, which is Columbus). Support, without which nothing could have happened resulted from the nature and makeup of the community. The county's population (16,000, with 10 percent minorities) is small, even for North Carolina. Possibly because of this, there's a community spirit that assures unequivocal commitment to its school population of less than 2,200. The area includes a number of private estates where people raise and ride horses for fox hunts and other sports. There are also a number of affluent retirees intermixed with working people who commute to nearby cities.

Almost immediately after the merger of the county and city districts, construction began on a modern high school with facilities that support outstanding programs in academics and arts. The current total of six district schools includes two K-5 elementary schools, one 6-8 middle school, two K-8 schools and one 9-12 high school.

Coinciding with the commitments for the merger and ensuing modernization, the district became a pioneer, in 1991, in implementation of the ICLE Management of Change process. As reported in Chapter 5, the community responded enthusiastically to the call for participation in the review and planing phases of the change program, with citizens crowding the largest available auditorium at the opening session. More than 90 percent of the teachers pledged support for the commitment to bring Polk County Schools up to a level of world-class achievement. Implementation of the change program was incremental, with completion of a five year, learning-oriented reorganization and operational improvement program in 1996.

Despite its relatively small population, the district has become a leader in installation and constructive use of computers for direct learning support. Every classroom has at least one computer and each school has at least one computer lab. All classrooms are networked to the library and have Internet access. The district was also chosen for participation in the Schoolbook 2000 program sponsored by Microsoft and Toshiba. A combination of state and local funding was raised to acquire 65 laptops. Leading edge achievement has also come with programs that base instruction on the arts and from an unequivocal commitment to a learning orientation in all schools. Specific descriptions of some outstanding programs and achievements within this district follow.

School for Preschoolers

The district's preschool facility is a good indication of the way things happen when top educators and community leaders are flexible and committed. Back in 1994, the idea for a preschool program surfaced and attracted strong community and board support. A dedicated supporter, Mrs. Margaret Forbes, purchased a building that had been used as an office for a power company and gave it to the district for use as a preschool. Subsequent donations and board funding supported refurbishing that led to opening of the Forbes Preschool Education Center in November, 1996.

The Center provides a unique, comprehensive service for all families in the county. That is, the facility is open to all four-year-olds as a standard district service. Its intent and reach thus go far beyond such programs as Head Start (though some support is derived from funds allocated on the basis of economic status). By the spring, 1997 semester, some 45 youngsters attended the Forbes Center daily. They were divided into three groups, one for handicapped and learning disabled children. The center conducts a full program of early childhood activities aimed at preparing the students to enter kindergarten. The preschool students also can be dropped off before the start of the school day and kept afterward as a service to working parents.

The facility and its kids have become a source of pride for the community. Among other activities, field trips are planned with some regularity to the retirement home where Mrs. Forbes resides. The children are a source of joy to the residents, with some residents behaving like honorary grandparents and great-grandparents, providing valued affection and hugs that the kids enjoy. The net effect is a significant increase in the "family" feeling that permeates relationships between schools and community, and which becomes a solid stepping-stone to quality education in the K-12 grades.

Art and Technology in Elementary Education

The published work contains 56 pages graced by 72 illustrations. Its "Forward" [sic] is self-explanatory and plainly unedited, telling, among other things, a good deal about quality education in a rural American school:

> We are fourth grade students from Saluda School in Saluda, North Carolina. We have written this book called *Mountain Reflections*. It is about the early years of Saluda. Since Saluda has just been added to the

National Register of Historic Places, we studied the buildings in the historic district. We went downtown and took pictures you will see. By doing this we have learned what Saluda was like in the past. We have also interviewed people who have lived in Saluda all their lives. In this book, you will find memories of long ago and stories in which we imagined living in the past.

We want you to know that all of the work done on this book was done by fourth graders. Making this book helped us learn more about computers. We learned about saving and moving pictures. We got to print and have our own files. We learned how to scan pictures and take pictures with a digital camera.

We have made this book for all the people who would love to hear about the North Carolina Mountains. It is part of our social studies lessons and our narrative writing. In this book we share our mountain culture, how much it has changed and how much it has stayed the same. We put a lot of effort into this book because we love North Carolina. When you read our book, we hope you will, too.

We are selling *Mountain Reflections* to help raise money for a trip to the North Carolina Coast where we will study the culture of the people of our coast.

The bottom of the page bears the names of the 12 students who put the publication together, along with the name of a current natural treasure of the area, fourth grade teacher Carlann Osborn, who earned National Board certification in 1997. One of the prominent contributors to *Mountain Reflections* is 10-year-old Charles W. Pearson, who writes about the building of the railroad line through Saluda in 1876 and about his-great-great-grandfather, Captain Charles W. Pearson, who oversaw the job. The same author also contributes an interview with Charles W. Pearson, Sr., his grandfather, who had a dog named *Pete* as a child.

On visiting Saluda School, one of the included highlights was a chance to observe the same computer lab where *Mountain Reflections* went together. On this day, the lab was peopled by second graders whose faces came barely to the bottom of the computer monitors. They were reacting to an exercise in a software program called *Stories and More.* The current assignment asked students to write a story of their own. One of the young authors, a seven-year-old boy, started his story, "Wants apon a time ..." All were fully comfortable at the keyboards and, as second graders go, quite fluent in reading materials at their grade level.

A fourth-grade art class was working on sheets of paper

wider than each of them was tall. These were illustrated time lines showing the history of communication through pictures, words, and electronics. The walls of the main hall were festooned with paintings by some of these same kids carrying slogans like *End Racism; Be Cool, Don't Litter;* and *Join Hands to Fight Racism.* All this—and test scores to be proud of as well (Polk County placed twenty-fifth in the state in grades 3-8 student growth for 1996-97)—adds up to a conclusion that at least some American kids are well launched to a quality education.

High School, High Standards

At Polk County High School, Principal O. Jay Freeman is turning in an encore. He moved up recently from a hitch in which he helped Saluda School immerse itself in computers and creativity. Now, he's turning in the same kind of performance at the district's ultramodern high school. The facility, opened in 1992, held its first graduation in 1996.

Through participation in the Schoolbook 2000 program, the high school now employs 65 laptops for instruction in writing in its ninth grade English classes. Ninth grade students write on a series of assigned and elective topics, producing a continuous stream of written materials. All assignments are captured on laptops, with floppy disks turned in to teacher Jane Kinchloe, who uses software with editing capabilities to highlight passages and to recommend revisions or improvements. The laptops and the ability to exchange floppy disks make it possible to monitor revision of student work in keeping with Ms. Kinchloe's conviction that the real learning in a writing program comes from constructive review, criticism, and revision.

In part, the ability to give students time for in-depth instruction in writing results from the school's block scheduling technique. The school day is divided into four 90-minute periods, each of which is dedicated to one unit per semester of instruction credit against a graduation requirement of 28 units. This means students can earn academic credits needed for graduation in seven semesters and can apply up to four additional units for enrichment, reinforcement in subject areas where they are weak, advanced placement work, or dual enrollment with a local community college for direct college credit.

Retaining the family-like feeling of responsibility to serve students, the district, beginning in sixth grade and carrying through to twelfth, assigns each student to a member of the staff who serves as an advocate. Each advocate meets daily with the small group of students assigned to him or her to discuss current assignments and deal with any special needs or problems. The same advocate follows the student through the three years of middle school. New and ongoing relationships are then formed to encompass the four years of high school. Students accumulate and maintain portfolios throughout their high school careers to help monitor their progress and to prepare, with the help of advocates and counselors, for college or work careers. Each student develops a four-year high school plan in eighth grade. This is then reviewed and updated annually.

Capping off the high school experience in Polk County, each student now has to turn in a senior project. The program requires at least 15 hours of research and delivery of a paper at least eight pages long. Each student's work is judged by a committee of faculty members and community resource people.

Students who experience difficulty in keeping up with their studies can take advantage of either after-school tutorial "Learning Lab" sessions or a four-week summer workshop. Throughout a student's school experience, the district issues four interim reports to his or her parents at three week intervals, then detailed report cards every six weeks. Faculty and administrators are available any day, any time, to counsel with parents and their children. In Polk County, academic success is regarded as every student's right.

The achievements at Polk County Schools speak eloquently for themselves. However, the authors feel compelled to comment on the conditions, the commitments, the dedication, and the plain hard work without which educational achievements of this caliber cannot happen. These achievements comprise an eloquent tribute to the local leadership that has been clearly and resonantly committed, consistent throughout the ongoing effort, and focused steadily on program goals that reflect the quality and excellence the entire community set out to accomplish.

In particular, special recognition is due to Polk County superintendent and lifelong community resident, Dr. Susan S. Leonard, whose clearly focused leadership has inspired outstanding, loyal performances by students, faculty, and administrators, as well as unstinting support by the entire community.

WINNING THE BATTLE WITH TIME

American kids are shortchanged, according to a widely enunciated theory, because they attend school only 180 days a year.

This is, by far, the shortest school year in any developed country. Japanese kids get 243 days per year. In other countries, attendance opportunities range from 200 days and up.

But there are also some disturbing questions associated with this school-year debate:

❏ If kids aren't learning to read and do their numbers in 180 days, what guarantee is there, given continuity of the same system and instructional methods, that they will learn more in 200 days?

❏ Experienced educators know well the phenomenon of student burnout. It hits somewhere around eight or nine weeks into each semester. They become tired, unfocused, bored. How would they handle themselves if the system added two more weeks to each semester?

❏ What purposes might best be served by extending the school year? Is it about improving student achievement or about real estate, about making better use of facilities to reduce overcrowding?

That last question holds the real test of truth. *Is year-round schooling about facilities or learning?* For a substantial number, possibly most, of the million-plus kids now on year-round scheduling (including 40-plus percent of students in the Los Angeles system), it's about real estate. Kids and teachers are assigned to one of three "tracks" that attend schools on overlapping schedules. In effect, school capacity is expanded by one third without added construction costs. This arrangement works well in some instances, as it does in Wake County, North Carolina, where a tracking plan is applied in magnet schools that deliver strong advantages in exchange for any inconveniences that result from altered schedules. However, in places where tracking is arbitrary, as has happened in Los Angeles, the frustration and ire brought down upon district officials by this arrangement can be substantial.

Of great relevance, however, is the plan introduced in Mooresville, North Carolina, and 100-plus other districts across the state. The aim there was to revise schedules for the benefit of students by expanding and enhancing opportunities for learning. Subsequent experience has established that kids can benefit from creative adjustment of schedules and application of resources.

The notion about extending the school year was an outgrowth of the civic spirit of one of the authors of this book, Dr.

Sam Houston, who was superintendent of Mooresville Graded Schools in 1990, and also an active member of the Mooresville Chamber of Commerce. At a Chamber meeting, Houston encountered representatives of Japanese firms interested in locating facilities in the area. The foreign visitors inquired about local schools and expressed concern about length of the school year as well as flexibility that would permit some native-language instruction.

The topic of an extended school year hadn't come up before and nobody in Mooresville knew what was involved or how to go about it. So the superintendent dispatched a team headed by one of the district's elementary principals, Mrs. Carol Caroll, to a San Diego meeting of a year-round schooling group. Caroll and her accomplices proved to be quick studies. On the return flight, she started drafting a grant proposal for funding of a year-round program to begin in the elementary school where she was principal to the RJR Foundation's Next Century Schools program. The district was awarded $500,000 for a three year program.

The winning formula behind this program resulted from consideration of learning patterns of American schoolkids. Several problems were noted and attacked:

1. Most kids forget much of what they learned during long summer vacations. As a result, several weeks at the beginning of each fall semester are used nonproductively in reviewing lost content and getting the kids back up to speed. Overall progress is inhibited.

2. Toward the middle of the typical 18-week semester, kids suffer a natural burnout, sink into a state of doldrums, and turn in work of notably lower quality. The effects can be particularly critical in elementary schools where students may have same-teacher continuity through a full year.

3. If a student falls behind because of absences or simply doesn't understand a unit of work, there is little or no chance during an 18-week semester to identify and deal with the need. It's too easy for students to slip through the cracks of a long session without interim assessment and grading— as well as time for any needed remediation. Again, the problems can be particularly acute in elementary grades, where students can lose ground they may never make up if their troubles arise in basic knowledge areas such as reading, language arts, and math.

At Mooresville, a highly satisfactory answer has evolved under an "optional year round" (OYR) plan. Note the reference to optional. Parents are informed about the availability of the year-round schedule and must apply for admission. Some 49 percent of K-8 parents enroll their children in OYR. The year-round schedule focuses on nine-week (45-school-day) terms. The approach is also known as the 45-15 schedule, indicating that kids spend 45 school days in session, then take 15 days for an intersession. There are three intersessions between the four terms. The schedule has been adjusted recently to create two three-week and one two-week intersessions.

The intersessions make the difference. Kids get a breather right about the time when they would normally be suffering burnout. Both the intersessions and the truncated eight-week summer break are short enough to eliminate the formerly routine back-to-school memory lapse in September.

But the most significant benefit of the OYR plan lies in constructive use of the intersessions. Implementation of OYR has corresponded with introduction of learning-oriented, problem-based methods throughout the Mooresville district, but particularly in classes of the OYR program. These efforts stress integral, real-time assessment of student progress through problem-based materials. By the end of each nine-week term, teachers have a clear fix on the kids who've had trouble and will need help during the intersession time, which is put to busy, constructive use.

The main benefits from the intersession time result from supplemental instruction for students who require extra help and for enrichment opportunities for academically current students. Remedial work during the intersessions is underwritten through allocation of the state's normal summer-session funds, usually applied for repeating coursework. Reinforcement or supplemental work is offered during one week of each intersession. Students attend five full days, with lunch provided routinely because the traditional-schedule students are still in session. With the shorter terms, the one-week sessions are almost always enough to bring students up to standard achievement levels. If further work is needed, students can receive after-school tutoring as appropriate throughout the school year. Interestingly, the attitude in OYR programs is so positive that many students actually request the extra help of after-school tutoring or remedial intersession programs.

Another special benefit derived from the intersession breaks lies in the enthusiasm generated by a full menu of enrichment experiences offered. These activities are both cultural and recreational. Included have been ski trips to nearby mountains; food preparation and travelogue sessions on foreign travel, including study of the customs and cultures of other countries; nature study programs that include overnight camping experiences; and instruction in team sports and swimming.

One of the questions that has to be anticipated when this type of program is introduced come from parents who work and who count on having children in school. For these parents, the district arranges study, sports, and other activities to provide continuous attendance. Parents who opt to have their children stay in school when they have no scheduled classes to attend pay a nominal fee, based on their financial circumstances.

Part of the philosophy at the Mooresville district stems from the old saying: *If you find yourself with a lemon, make some lemonade.* Some years ago, the district closed down an old building, a carryover from the days of segregation, that was unsuitable as a modern educational facility. Plans to tear down the structure were thwarted when it was declared an historic site. So, the district proceeded to convert the building to an ultra-modern, highly productive Advanced Technology and Arts Center.

Included are a series of shops in which students prepare to qualify for productive jobs on graduation. In one shop, students learn carpentry and construction, with participation by local unions. Another shop specializes in heating, ventilation, and air conditioning, imparting critical and profitable skills for students graduating into a torrid southern summer climate. In one of three computer labs, students master computer-assisted drafting and manufacturing methods.

There's also a computer lab that specializes in electronic assembly and still another that deals in business applications. Instruction to prepare students for health-care jobs is conducted in a room that has a number of special facilities, including a hospital bed, and medical lab facilities, as well as a commercial kitchen.

Modern communication-industry careers can begin in a fully equipped TV studio where students produce a variety of show materials and transmit daily newscasts over a local cable network. Other communication specialties include computer animation units and a commercial art studio.

School buses run between the high school and the technology center every period, providing a continuity of academic and job-preparation opportunities.

These capabilities and, in particular, the community's attitude about education have contributed directly to growth in the Mooresville area, which lies within commuting distance of Charlotte, one of the fastest growing cities in the country. Adding educational excellence to an area already endowed with scenic beauty and recreational amenities has improved opportunities and quality of life for all citizens.

THE ATTRACTION OF POWERFUL MAGNETS

The wakeup call came in 1975. The U.S. Office of Civil Rights withheld $1 million that had been earmarked for Raleigh (North Carolina) City Schools. Reason: Desegregation wasn't happening as it was supposed to. Instead, there was white flight from older residential sections in Raleigh to rapidly developing suburbs in suburban Wake County. The court-ordered solutions that were happening elsewhere in the country didn't look attractive. So, the North Carolinians devised a solution that would work for them, a solution something like the plot of the movie, *Field of Dreams*.

The plan was to merge the Raleigh and Wake County school districts, then make the best, highest quality education available primarily in inner-city Raleigh neighborhoods, assuming that quality-directed parents and students would show up. They did. In effect, Wake County Schools has marketed education by studying and appealing to its consumers. By 1997, 34 of the county's 105 schools offered a wide range of magnet programs, with a high proportion of these special-appeal facilities situated in or near central Raleigh.

The plan has worked, quite simply, because experience has shown that parents in North Carolina, as elsewhere, really care about the quality of their kids' education. The attraction of superior education is far more compelling than any objections to the racial or ethnic makeup of a student body. The marketing orientation of the district also follows a pattern of proven success: District officials have researched and experimented to determine what kinds of experiences appeal to population segments. Curricula are packaged accordingly, with special content emphasis established for magnetic appeal in a series of separate, distinctive schools. A sampling of the programs is described below.

❑   An ***extended day*** program opens a school at 7 a.m. Before normal school hours, students take part in supervised activities that can range from play to completion of home-work. The same happens after normal school hours end. Students remain in school until they are picked up by parents, with closing scheduled for 6 p.m. In between, a normal school curriculum is conducted. Parents support the extra care by paying nominal fees that are significantly under commercial child-care services. All services, including the extended-day operations, are overseen by licensed, credentialed personnel.

o   A **Montessori** school offers a program that follows this popular, early-childhood model for students in the pre-kindergarten through second grade age ranges. Teachers at this facility have all received special training in Montessori methods.

❏   Special work in **language arts and communication** is offered at the elementary level. This facility covers the full core curriculum but places special emphasis on striving for excellence in use of language and in interpersonal communication.

❏   A K-5 elementary school features special work in **arts and science.** For one hour each day, students at this school attend a special class in one of four arts areas: graphic arts, music, drama, and dance. This work is related to the standard curriculum at each grade level. These activities are part of a statewide arts program known as A+ schools. The A+ program is covered in the chapter that follows. Within this same framework, students use computers and multimedia techniques to enrich their science classes.

❏   A **classical studies** school features a two-hour daily class that stresses classical literature through participation in the Junior Great Books program.

❏   A number of schools are devoted to **gifted and talented** programs. These feature intensive academic achievement curricula. Content encompasses a wide range of subjects aimed at exposing students to opportunities and helping them set future directions. At the secondary level, emphasis is on advanced placement work.

The plan has worked well largely because it provides natural affinity groupings for students who are motivated academically and/or intellectually—kids who come to school for achievement and welcome the presence of peers from any background.

Relating Time and Space

Through a combination of favorable geography, extensive development of infrastructure, governmental hospitality, and also availability of quality schools, North Carolina has enjoyed rapid economic and population growth for several decades. One consequence of this growth has been severe crowding in schools. As growth continued and accelerated, it became plain that it was patently impossible to build sufficient school capacity fast enough to meet needs if all schools were to maintain minimal 180-day schedules.

Wake County Schools did undertake monumental programs for building and physically expanding the area's schools. But the administration also met its needs by pioneering year-round use of schools in crowded areas. Rather than attempting to mandate alternate, year-round attendance, the Wake County district folded year-round programs into its already successful magnet schools program.

Year-round schools in Wake County follow a 45/15 schedule pattern like that in Mooresville, described above. However, the Wake County schools operate under a four-track system that alternates use of facilities and enables each participating school to accommodate one-third more students than on a traditional 180-day schedule. The magnet features of the year-round schools include high instructional quality through a favorable (1:8) teacher-student ratio and special enrichment or reinforcement programs during the intersessions that can make for a total of up to 192 days of schooling per pupil.

To avoid conflict or undue inconvenience, year-round attendance is treated as an option for qualifying families. Given the quality of the work and the advantages to the children, fewer than 25 percent opt out of year-round programs.

To summarize, the experiences described above establish, the authors submit, that constructive change and performance enhancement in American schools are both feasible and desirable. The descriptions in this chapter deal with a single-state microcosm and are limited to public institutions. The chapter that follows continues to focus on North Carolina advancements but spreads its topical coverage to include private and joint private-public programs.

Chapter 16
Doing Educational Change—Part 2

You've read many times, including in this book, that the mission of a school is to prepare students to function successfully in the **real world.** If you subscribe to that idea, the notion that follows is logical and desirable: Alliances should be formed between schools and real-world entities to bring lessons applicable in the world of work into the classroom.

Carrying this idea further, you've read and heard that, in the real world, "experience is the best teacher." So, why not build the lessons of experience into encounters organized for classroom presentation?

The programs described in this chapter are built around the premises cited above. They are designed to capture and/or replicate lessons from the world of work and package them as student learning experiences. As with the examples in the previous chapter, implementation of the programs described here was facilitated by the friendly climate and active support for innovative education that exists in North Carolina.

MAKING LEARNING EXCITING AND RELEVANT BY CHALLENGING STUDENTS TO SOLVE PROBLEMS

Doctors do it. The majority of medical schools in the United States make at least some use of instructional case studies. And they generate graduates with whom we willingly trust our lives. So, why not apply the successes experienced in medical schools, aviation training, and graduate schools of business to the promotion of learning in K-12 situations? Why not indeed? It's actually being done in Winston-Salem, North Carolina. And it's working and generating high levels of student excitement.

The program goes by the name of Problem-Based Learning (PBL) and is being applied by an organization named the Center for Excellence in Research, Teaching, and Learning (CERTL). This organization, in turn, is a joint venture of the Winston-Salem/Forsyth County Schools, the Wake Forest University School of Medicine, and Winston-Salem State University. Ann Lambros of the medical school staff serves as coordinator of CERTL. The consortium's PBL program was funded, beginning with the 1995-96 school year, by a $2.5 million grant from the National Science Foundation. CERTL is a subcontract of that grant jointly funded by the National Institutes of Health and the National Science Foundation. In 1998, an additional grant of $180,000 was awarded by the Burroughs Wellcome Fund.

The principle behind the initial grant award was that traditional methods of teaching science and math tend to be too abstract for many students. The traditional approach to K-12 education, it was suggested, fails to stimulate serious math/science commitments among minority students. By appealing to these students through a case-based approach, the problem-based approach involves them in a learning process that is more natural for most students.

This principle is based on findings about how kids learn in response to alternate presentation approaches. The PBL program is particularly concerned with math/science because pedagogy for these subjects has traditionally followed a path to learning that most students find unnatural. That is, most math and science instruction has followed the specific-to-general route, with students learning about rules, theorems, or number/physical structures first, then getting around to applying those basics later.

The other approach, used more commonly in language arts or social studies (and lately in some natural science programs) proceeds from the general (known or familiar) to specific application, filling in unknowns as students search for answers. In history, for example, the current status of the local state or the U.S. as a whole will be apparent to kids who then go back to sources or origins to find out how things got the way they are. In other words, students cover context first, then fill in details.

The PBL method applies the same logical learning structure to math and science. For example, students in North Carolina are all too familiar with the natural phenomenon of hurricanes as California students are apt to be aware of earthquakes. These known conditions, then, make more logical starting points for studies of climatic conditions or geophysical structures than beginning with abstract scientific principles.

Convincing Precedents

The belief that the problem-based approach would enhance performance of K-12 students stemmed from experience at Wake Forest University School of Medicine and other institutions of higher learning that have used case-centered instruction for some four decades. Western Reserve University is credited with initiating this type of instruction as a mainstream technique during the 1950s. Since then, the case method has been used extensively at most of the country's medical schools. Harvard was an early innovator in this movement.

The Wake Forest University School of Medicine has used the case method for first- and second-year medical students for more than 10 years. The case methodology replaces traditional book-and-memorizing methods in courses like biology, anatomy, pharmacology, and other subjects with study assignments derived from cases selected from the hospital's extensive medical files. Cases are constructed to require students to seek out and study the basics they will need in the practice of medicine.

Over a two-year period, proponents of this method feel, students can cover all of the basic knowledge acquisition included in a traditional curriculum and also gain superior skills in analyzing, dealing with, and treating patients. When asked whether the case method imparted sufficient mastery of the basic knowledge required to practice medicine, Dr. Jay Moskowitz, senior dean for research at the Wake Forest University School of Medicine, replied that the case method is about dealing with and treating patients. The anatomical and medical information doctors need, he explained, is readily available in reference books.

Adapting to the K-12 World

This same philosophy, according to Dr. Stan Hill, science coordinator at Winston-Salem/Forsyth County Schools, lies behind the PBL approach. Learning, he feels, will be more thorough and more relevant or applicable to real world situations if students are challenged to forage for information on their own rather than being spoon fed with rationed dosages of factual material.

There are multiple-but-related keys to making PBL work, according to Hill. The most critical dimension of success comes from in-depth training of motivated teachers who volunteer and are willing to devote their skills and time to this program. The second element for success lies in devising the tools and methods those teachers will need to make the program successful. A third, overriding requirement is communication with the program's diverse publics, including parents, students, educators, the public at large, and potential sponsors needed to maintain the rapidly accumulating momentum that builds quickly following successful program launch. (Students in the PBL program have, so far, performed better than their counterparts in traditional classes on statewide tests.)

A New Kind of Teaching

PBL involves a different type of instruction that, in turn, has to be delivered by teachers with newly developed skills and a different outlook on what to expect from kids and how to stimulate them to those greater levels of achievement. Thus, the in-service program that supports PBL is both more extensive and intensive than the typical course covering curriculum revision. Teacher indoctrination to PBL is through a one-week seminar, plus a series of followup sessions throughout the school year. These sessions deal with the principles, methodologies, and classroom presentation and management skills needed to make PBL happen.

Teachers admitted into the program also receive stipends for development of study cases that become the heart of PBL instruction. During the first year of the program, some 100 cases were developed. These, in turn, are being packaged into classroom kits that include problem statements, teacher and student guides, and sets of classroom resources or keys to on-line research sites. A challenge common to all PBL problems is that, at the outset of a study unit, students are never given all of the information they need to develop solutions; additional research for further knowledge acquisition is essential. For each case, it is also stressed that there is no single, specific answer to be delivered by all students. Rather, students are to identify individual goals for each study assignment, acquire knowledge needed to reach a conclusion, then present and explain conclusions—which do not necessarily have to match those of other students or study teams.

APPLYING KNOWLEDGE—A PROCESS

The idea of PBL is to help students acquire the kinds of logical, problem-solving skills needed to take stock of their existing knowledge, determine what they need to know to deal with a problem, then think their way through to a proposed solution. PBL assignments should promote learning by replicating real-life situations. Students can be assisted with guidance toward forming constructive habits for dealing with and resolving logical and tactical problems. To help form constructive habits, and also to facilitate work on PBL assignments, students are given copies of worksheets that resemble the one in Figure 16-1.

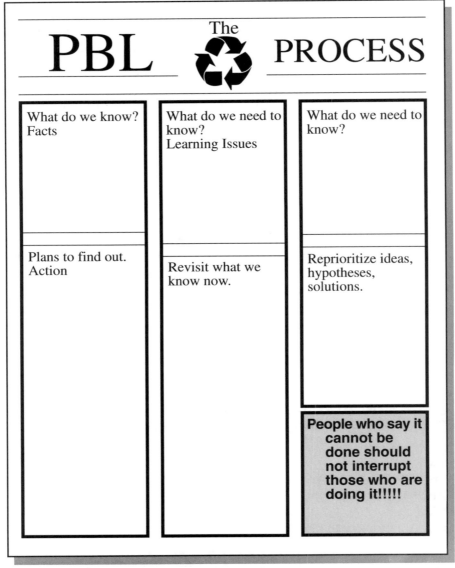

FIGURE 16-1. PBL STUDENTS USE A FORM LIKE THIS ONE TO GUIDE THEM FROM PROBLEM STATEMENTS TO CONCLUSIONS THEY PRESENT.

The form in Figure 16-1, backed by guidance from a teacher to individual study teams that attack the assignment independently of one another, leads students through all or a subset of a six-step process:

1. Students receive their assignment, usually in the form of a problem statement that outlines a life or job situation and presents an initial description of the conditions and facts they are to deal with. The PBL methodology calls for presenting open-ended problems that will require students to gather information that has not been provided. The potential answers or solutions are also open-ended; there is no single "correct" answer to a problem.

2. Under a heading "What do we know?" students list any information they can recall about the subject under study. Note the similarity to the study methodology outlined in Chapter 3. Existing knowledge forms a basis for future learning.

3. From their preliminary assignment, coupled with any existing knowledge they may have, an individual student or members of a collaborating team prepare a statement describing the problem to be solved or the result to be attained. At this point in the process, the statement may be tentative, subject to expansion or revision as the student or team learns more about the task.

4. Students list "What we need to know," a first guess at the information or facts they need to supplement existing knowledge and to fulfill the mission or the problem. The listed items then guide research that follows.

5. Students list possible actions, recommendations, solutions, or hypotheses under a heading "What should we do?" In effect, students formulate and apply preliminary tests to hypotheses developed on the basis of information gathered thus far.

6. Steps two through five may be repeated as often as necessary until the student or team feels they have a conclusion they are ready to present. Presentations can involve different degrees of rigor, depending on the progress of the class through the semester and the importance accorded the topic of the study. Final activities can include documentation of the research and findings, a written statement of the proposed solution, and an oral presentation to the class as a whole. On extensive projects, students may present art posters or multimedia computer displays.

In gathering information on PBL for this book, our observer sat in on a seventh grade science class of one of the lead teachers of the PBL program, Jay Atkins. This session was preliminary in nature, devoted to presenting a problem and acquainting students with the work ahead. The topic was a natural for North Carolinians: Students were to think of themselves as employees of the National Hurricane Center in Miami. They were given atmospheric information about the location and characteristics of a climatic disturbance. Their job was to determine whether the conditions warranted a hurricane warning to residents of Caribbean islands or coastal areas of the United States. Immediately, some students were searching maps to pinpoint location while others were on-line to an NHC website, initial steps in an exercise that would occupy one to two weeks and would impart vital lessons on ecology, climate, and the ecosystem.

PBL Sample

Because the authors feel problem-based learning has great potential interest for educators committed to creating a learning environment, a complete, multi-task learning problem is presented. The title of this problem is ***Extra, Extra ... The Pen, Ink, and Paper Chase is Here!!***

TASK 1

You are good friends with Omar. He is a very dependable student. Omar's teacher has given him a science assignment. The task is to write a two-page report on how paper is made.

Omar found all the information needed to write the report. In the library he found books on the history of paper. On his computer he located additional information on how paper is made. Omar was ready to complete his assignment when he made a shocking discovery—he didn't have any paper. He also realized he didn't have anything to write with. He has called you for suggestions.

What would you do if you were Omar?
What excuse do you think Omar will tell his teacher?

TASK 2

You and Omar think for a while about his problem. He still wants to complete the assignment. He does not want to disappoint his teacher. He is always such a dependable and hard working student. You both decide he will just have to go to the store and buy more paper.

At the store, Omar discovers there is no paper. In fact, there is no more paper in the city, state, country, or even the entire world. All of the clean paper and writing tools (pens, crayons, and markers) have mysteriously disappeared. Now what can Omar do?

What should Omar do now?
If there is a way to complete the assignment, what could Omar use?

TASK 3

Omar tells you that he remembers in the research books and information he found on the computer that paper can easily be made. But, he has no information on how pencils, pens, or ink are made.

What would Omar need to make his own paper?
What could he use as a writing tool?
If Omar needs ink, what can he make it from? Are there things at home he could possibly use? Make a list of some things you can think of.

TASK 4

Find out how paper is made. List the materials needed to make paper.
If you wanted to make a writing tool from something found in your home, what would you use? Make a list of items you might use.
If you wanted to make ink from things in your house, what might you use? List these items. Decide as a group which item might be best for making ink. Why did you choose this item?

CLASS ACTIVITIES (This document for the teacher.)

1)   Paper making using recycled materials.
2)   Making ink from kitchen products.
3)   Making a feather pen.

MAKING RECYCLED PAPER

You will need: a sheet of newspaper
sheets of toilet paper, napkins, and paper towels

wire mesh screen
a jar with a lid
about 2 cups of water

Directions:

Tear up the newspaper and other papers into tiny pieces. Place them into a jar. Then pour the two cups of water into the jar and replace the lid tightly on the jar. Shake the jar vigorously for about five minutes. Next, place the screen over a sink or washtub or something where a mess won't be made. Pour the jar's contents onto the screen. Then spread the mixture evenly onto the screen. Use paper towels to soak up some of the water. Allow the mixture to dry and you will have a sheet of paper.
Make inks by crushing different types of berries into bowls. Remove any peels and seeds. Add 1 teaspoon of alcohol. Try each to see the final results.
You may wish to consider other foods such as beets, egg yolk, and food coloring (mixed) to create other interesting inks. Add alcohol to these items as well.
A quill pen can be made by cutting the tip of a feather at an angle. Cut the tip slightly lengthwise. Dip it into the ink you made and have fun writing.

(**NOTE:** An adult should cut the feather with an Xacto knife or razor blade.

A classroom package of each learning problem comes in a specially made box. Included are a quantity of the assignment sheets, instructions for the teacher, and reference materials for class use. Teacher instructions also identify Web sites on which additional references and/or instructions can be found.

Building and Maintaining Momentum

The enthusiasm that applies momentum to a program of this type typically begins with teachers who anticipate the effectiveness and achievements they will promote. Quickly, it spreads to the students, reflecting the fact that they are challenged first and that their explorations lead to exhilaration of discovery. They will certainly remember and be better able to apply information they have discovered and used themselves than they could ever have done with lessons spoon-fed under a lockstep curriculum.

KINDLING AND CAPITALIZING ON CURIOSITY

The last answer to the last question asked during a visit to the Exploris Charter School in Raleigh, North Carolina, was perhaps most pertinent to the immediate success of that new educational venture. A group of sixth graders was asked how they liked the new school, as compared with the fifth-grade school they had graduated from the previous year.

"In the other school," one boy answered, "they told you what to do all the time. Here we make the rules."

The message behind this answer: The teachers at Exploris are masters at involving students in their own educational processes. The kids know where they're headed and what's expected of them at all times. And where they're headed is toward a world view of people, places, and living conditions—a goal that fulfills the ambitious vision of the school's parent organization.

Exploris is a combination children's museum and learning environment currently rising in downtown Raleigh, North Carolina, a fulfilled dream of prominent local entrepreneur and world visionary Gordon Smith III. Now a successful stock broker and real estate developer, Smith formed a major portion of his personal belief system as a Peace Corps volunteer serving in India following college graduation. When his family sold an established, valuable publishing property to Time-Life in 1985, he was freed to begin developing his vision of a facility in downtown Raleigh that would bring the world to the kids of North Carolina and give them a vision of their relationship with the rest of humanity.

Smith is the driving force behind development of the $36.5 million museum and learning center to be called Explor*i*s. (The *i* is always printed in a different font from the rest of the word to demonstrate the outreaching, exploratory intent of the organization.) The completed facility, due to open some time in 1999, will include study kiosks connecting users in Raleigh to distant lands and exhibits featuring worldwide lifestyles and customs. Smith is CEO of Exploris and Anne Bryan, a former state education administrator, is president.

When North Carolina passed legislation permitting formation of charter schools, Smith envisioned a perfect synergy between eager middle school students and the Exploris staff, which was already busy developing plans for facilities and exhibits. The Exploris Charter School that opened in the fall of 1997 will ultimately serve youngsters in sixth through eighth grades. The first class consisted of 52 sixth graders. Fifty-two more students will be admitted each year, creating a student body limited to 156 students to be guided by a faculty of 12 full time people whose services will be supplemented by specialists in fields such as crafts, Spanish, or health and well-being. Enrollment in the school is open to students throughout the area served by Wake County Schools. When applications outnumber available positions, lotteries will be conducted.

The synergy Smith envisioned started happening almost immediately as museum staff members previewed exhibit plans with the students and used the kids' reactions as market research. Capitalizing on this involvement, the faculty set up a first-year project under which the students, using a variety of blocks, clay, and other materials, developed models of what they thought a museum should look like.

The charter school, envisioned as a "community of learners," operates on nine-week quarters with two-week intersessions, time the teachers put to good use for planning and development of learning aids. The notion that the kids make the rules at Exploris comes from the activity schedule of the school. Each day begins with a class meeting at which plans and any community issues or student questions are covered, sessions from which students leave with the feeling they make the rules. Teachers also brief the kids on their learning assignments for the day. Instruction then takes place in "minilessons" limited to an hour that feature interactive presentations by teachers with student participation. Then, two hours are devoted to learning/study projects in which students break into teams to complete knowledge-acquisition assignments.

Students bring their lunches and eat anywhere they wish, including in hallways or on staircases, where they typically discuss study projects or read books. Reading requirements are relatively heavy, with a target set at 900 pages during each nine-week quarter. Students turn in summaries and critical essays on completed readings. Afternoons can be spent on joint study projects with members of the museum staff or in Spanish lessons, held regularly.

During an observation visit on behalf of this book, one class got a close-up personal look at geometric shapes as they wandered across a pattern of lines, shapes, and angles taped to the classroom floor by the instructor, then wrote summaries of the principles and knowledge they had acquired. Another group selected and mounted photographic prints from images created by pinhole cameras each of them had made. A review of the geography and ethnic makeup of the Middle East was guided by a teacher who had worked in the region for two years.

In between, there were private times during which the kids positioned themselves comfortably on the floor and concentrated on wading through as much of their pending reading assignments as they had time for. A basketball backboard in the backyard provides one locale for exercise. A large park across the street with plenty of running-around room satisfies the rest of the need for exercise facilities. Wandering further afield, faculty and students use downtown Raleigh as an expanded classroom, to be supplemented by exciting museum exhibits shortly.

As one faculty member put it, "The idea is that these kids are living their education. It's about more than studying from books."

CHOOSING ART AS A KEY TO LIFE AND LEARNING

It was the kind of scene that could happen in any American home, any day, any evening after dinner. Homework was done and put away. Then it was time for mom to nag her 10-year-old daughter about cleaning her room before bedtime. But here's a different twist. Mom says: "You get this room cleaned up young lady or you can't go to school tomorrow morning."

This really happened. Jim Fatata, principal of Bugg Elementary School in Raleigh, North Carolina, learned about the incident because a delighted grandmother, the mom's mom in this case, called to share the story. This kind of story can, understandably, be a mind blower for an elementary principal who believes in what's happening in his school. But it's not unusual. With equal pride, Jim Fatata reports that his school's average daily attendance for the past year has been 97.3 percent.

Bugg Elementary is one of 27 schools in North Carolina with similar anecdotes to share. Without exception, faculties and kids of the elite A+ schools, all located across North Carolina can share satisfaction and pride in similar occurrences. The A+ Schools Program applies instruction in arts as a catalyst to promote multidisciplinary academic learning through interconnected activities. The program is sponsored by the Thomas S. Kenan Institute for the Arts, headquartered in Winston-Salem, which enjoys support from more than a dozen other corporate and foundation sponsors.

The A+ program implements a philosophy derived from 15 years of research at Harvard and elsewhere by Howard Gardner. This approach is based on the belief that students learn through use of "multiple intelligences," and that the learning experience is more enjoyable and effective when varied-but-related experiences focus on the content to be mastered. The Kenan Institute was set up in 1992, beginning largely as an activity carried out by Jeanne Butler when she moved to North Carolina after a stint as director of the National Endowment for the Arts. The program was launched in two schools whose staffs worked directly with Butler. That experience led to expansion of the Institute's activities in 1994. A year later, after a search and selection process, 25 additional schools were added.

In each A+ school, one hour a day is devoted to instruction in one of four art-related classes—visual arts, music, drama, and dance. This instruction is handled by specialists, who coordinate with the regular grade teachers to relate the arts experiences to specific segments of the North Carolina Standard Course of Study. In the fall of 1997, the A+ program encompassed approximately 12,000 students in the 27 participating schools. Some 1,100 teachers and other staff members were especially trained for work on this curriculum.

At the Bugg School, for example, a class studying space exploration might experience a music composition intended to depict the vastness of the universe. In visual arts, students would illustrate or build models of space travel experiences, while the dance class might interpret the same music, and the drama class would construct skits around the same theme. One of the school's two computer labs might be working on time-and-distance-related math applications while, in the other, students compose written descriptions of the information they have gathered, along with their feelings and reactions to the lessons. In one fifth grade class, students write a letter to their parents every Friday morning telling about their experiences and summarizing what they have learned during the week.

When 25 schools were added to the A+ program in 1995, the Kenan Institute initiated a four-year developmental and evaluation program designed to track progress largely through surveys of participating students. A critical element of the overall program has been a series of summer institutes for all teachers and aides actively involved in A+ schools. These are one-week residential sessions during which teachers work with selected participating students. Program coordinators then visit the schools for additional workshops throughout the school year. Faculty networking also carries on during the school year through local conferences, publications, and an on-line exchange.

Evaluations of program progress are performed continuously by a consultant, with status reports published annually. The focus of this study has been on the impact upon the students themselves. No formal note has been taken of grades on standardized academic tests, since these measures fall within the purview of the school districts and the state's education agencies. Rather, student reactions are measured by responses to such questions as:

- ❏ How do you know you are smart?
- ❏ What makes you work (not work) in school?
- ❏ How do you learn best?
- ❏ I like/don't like doing art (music, dance, drama) in school.
- ❏ I feel this way because ...

Performance-based criteria, though not used as justification or claims for success, are nonetheless effective. Attendance records are vastly improved. Discipline referrals are way down. (At Bugg, there were 70 referrals the year before the A+ program was introduced, three during the first A+ year, zero during the second A+ year.) Student attention to classwork is way up, as is parental involvement.

On the day when information for this book was gathered at Bugg Elementary, Jim Fatata assigned a fifth-grade student to conduct a tour while he met with a parent of a fifth grade student and teacher. The meeting had been called by the teacher, who felt the curriculum at Bugg was not challenging the extremely bright fifth grader sufficiently. After a serious discussion during the afternoon, the child's needs came up again at a faculty meeting after school that day. The entire faculty focused on devising ways to enrich the student's learning experiences during the remainder of the current school year, including options for placement in other schools and for special programs after the student's graduation from Bugg, which is a K-5 school.

This kind of conversation among teachers in a school with an enrollment of 465 was more than enough, in itself, to gratify the visit and to validate the quality of what's happening under the A+ program.

A MAJOR COMMITMENT

Early on, this book proposes that prospective employers are prime customers for the outputs of the country's educational system—at least when it comes to evaluating and acting upon the capabilities with which students leave our schools. That posture could be viewed as placing future employers in the role of critics, enabling them to tell schools what they are doing wrong without demanding positively oriented investment or commitment from them.

Fortunately in this instance, reality points elsewhere. The commitment in financial and intellectual support of the Kenan Institute, described above, is one example of the extensive investment private-sector organizations are making in public education. The Schoolbook 2000 program that's placing thousands of laptops in public schools is another kind of example.

Still another type of commitment to education from the private sector, the kind of investment that could be classified as a blue-chip bet on the potential of American kids, is represented by the Cary (North Carolina) Academy, which admitted its first students in August, 1997. The Academy is a from-the-ground up commitment to bring twenty-first century thinking and technology into the education of sixth-through-twelfth grade kids, a commitment that adds $15 million for facilities and equipment to the already-major gift of the 52-acre site on which the school sits.

Cary Academy is an outgrowth of the success and vision of the founders of the SAS Institute, the country's largest privately owned software developer and supplier. SAS employs some 5,000 people, about half on a campus in Cary, North Carolina, that initially included the land from which the school site was subdivided. The founders and principal owners of SAS—James Goodnight and John Sall along with their wives, Ann and Ginger—have donated the great bulk of the costs of creating and donating the school to a nonprofit foundation that will operate the facility. This assures that the commitment is to children and to educational processes, since the school will never return a profit to its benefactors.

The Cary Academy is housed in an ultra-modern campus that may well represent the most modern educational facility in the country, certainly among preparatory institutions. Separate buildings are provided for a middle school, a high school, a fine arts building that includes a 500-seat auditorium, a library/media/administration building, and a range of indoor and outdoor athletic and sports facilities. Furnishings include "at least" one computer for every two students, although some rooms, such as those set up for instruction in English, have one computer for each student. The school will ultimately accommodate 70 students per grade for a total enrollment of 630 or thereabouts. In full operation, the plan calls for at least 500 computers on premises and open access to the school's intranet from students' homes. (Each student receives a private password for access to the school's intranet on enrollment.)

Despite the strong presence of computers, however, the curriculum is heavily weighted toward core academic subjects and to the assumption that virtually all Cary students will go on to leading universities. Specific computer-oriented instruction is limited to a few programming courses that offer minimum academic credit and one advanced placement course. Pointedly, a heavy emphasis in the student program is on a composite Humanities course that includes interrelated instruction in literature, history, and arts, combined with rigorous writing assignments that include work on essays, creative writing, report and technical writing, and scripts. Also required are studies in math and science, a foreign language, and art.

Within this spectrum, the main purpose of computers is for completion of writing and research assignments. Educational software was available and utilized from the opening of the school. In addition, SAS Institute has created an educational division whose staff will interact with the faculty and students of the Academy in a continuing effort to develop new, innovative ways to use computers as learning tools.

A visit to the Cary Academy aimed at gathering information for this book noted a ninth grade class at work on a final examination that required writing of a series of seven essays summarizing content of works of classic Greek literature. Another ninth grade class studying ancient history was at work on clay-sculpted bas relief models of ancient architectural structures. Following completion of the basic models, the students were to fire their work in high-temperature kilns, then add color glazes and fire them again.

In the middle school, a seventh-grade science class was busy on an "adopt a galaxy" project. Two-student teams each chose one galaxy within the solar system. Each team was responsible for turning in a graphic representation or model of its adopted galaxy, along with a written presentation and an oral recap. The intent of the designers of the curriculum is to require students to look at every learning experience from multiple vantage points.

Although the Academy is private and charges tuitions in line with other private schools in the area, provision has been made for greater-than-average funding of scholarships. The intent is to attract and nurture students motivated to make the most of natural talents by stimulating them with exceptional opportunities.

TAKING STOCK

The sources and concepts covered in this book are, admittedly, anecdotal and selective in nature. But, the authors maintain, that's as it has to be. There is no reliable way to do convincing statistical analysis of innovation, particularly if the innovators are operating on an ad hoc, highly individualistic basis.

At the moment, we submit, that's the way things are in American education. Further, we hope, fervently, that they stay that way. We truly believe that American schools cannot be brought to heel under a single set of curriculum standards aimed at imposing national, discipline-specific, multiple-choice tests. If the studies and findings in this work prove anything, it is that a one-size-fits-all approach cannot and will not work in America—possibly not in any given state, county, or school in America.

The most positive finding from our efforts, the authors feel, is that American schools are well along on a road leading to an orientation toward learning as a replacement for centuries old, discipline-oriented teaching methods. Another source of satisfaction is that more listening and less didactic defensiveness is happening among administrators and teachers. Schools are once again becoming service-oriented community institutions.

As educational veterans, we have learned that you have to take your good news wherever you can find it. We have found significant pockets of good news and it has been delightful to share the resulting pride and happiness.

A

Using this Book in Planning and Development

We at ICLE were flattered to learn that a number of copies of the first book in this series, *Education Is NOT a Spectator Sport,* were judged to be sufficiently interesting so that a number of copies found their way into study or in-service sessions for district board members, volunteer groups, and professional development programs for teachers. So, we decided to anticipate more of the same for this work.

Following our own advice on how to build a learning-oriented system, we've developed a series of questions that might be potentially profitable as the basis for study sessions. For each question, we've provided some text references and additional topics you may find worth pursuing—all aimed at helping you to apply the information in this book to your own needs. If there are additional questions, or if the staff of ICLE can be of further help, please call. We will value your inquiries and/or suggestions.

If you'd like recommendations for a format, or organization plan, for your study sessions, we suggest you consider the following algorithm.

1. For the topic under review, identify your present position in terms of policies, capabilities, and results delivered.
2. Based on the image of your present position, define where you'd like to be in each of the affected areas.
3. Identify the points of difference between where you are and where you should be.

4. Apply Functional Analysis to separate elements of your status so that they can be analyzed individually, then interrelated.
5. Develop an algorithm to deal with each element of your situation, aimed at moving from the present to the desired status.
6. Establish a plan for modification or change by combining the situational elements you have considered separately into a coherent, improved approach.

What is Functional Analysis and how is it applied?

Functional Analysis is a management planning technique used to diagnose and deal with complex situations that present problems beyond the scope of traditional problem solving or decision making methodologies. The example used in this book is the undertaking to explore space and send a manned mission to the moon. There were multiple unknowns. So, the assignment was handled by breaking the overall, complex task into a series of separate studies that could be analyzed and dealt with individually. Many managerial challenges faced by educators are complex enough to warrant this approach. ICLE is using this method to analyze educational curricula and evolve an approach designed to help establish more realistic educational content outlines that can help enhance the ability of students to apply knowledge they acquire in the course of their studies.

For a brief introduction to Functional Analysis, see Chapter 13. For an in-depth discussion of how students can relate existing knowledge elements to a given situation or requirement and apply what they know to improve study habits, solve problems, or reach decisions, see Chapter 3.

Functional Analysis is seen as one of the cornerstones of continuing education for teachers who are to take part in multidisciplinary instruction programs and in building assessment instruments for basing measures of student progress on their ability to think, taking them beyond traditional standardized tests that measure their recall of specific items of knowledge. One reason for going beyond traditional testing is that it is basically unhealthy for students to go all the way through an educational experience being trained to believe there is only one answer for every question. The Functional Analysis process promotes creativity and initiative for teachers and, through them, for students.

What is a learning transaction and why do you say education is a service business?

Basically, a transaction—in business or between individuals—involves a fair exchange, presumably of goods, services, or sums of money that represent equal values. The opening chapter establishes the transaction as a theme by describing a successful modification of the business education program in New York State, based on using the transaction as the focus for learning about how business works. Chapters throughout the book enlarge on this perspective.

Chapter 2 deals with the ICLE Relational Model and its application as a means of establishing quality goals for educational programs and for monitoring actual learning achievements.

Chapter 3 deals with processes for the application of acquired knowledge.

Part II of this book—Chapters 7 through 13—deals with a series of separate, specific educational areas in which learning transactions occur. The series of chapters begins with a discussion on the elements that comprise a learning environment and goes on to deal with critically important content areas.

The final three chapters deal with implementations of educational transactions within learning-oriented situations.

Imparting the concept of education as a series of transactions between students, teachers, and peers can play a major part in conditioning students to understand and prepare for the adult roles in society for which modern educational programs avow to prepare them.

What is the Relational Model and how is it used in planning educational change, including in curriculum design and development?

The ICLE Relational Model is a multi-dimensional taxonomy used to describe both the mastery of educational content and the student's ability to apply acquired knowledge. The structure and creation of Relational Models is covered in depth in Chapter 2. This tool is introduced early in the book specifically for its usefulness as a means of concurrently evaluating levels of learning and capabilities of application of knowledge through use of this single tool. In turn, this ability to identify, qualify, and express related achievements in knowledge acquisition and application becomes the basis for understanding and communication about the principles of establishing a learning environment and measuring student achievement.

Chapter 12 uses the Relational Model as a foundation for discussions on learning assessment. The Model provides a universal basis for evaluating the degrees of knowledge and skill stipulated for an assessment exercise and also as a basis for grading student performance.

The Relational Model is a unique tool devised by ICLE to help create learning situations based on application of knowledge rather than simple measurement of acquired bodies of information. This capability, in turn, should become a major guide for teachers working to create and implement learning-based education programs.

How can we help to assure that students build skills essential for learning success, particularly in the areas of English language arts (including reading) and math, before they complete third grade?

Chapter 13 points out that the typical student enters first grade with a spoken vocabulary that can run between 2,000 and 4,000 words. The logical place to begin assisting that student to learn to read and write English is to build upon his or her existing command of language. Chapter 13 suggests a methodology that involves students in the selection of the words they are to learn to read and write. The description includes a recommendation for use of computers to impart this basic language instruction. Vocabularies of letters, words, and phrases are displayed by the teacher-facilitator in response to words introduced by the children. The computer entries can then be printed out and used as personalized readers for individual students or study team groups. Reading progress will generally be more comprehensive and faster than with traditional readers.

In the math area, one approach suggested in Chapter 13 is to regard arithmetic as a language. Lessons should be described in words as well as numbers. This approach helps to bridge the transition into word problems when they are introduced.

Chapter 11 discusses English as a learning platform on which teachers can build interdisciplinary instruction. It is pointed out that all learning stems from language proficiency. Instruction can be more effective and can more closely resemble real-world conditions if disciplines are combined instructionally. However, transition to interdisciplinary instruction requires care in the selection and coordination of teachers who will work as teams.

A report within Chapter 16 describes the A+ program, a methodology for integrating study of the arts with prescribed curriculum content. The creativity and challenges of expression and communication inherent in use of the arts—visual, theatrical, musical, or dance—makes the learning experience more enjoyable while reinforcing acquired knowledge through tactile artistic expression. Building entire learning experiences around the arts is seen as an important, growing area of elementary and secondary education.

Note that the topics cited above involve two different educational levels. The introductory reading program represents an ideal challenge for elementary teachers. The principle of teaching on the basis of existing language levels needs to be introduced and discussed. Then workshops can be created to build proficiency in use of a computer for elementary reading and writing instruction.

Interdisciplinary instruction also applies at elementary levels. But the team teaching methods covered in Chapter 11 deal more specifically with middle and high school programs under block scheduling. Teaching in the block leads naturally to introduction of interdisciplinary instruction.

Throughout discussions of language and math skills and interdisciplinary instruction it should be stressed that curriculum design and syllabus decisions should be based on what is best and most natural for the students.

We're interested in undertaking a full-scale program for educational change through emphasis on learning rather than teaching. Can you suggest some references within this book?

Chapter 7 addresses a series of typical questions related to creation of a learning environment. Each question holds a potential for an in-service training discussion. In particular, the questions and answers can be helpful in explaining learning transitions to parents and community leaders.

Chapters 4 through 6 cover the transition to a learning environment within the ICLE Management of Change process. The six-step process is aimed at establishing the need for change and forming a coordinated, community-based program that leads to defining new curricula and implementing new instructional philosophies and methods.

Our computers are being used primarily for Internet-type references and for instruction about computers and their use in organizations. We are interested in learning about use of computers for direct student instruction in curriculum content areas. Where do we look for help?

Surveys indicate that many schools and districts are installing computers primarily in middle and high schools, where they are being used primarily as network references and for instruction in business-type applications such as touch keyboarding, word processing, spreadsheets, and databases.

At this writing, the greater potential for use of computers for direct instruction of students probably exists at the elementary levels, where standard programs are available to lead students through instruction in reading and practice in writing. Creative math instruction programs are also available. These typically are well proven tools that have worked for tens of thousands, possibly hundreds of thousands, of students. With the advent of inexpensive network or other low cost computers, elementary education could be upgraded significantly by providing computers—backed by competent technical support—at elementary schools.

To date, the most significant contribution of computers to instruction in middle and high schools is for writing instruction. With access to computers equipped with editing-type software, teachers can efficiently and effectively comment upon and monitor quality of student performance as writers.

Note that the discussions in this book stress that, to achieve improved performance in writing and other academic subjects, teachers are going to need more review and prep time than many have had in the past.

Chapters 9, 10, 11, 13, 15, and 16 contain discussions and/or case descriptions about computers in education. As part of any program review involving computers in a given school or district, we recommend taking stock of your current situation. Establish a consensus on whether your school is adequately equipped and staffed to implement use of computers for instruction. Ask whether you are getting your money's worth out of computers in terms of actual student progress. Be honest. Every school or district can use computers more profitably than is now being done. Viability of your educational program may well depend on how constructively you deal with these questions.

We'd like to increase our use of performance-based assessment. We're particularly interested in tradeoffs and decisions between standardized testing and performance-based, analytical assessment. Where do we look for help?

Chapter 12, which deals with testing and assessment, states a conviction that, as long as colleges and state boards base evaluation of school and student performance on results of standardized tests, there is no choice but to continue to administer these tests. However, it is also pointed out that student scores and/or responses on standardized tests are of little or no value when it comes to adjusting or revising curriculum. Typically, standardized tests are machine scored at an off-site location, with results returned well after instruction has been completed in the corresponding subject. Further, machine scoring typically reports only gross scores, without indicating which questions were answered correctly, thus providing no potential guidance for instructional adjustment.

Performance-based assessment, by contrast, is integrated with instruction and serves to provide immediate feedback that can be applied to adjust instruction. Chapter 12 notes that standardized tests provide an indication of what students know while analytical assessment provides an indication of how they think.

Chapter 12 describes the principles of analytical assessment and covers a process for development of assessment instruments. The ICLE assessment process includes evaluation of degree of knowledge and skill required for an assessment exercise through use of the Relational Model. Also presented is a process to be followed in developing assessment instruments.

Be aware also that a potential problem may result from emphasis on use of problem-based learning and corresponding performance-based assessment. Students whose classroom performance is based on knowledge application and problem-solving skills may turn in lower scores on standardized tests than they would deliver if the school stuck to fact-based instruction. There is no set solution for this dilemma. It is up to each school to consider the consequences and establish priorities and policies.

A point is made that heavy emphasis on testing can lead students through a complete educational experience in the belief that every problem has one, single solution. In today's world, some analytical capability will be demanded in the workplace.

This is a difficult area of educational transition, one that deserves serious consideration by faculty members, administrators, parents, and community participants. The deciding factor should be a clearly drawn profile of what students are expected to look like on graduation.

We've heard about and are interested in forming links between the arts and instruction in core courses. Where should we look for discussions of methods and benefits and help in planning changes?

Look at descriptions of programs in Chapters 14 and 16, particularly the description in Chapter 16 of the A+ schools program being implemented in 27 North Carolina schools. Arts based instruction appears to hold great promise, particularly for schools and communities anxious to build a sense of culture and rounded citizenship in their educational programs.

Arts-based education establishes an interdisciplinary basis for instruction. Students cover all standard academic content areas, enriching their learning with tactile experiences as they draw, sing, dance, or act out lessons, relating their learning experiences to the history, culture, and artistic expressions of the times and developments they are studying.

Arts-based instruction typically varies with grade level. At elementary levels, students are encouraged to picture or act out their impressions of the knowledge they are acquiring. At higher grades, learning becomes interdisciplinary as students relate the culture, interpretations, and impacts of events they are covering upon the people who were affected.

Index

Numbers in italics indicate pages with illustrations.